Boarding House Reach

North Carolina's Entrepreneurial Women

For Jill
Enjoy!
Alice E. Sink

Alice E. Sink & Nickie Doyal

Dram Tree Books

First Edition 2007
Published in the United States of America by Dram Tree Books.

Publisher's Cataloging-in-Publication Data
(Provided by DRT Press)

Sink, Alice E.
   Boarding house reach : North Carolina' s entrepreneurial women / Alice E. Sink and Nickie Doyal.
   p. cm.
   Includes bibliographical references.
   ISBN 978-0-9786248-6-6

1. Hotels--North Carolina--History. 2. Businesswomen--United States--Biography. 3. Businesswomen--United States--History. 4. Businesspeople--United States--Biography. 5. Businesspeople--United States--History. I. Doyal, Nickie. II. Title.

HQ1410 .S565 2007
331.4/0973--dc22

Volume discounts available.
Call or e-mail for terms.

10 9 8 7 6 5 4 3 21

Dram Tree Books
P.O. Box 7183
Wilmington, N.C. 28406
(910) 538-4076
www.dramtreebooks.com
Potential authors: visit our website or email us for submission guidelines

 ——— *Dedication* ———

We dedicate this book to our family members, who have demonstrated patience and loyalty during our past four years of researching and writing.

Boarding House Reach:
NORTH CAROLINA'S ENTREPRENEURIAL WOMEN

TABLE OF CONTENTS

Boarding House Recipes

Food Good Enough For The Boarding House Table

Foreword

My Grandmother Evans ran a boarding house within walking distance of all the factories and mills in Lexington, North Carolina. Jenny Alice Wood Evans' backyard adjoined ours. Her house stood tall and boxy and unheated. The downstairs living room remained unused and cold except on Christmas Day when a space heater gave out intermittent heat for our family gathering.

My grandmother's bedroom held her double bed, sagging with the same mattress that had served as a birthing place for her five children, one of whom was my father. A dresser with antique mirror and an overstuffed chair completed the furnishings. Her small bathroom contained a commode, lavatory, and tub that, for some reason or another, never worked and became storage space for a suitcase and extra blankets. She bathed at the small sink with water heated in a pot on the kitchen's wood stove and carried to the bathroom.

Grandmother's only female boarder, Blanche, occupied the room with the double French doors. I suppose she bathed and brushed her teeth at my grandmother's bathroom lavatory and used a slop jar during the night. I can see how, with careful scheduling, that sharing would have worked.

The dining room held a huge oak table, a dozen or more mismatched chairs, sideboard, china closet, and—near the open fireplace—an easy chair, radio, and overstuffed sofa.

Her roomy kitchen contained both wood and gas stoves, a single-base enamel sink, and a large table with marble slab for cutting mints and rolling pie crusts. In a freestanding cupboard, my paternal grandmother kept flour, sugar, spices, and jars filled with saved string and recycled buttons. A refrigerator, chilling quart jars of homemade buttermilk, stood in one corner. Between the dining room and kitchen two large pantries held shelves loaded with vegetables: bell jars filled with green beans, beets, soup mixture, squash, butterbeans, corn, and bread-and-butter pickles. A country ham hung from a large nail.

Upstairs, four bedrooms had a total of eight beds, four chests of drawers, and four straight chairs. One small bathroom with tub, commode, and lavatory served the male boarders.

These men (and Blanche) worked in the local furniture factories or cotton mills. They ate breakfast, dinner (the noon hour signaled for all workers by one loud blast from the town's fire horn), and supper at my grandmother's seven days a week. She raised her own vegetables and chickens and made her biscuits and cornbread from scratch. Staples, which she ordered from Michael's Store just two blocks over, arrived at her house via a delivery man, who entered her back door, usually without knocking, deposited everything on her kitchen cabinet, and sometimes left without a word.

Part Cherokee, Grandmother had an olive complexion, ink black eyes, long finely textured Native-American hair, and beautifully high cheek bones. She seldom ventured away from home during her boarding house tenure. A devout Christian, she attended First Baptist Church services every Sunday. As a die-hard Republican, she voted every time the polls opened. In addition to these two excursions, she made an annual pilgrimage to Michael's Store, just to say hello to the owners and take note of new products.

Born in 1940, I arrived during the last phase of Grandmother's boarding house days. By the late 40's all the boarders had left. Other than Blanche, my specific memories have faded, but I'll always remember all those people eating chicken and dumplings at Grandmother's table or swaying in oversized rockers on her front porch.

That image prompted me to write about North Carolina's boarding house phenomena, and research assistance appeared in the form of Nickie Doyal, a senior at High Point University, where I have taught English for the past twenty-six years. Nickie, a media major, appeared in my office with the news that the Honors Program had approved a stipend for her to work as my research assistant.

Our process went like this: We distributed flyers, announcing the project and urging anyone to phone with information, to various women's clubs. Soon we had more responses and leads than we had ever expected. Respondents referred us to boarding houses—a few still standing—in virtually every part of the state.

Some months Nickie exhausted all her long-distance cell phone allotment, telephoning people who knew descendants of former boarding house owners. We then began our road trips. With MapQuest guidance or scribbled directions on the backs of envelopes, we eventually found our interview sources. Yes, we got lost—a lot—but on the less-traveled back roads, we often discovered quaint country stores and scores of interesting and helpful people.

A dual interviewing system evolved. Usually, Nickie asked the questions and taped while I took notes with pen and steno pad. Our elderly interviewees sometimes replaced words with gestures. More than once, in the midst of conversation, someone would reach for a photo album or rummage through a drawer trying to find an old newspaper or memorabilia. We did not want to miss anything.

May 2003 Nickie graduated summa cum laude, and I signed on for an Early Retirement Plan at the University; consequently, the actual writing and rewriting of this manuscript began. We decided to continue with the program that had worked so well for us at the beginning: Nickie's expertise in making contacts and conducting interviews combined with my writing talents.

Having previously published nonfiction, I knew most of the rules and all of the pitfalls. I wanted each piece to present a different focus. Yes, all the women who ran boarding houses worked extremely hard. Yes, they supported their families. Yes, they exhibited tough, but compassionate, spirits—but what made them individuals and their boarding houses different? More often than not, we had to dig for that uniqueness.

Next, I envisioned pictures and memorabilia to enhance each narrative. Descendants trusted Nickie to make professional copies of old photographs, cookbooks, and journals, with her promise that all would be returned to the owners. She did just that. This facilitated our ability to borrow priceless family heirlooms.

While working on this project, I learned something. Both Nickie and I brought different talents to the table; these individual strengths combined to produce a professional manuscript, one based on painstaking research, polished writing, and a harmonious partnership.

I gained something else: I renewed a connection with Grandmother Evans. Now I can sincerely appreciate her hard work and astute management. I think of her every time I roll pie crust on her old marble slab.

Alice E. Sink

— *History* —

T he *American Heritage Dictionary* defines a boarding house as "a house that provides meals and lodging." The true boarding houses in this book present narratives so unique they extend beyond this rather limited definition.

Before the term "boarding house" originated, traveling men in North Carolina during the earlier Colonial period had two choices for accommodations: an ordinary (considered second rate) or a tavern (a first-class establishment). Upper-class travelers avoided ordinaries, usually a one-room log house, sparsely furnished, and often inhabited by insects and other snoring men; however, poorer men stopped at ordinaries seeing them as a refuge from the barren land, stormy weather, and dirt roads.

As early as 1715, the Colonial Assembly had issued certain guidelines for ordinary keepers, who, unfortunately, overcharged customers. According to Dr. Alan D. Watson, the following laws were established:

Ordinary keepers [had to] sell strong drink in English sealed measures, pints, quarts, pottles, and gallons...and the Assembly set a maximum price of 12 pence for a meal, ls. 6d. per gallon of home-brewed beer or unboiled cider, and a l00 percent profit on imported liquors...The profits allowed by the 1715 law encouraged extravagant prices...[so] five years later another law was passed allowing the precinct courts to determine the price of liquors, diets, lodging, and pasturage for ordinaries...[with] the table of rates...displayed openly in the ordinary.

By 1741, the Assembly required that all ordinary or public house keepers apply for and take out a license. The penalty for not doing this earned the perpetrator thirty lashes at the public whipping post (first offense) or, for subsequent offenses, thirty-nine lashes and a month in prison or a fine amounting to five to ten pounds. The license cost £2-£4 and a potential keeper also had to pay 30 pounds bond money.

Women, who needed to support their children after their husbands' deaths, took out a reported twenty percent of these licenses. Records indicate that many of these women kept their licenses for only a year or so because "they...became quickly disillusioned with the arduous task of providing service to the meanest sort of persons and enduring the roughest of the men calling at the ordinaries." Not so for Mrs. Fielder Powell, of Craven County, who operated one of these establishments for almost twenty years, from 1756 to 1775.

Both ordinaries and taverns proved an indispensable part of Colonial North Carolina society, and according to historian Watson, "Life in the towns revolved around these public houses, and as a result, many of the ordinaries evolved into establishments of high quality and good repute."

Ordinaries sprang up around ferries and towns, especially those near courthouses and jails. Someone had to board travelers and feed prisoners. The Assembly of 1767 passed a law requiring ferrymen to buy an ordinary license (and provide food and lodging) if they charged travelers more than 4 pence for a man and horse to cross the river. Most ordinaries provided little comfort and certainly no amenities.

Taverns, on the other hand, provided better food and spacious lodging with closets. Travelers also liked the diversity provided. Billiards, hazard, all-fours, backgammon, chess, draughts, whist, piquet, and quadrille were frequent gaming pursuits enjoyed by boarders. These places also served as centers of political discussions, were used by shipmasters for the leaving of mail, employed as locations for the sale of slaves, and used for vestry meetings.

Little has been documented about boarding houses during the 1800's. We do know several historical details. For example, as in the previous century, a widow usually opened a boarding house to provide for herself and her children. Even with occasional help, she stayed extremely busy. In addition to cleaning, cooking, washing, ironing, and sewing, she often grew her own vegetables and raised cows, pigs, and chickens. The early boarding house provided a place for guests to sleep and eat and also a social environment for young men—and later young women— separated from their families. In the evenings, guests gathered in the parlor to play games or on the front porch to talk and smoke.

In her book *Feeding Generations: Boarding House Fare and Family Oral Tradition,* Helen C. Gift reveals the reason why we don't have many specifics concerning nineteenth-century boarding houses and the women who ran them.

"...in a time when women were less well educated," she writes, "seen as too frail or incompetent to be employed at 'men's work,'...most women were...domestics, drawing on the skills they had developed in their own homes." Gift goes on to say that women "who had space in a house, family resources for property or 'start-up' capital had other options for income such as sewing, laundry or boarding transients...but little appears to be documented about the careers of these women."

She goes on to explain that married women seldom worked outside the home; furthermore, when they helped with family businesses, ran a boarding house, or labored on the farm, the Census Department rarely received reports of such employment. While there is little recorded nineteenth-century boarding house documentation, certain givens do surface. First, the women who ran boarding houses did so for a reason. Most of the time these women needed a workable way to support their children, whose father had died. They could earn money as well as stay home with their offspring. Or like some wives who opened boarding houses to escape drinking or abusive husbands, this option proved a socially acceptable way to break from a doomed marriage.

Whatever the reason for starting their own "home business," these women—who practically always lived in the same house as their paying guests—worked diligently from sunup to sundown, preparing and serving nutritious and filling meals, baking special cakes and cookies to sell to the general public, cleaning, changing bed linens, doing laundry (often times by hand), raising vegetables and chickens and often a cow in their back yards, and enforcing rules that guaranteed the civility and morality of the boarding house.

Nineteenth century women's recipes—passed down verbally from grandmother to mother to daughter—were seldom recorded. Because of their limited reading and writing skills and lack of treasured paper, women did not write ingredients or directions for their favorite dishes, which often included biscuits, turkey dressing, sweet potato pudding, top-of-stove pot roast, and fried chicken. They memorized them. The following is a record of food served at an 1830's boarding house:

All meals: meat, hot vegetables, hot "new" bread, rolls, butter.

Breakfast: hashed or minced left-over meat with cold vegetables "served hot"; pork or mutton chops, beef-steaks or sausages. Occasionally salt mackerel, shad or other fish, apple sauce, sometimes peach sauce, seasonal radishes, peppergrass, onions, cucumbers, boiled beet-root plain or in vinegar, coffee.

Dinner: stewed meat joints with fish or poultry, many and diverse vegetables including sweet potato, squash, Indian corn, eggplant, pies, puddings, tarts, apple sauce, sometimes peach sauce, seasonal radishes, peppergrass, onions, cucumbers, boiled beet-root plain or in vinegar, coffee, never beer.

Supper: cold meats from dinner, dried or smoked beef, salt fish sweet cakes, sweetmeats, stewed peaches, pears and other fruits, apple sauce, sometimes peach sauce, seasonal radishes, peppergrass, onions, cucumbers, boiled beet-root plain or in vinegar, tea.

The twentieth century saw the opening of more and more boarding houses. By 1935, North Carolina had begun recovering from the Great Depression. In many towns, mills and factories re-opened, so men and women looking for work left their homes and migrated from neighboring rural areas. They needed a place to live.

Again, widowed women opened their homes to these workers. The typical residence, a large, unheated two-story house could accommodate as many as a dozen paying guests. The downstairs most often consisted of a parlor, dining room, kitchen, and the family's living quarters. The upstairs usually had four bedrooms with as many as three double beds in each—always two people to one bed. A bathroom at the end of the hall contained a toilet, sink, and tub, but no hot water. The cost to these textile workers: three to four dollars a week. This included three bountiful meals a day, served family style. Boarders helped themselves to bowls filled with vegetables, platters of meat, and baskets of homemade biscuits—all placed in the center of the table—hence the term, "boarding house reach."

The April 1908 issue of *The Ladies' Home Journal* offered several articles to assist women in their duties. "The Normal American Woman," "Summer Boarders," and "What Would You Do If Your Husband Died?" were geared to inform women, give them advice, and offer suggestions to make their lives a little easier. The advertisements in that issue of *Journal* strove to educate women concerning household chores, laundry practices, and sewing habits.

The lead article, "The American Girl," in the May 1908 issue of *LHJ* addresses the many responsibilities "the average American mother" faced. Other articles addressed subjects like "How to Make Vegetables Go Farthest" and "Personal Experiences Which Suggest New Ways to Increase an Income." Women—especially those who ran boarding houses—found kindred souls with whom they could identify.

One North Carolina boarding house, Old Kentucky Home, became famous when Thomas Wolfe fictionalized his mother's residence in his novel *Look Homeward, Angel*. The Thomas Wolfe Memorial State Historic Site staff has recently renovated and restored the original Wolfe house and re-opened it to the public.

During the twentieth century teacherages opened to accommodate unmarried females who taught in the local schools. Other boarding houses specialized in housing orphaned babies, baseball teams, prominent lawyers and judges, German prisoners of war, Scottish immigrants, university students, working girls during World War II, and other unique clientele.

Today, few North Carolina boarding houses remain. Anyone running a boarding house today must abide by the forty-three pages of single-spaced rules issued by the State. A few of the dictates governing boarding houses include:

5:27-4.2 Facilities

(a) Every boarding house shall contain a kitchen sink of nonabsorbent impervious material.

(b) Every...boarding house shall be provided with a minimum of one flush type water closet, lavatory, and a bathtub or shower for every eight persons....

(c) Every water closet, lavatory, and bathtub or shower shall be accessible from within the building without passing through any part of any other rooming unit and shall be located no further than one floor above or below the rooming units served, provided that no resident shall be without ready access to any such facility by reason of physical disability. Such water, lavatory and bathtub or shower shall be contained in a room or rooms which are separated from all other rooms by walls, doors, or partitions that afford privacy.

And the list goes on!

No wonder brick bank buildings and urban parking lots have replaced those long-ago structures. Gone also are the huge dining-room tables laden with turkey, dressing, candied sweet potatoes, green beans, and homemade biscuits. Gone are the crowded unheated bedrooms and shared baths. Gone, also, are the summer evening gatherings on the wrap-around front porch and the nudging of the proprietress who insists, "Now, how about another dish of hand-turned ice cream?"

Information for this piece comes from the following sources:
- Gift, Helen C. *Feeding Generations:Boarding House Fare and Family Oral Tradition.*North Carolina: Brevard, 2001.
- Watson, Alan D. "Ordinaries in Colonial Eastern North Carolina." *The North Carolina Historical Review.* January, 1968, Volume XLV, No. 1.
- "Ladies Home Journal" articles. April 1908 and May 1908.
- Internet printout of Amended 1981 Boarding House Rules and Regulations.

The naked chimneys of old Rockford mark the site today.

Rockford

Rockford's Early Boarding Houses

In earlier times, perhaps every structure in Rockford, called by whatever name— home, hotel, or inn—provided lodging and meals for guests. Research provides only sketchy profiles because early papers and documents do not reveal definitive information about the service or the servers of Rockford boarding houses. Historical and literary accounts present only snippets, so hopefully, the Rockford scenario will unwind without excessive poetic license.

This we do know: In 1789, the year George Washington became President of the United States, the North Carolina Assembly created Surry County and named Rockford as the county seat. A newly built wooden courthouse, constructed with nails made at the local forge, served those who came to this little northwestern North Carolina town to attend to county business.

Rockford citizens soon began offering various accommodations for the influx of judges, lawyers, and jurors who traveled by boat on the fluctuating Cape Fear River to decide legal matters at the Courthouse. Citizens throughout the state, interested in local political trends, mainly Whig-related, found traveling to Rockford for political rallies and public meetings more expedient than relying on newspapers of the day. These men needed lodging.

Rockford dates back to the earliest days of the nation.

The Grant Hotel, built in 1796, probably provided Rockford's first room and board. Rom Folger, who kept a journal of the early days of Rockford, tells the following story about the hotel proprietor, Reuben Grant, and one of his famous guests:

> *Grant had in his employ a boy by the name of Watson Holyfield, about the size of his own son (This was told me by said Holyfield, in his old age)...While he was staying with Grant, Aaron Burr on his return from a trip south, put up for the night with Grant, and seeing young Holyfield, offered to take him with him and give him an education, but the boy would not go.*

Rockford became a busy little town. A Masonic Hall lodge, now believed the oldest in northwest North Carolina, moved from Huntsville to Rockford in 1797; the original building still stands. Salesmen, called "drummers," arrived in Rockford to sell their wares. They boarded at the Grant Hotel, and often had to extend their stays because of the swollen river. Locals opened forges, where pig iron became wrought iron in furnaces and hearths; interestingly, the state capitol's iron fence came from metal forged at Rockford. As the town grew, so did the number of ferries, grist mills, tanneries, and taverns.

Mark York opened and ran the ever-popular York Tavern, providing a place for the gentlemen who came to Rockford to engage in conversation while they enjoyed their evening toddy, but not all adult beverages came from licensed establishments, according to an early account written by Rom Folger:

There lived south of the river an old man named Jenkins who, for some meritorious service to the county...was granted privilege of retailing "spirits" in small quantities without license. On Sunday evening before each court session one could see Jenkins winding his way through Rockford to the lot known as "the devil's half-acre." It was thus named because a "grog shop" was operated there by an old woman, and with its attendant evils [sic] the place was notorious. Early Monday morning Jenkins would procure four forked sticks, drive them in the ground, lay his crossed pieces on with a board on these, and, setting his jug and a half-pint cup on his improvised counter, he drew up a white flint stone upon which he sat and was ready for business...and anxious to wait upon the thirsty public.

In 1830 a brick courthouse replaced the earlier wooden structure. This new building, constructed on property overlooking the town and river, had offices on the ground level and a court room on the second floor. Lawyers built a row of log offices nearby.

Other professionals soon joined the lawyers. Dr. Milton Young Folger moved his practice of medicine to Rockford in 1844. Before his wife and children arrived by stagecoach to join him, records indicate that Folger boarded at the Grant Hotel. John Hamlin opened a general store and tobacco factory. In 1848 Judge Richmond Pearson founded Pearson Law School across the river from Rockford. Young law students lived in Rockford's private homes or boarded in a hotel owned by Col. Frank Armstrong, Clerk of the Court. The following documentation reveals details about the life of a slave once owned by Armstrong:

He [Armstrong] owned a young slave by the name of William Armstrong whom he depended on as waiter of tables, cook for special occasions and coach driver. According to William's grandson, Graham Armstrong, William remembered being sold three times on the steps at the courthouse in Rockford...William drove a coach which transported students to and from the Pearson School daily. It is said that William was allowed to sit in on sessions of school and that he listened to the students talking en route thus learning a great deal of law which came in good through the years. It is also said that Judge Pearson became quite fond of William and willed him a tract of land at Rockford.

[Later] William Armstrong bought land on the Rockford Road...where he operated a blacksmith shop and a small bar room. He later built a two-story log house on other land which he bought from an old lady called Aunt Tildie Barney.

A model of the Grant / Burrus Hotel.

She had a cabin on top of the hill where she sold brandy and whiskey, and it was a good place for a rest after pulling up the long hill from the river.

In 1850, the Assembly divided Surry County and named Dobson as the new county seat. Some residents moved to the new capitol, some left for more prosperous communities, and others went to the frontier land of Tennessee. The old courthouse eventually became The Rockford Male and Female Seminary to a hundred students, many of whom boarded in private residences.

Rockford men took their politics seriously. One story still circulates about an early political rally:

...one Mr. Settle, a Republican [had been designated] as speaker...and the Democrats were very unhappy because they did not have anyone to oppose him. And they were saying, "Oh, if we only had Joe Dobson!" A great whoop went up when they looked down the road and saw Mr. Dobson riding up on his horse, and they immediately demanded that their man be given time for speaking...Settle made his speech and Dobson followed. When he was about half way through, a man arose in the back of the court room and picking up his chair, walked down to the front of the speaker and set it down, saying, "Set down, Joe, you've done whupped him!"

Also in the late 1850's, William M. Norman, who had been a prisoner on Johnson Island during the Civil War, came to Rockford to board and study law in the home of Dr. Milton Young Folger. After marrying Miss Letitia Holyfield, he practiced law and also taught at the Rockford School. William Norman liked to tell this interesting true story about the War Between the States:

...some Union soldiers from an encampment some distance away...came to Rockford looking for a doctor to attend an officer who was seriously ill. They took Dr. Folger riding on his own good horse. He ministered to the sick man and was released, but he returned home on a poor horse much inferior to his own which had been confiscated. Little Molly Folger, who was at that time about six years old, never forgot the soldier who took her upon his knee and told her of his own little girl while waiting for Dr. Folger to get ready to accompany them.

As time passed, the Grant Hotel became the Burrus Hotel in 1890. Mr. John G. Burrus, the new owner, liked to tell visitors that the logs used in building the hotel's stable came from the torn-down law office of Andrew Jackson. Jackson often rode horseback from Tennessee to attend circuit courts in Rockford and had a law office across the street from the Burrus Hotel. In her book *The Story of Rockford,* historian Lucy Hamlin Houck reveals rumors of Jackson's "unpaid board bill...canceled after the Battle of New Orleans" and Dick Burrus, one of the heirs to the hotel, having "a pair of old ice skates with initials A. J. on them which are believed to have belonged to Jackson."

After the railroad arrived about 1890, the town boasted a busy station which served passengers and handled freight. Subsequently, townspeople opened various stores, built churches, and established a Rockford post office.

In 1907, the Rockford Academy Surry Association School opened. Frank and Elizabeth Bland offered room and board in their home to musically talented students from the private school. While Frank gave piano lessons and supervised practice sessions for recitals, Elizabeth took on a surrogate mother's role of providing comfortable beds, nutritious food, and loving attention.

While local documents, notebooks, and account books give only glimpses of boarding house life in Rockford, some significant details do surface. Central heat, indoor bathrooms, and kitchens, as we know them today, did not exist. At the Burrus Hotel, huge chimneys—with room-to-room open fireplaces—ran from basement to roof level. Today they tower like lonely giants amid the ruins of the building. In earlier days, servants prepared food and drink for boarders in a separate kitchen beside the main building. A double privy, the only facility available for guests, still stands behind the ruins of the old Burrus

Hotel. While the days of glory and commerce have long ago faded, the quaintness and beauty of Rockford remain.

The town of Rockford was placed on the National Register of Historic Places in 1976, and the Rockford Preservation Society, Inc. was organized in 1972 for the purpose of stabilizing and preserving the town. All of the properties owned by the Preservation Society, as well as many other privately owned properties, represent Rockford's unique history.

Information for this piece came from the following sources:
• All direct quotations and much valuable information came from Lucy Hamlin Houck's *The Story of Rockford.* 1972.
• Nickie Doyal and Alice E. Sink's tour of Rockford and Interview with Hannah Holyfield of the Rockford Preservation Society. September 26, 2003. Note: Just about every home we saw on this tour had at one time been a boarding house.

WANT TO GO?

Visitors to Rockford can enjoy looking at the antiques, candy, and odds-and-ends that fill the Rockford General Store. Operating Hours: Closed Tuesday; open Monday and Wednesday-Friday, 10 a.m. - 5 p.m.; and open Saturday, 10 a.m. - 6 p.m. and Sunday, 12 - 6 p.m. For more information, call 336-374-5317.

Southern Grits

l-cup course, stone-ground grits • 4 cups water
2-4 Tablespoons chicken-base paste • 2-4 Tablespoons butter
Milk or half-and-half, as needed.

Combine all ingredients. Cook over low heat for about an hour, stirring ocasionally. Cover and put into refrigerator overnight. The next morning, resume cooking. Add milk/half-and-half until desired consistency is reached or as needed. Cook over low heat for about an hour. Yield: 6-8 servings. From *Low Country Delights: Cookbook and Travel Guide*, Third Edition. Maxine Pinson & Malyssa Pinson. www. the food scoop.com.lcd.html. Phone (888) 717-4040.

Boarding Schools in Warrenton

As early as 1802, William and Sarah Falkener, London natives, moved to Warrenton and opened The Falkener School for the education of young women. The boarding school, located on the corner of Main and Franklin Streets, enjoyed success from the beginning. On December 17, 1804, The *Raleigh Register* printed Mrs. Falkener's advertisement, as follows:

YOUNG LADIES BOARDING SCHOOL

MRS. FALKENER Acknowledges with lively gratitude the Pleasure she received in the expressed Approbation of her pupils Improvements at their last public Recitations. She proposed to devote her attention the ensuing Year to such young ladies as may be confided to her Care; and assures the Parents and Guardians who may intrust their Children or Wards to her Management, that every exertion may be used toward accomplishing them in Literature, and moral and domestic economy. The first day of January next is fixed on for the Reception of Boarders and pupils; and as Mrs. F. has great Reason to expect a full School, she takes the Liberty of intimating that the earliest Applications will command Preference.

Warrenton, Dec. 10th, 1804.

The extraordinary Prices of Provisions compel a small Advance on what was formerly paid for board, etc. The terms will therefore be, for Board and Tuition one hundred and five dollars...one half of which must be paid at Entrance and the Remainder at the Expiration of six months.

The Falkener school proved a success and eventually required five assistants; however, by 1819, both Sarah and William had died, within a few months of each other, and the school closed.

In the meantime, Jacob and Judith Myers Mordecai had moved to Warrenton and made such unwise investments in tobacco they sought a new line of work. He signed on with the Steward's House of the Warrenton Academy and for two years managed the boarding aspect of this boys' school. In 1809 he opened his own school for girls, placing the following advertisement in the newspaper:

FEMALE EDUCATION IN WARRENTON

...I propose to open an instruction for female improvement, on the lst day of January next...The domestic arrangement for an efficient accommodation of my school will be an object of primary concern, and placed under the immediate inspection of Mrs. Mordecai. Believing it to be no small part of the education bestowed on females to cultivate a taste for neatness in their persons and propriety of manners, they will be placed under a superintendence calculated as much as possible to alleviate the solicitude of parents. In my Seminary will be taught the English language, grammatically; spelling; reading; writing; arithmetic; composition; history; geography, and the use of the globes...Terms for board, washing, lodging and tuition (drawing and music excepted) $105 per annum; an additional charge will be made for necessary books, paper, quills and ink.

Jacob Mordecai
Warrenton, August 18, 1808

N. B. Parents are requested to furnish a pair of sheets, a blanket, counterpane, and hand-towels; which without inconvenience to them will render the accommodation of their daughters more easy and comfortable.

Mr. and Mrs. Jacob Mordecai's luck again turned sour. Before they had completed even one year at the boarding school, the house he had bought in the center of town fell to the ground as the result of a violent wind storm. He rebuilt, and finally in April of 1811, with all new buildings completed, a fire consumed each and every one. According to historical records, "it was through the disobedience and carelessness of one of the [boarding pupils] that this calamity took place."

"It was the custom, and one of the inflexible rules of the school," the account says, "that at a certain hour a colored woman went to each room or dormitory to collect the lighted candles, and carry them below stairs. One young lady, engaged in sewing on a dress that she was anxious to complete, begged that the light might remain, but the servant would not consent. After she was left in the dark she remembered that she had brought a candle from home in her trunk; she had no candle-stick, so she stuck it in a hole in the wall between the laths, and while sewing she dropped off to sleep. The candle burned down, catching the laths on fire, and when the family were retiring an hour later they saw the wing in a light blaze.

Kind citizens of Warrenton, who sympathized with Mr. and Mrs. Mordecai, invited the girls to live in their homes. Dr. Glouster, friend of and physician to the Mordecais, offered his home as a temporary residence for many of the ninety girls who needed lodging. Mr. Oliver Fitts volunteered his residence as a new school which ultimately became the permanent home to Warrenton's Mordecai School. Mr. Jacob Mordecai's two daughters, Rachel and Ellen, and his son Solomon donated their services as teachers and soon joined other knowledgeable instructors in French, music, painting, drawing, and "plain and fancy stitch" sewing. Daughter Ellen also supervised the cooking and serving of meals.

Quaint customs and rules of the Mordecai School concerned daily hair care and are described as such: At a certain hour each pupil was required to go to the room of "Mammy," an old colored women, who lived in the old dormer windowed house. The pupil carried her own "fine-toothed" comb and brush, also a small wooden block with her name on it. Mammy carefully combed and arranged the hair, then dropped the block in a box to be later opened by Miss Ellen." If there were any delinquents they were called to task for it.

The primitive nature of the girls' morning bath rituals, described in detail, also causes one to wonder if the act of bathing actually involved torture: Each girl went to the well, in the yard, with her tin pan and towel, and took her bath, even when the water would freeze as it splashed on the well top.

Accounts of ancestors of former students reveal Jacob Mordecai's business sense after he had accepted his limit of ninety girls at the boarding school. One account vivifies his pragmatic attitude. Two of the girls boarding at the school had written home complaining about the poor food and meager servings. Their father decided to pay an unexpected call at the school, arriving at the mid-day dinner hour, and after careful observation believed the fare adequate—and made a point of telling Mr. Mordecai he had decided not to take his daughters home. Mr. Mordecai replied: "Yes, you will take them home, as I do not care to have such girls in my school."

When Jacob Mordecai discontinued his school in 1818, he moved to Richmond. During his ten years as boarding school owner, he had made a great deal of money, so he purchased a farm. He died in 1838. Another daughter, Caroline, stayed in Warrenton and married Achilles Plunkett, a teacher, in 1820. They opened another school in Warrenton about 1822. After Mr. Plunkett's death in 1824, Mrs. Caroline Plunkett and her stepson John D. Plunkett continued the school until 1829.

Mr. Oliver Fitts gave his home to Jacob Mordecai for use as a permanent boarding school after fire consumed the other one.

In 1828, when she was only eight years old, Ellen Mordecai, granddaughter of Jacob Mordecai, was sent by her stepmother to their Aunt Caroline's boarding school. Although Mrs. Caroline often showered her student boarders with kindness and affection, she also meted out discipline for those who refused to obey or to study diligently. She demanded perfection, insisting that her students memorize Murray's Grammar rules, learn geography by finding every city, lake, river, and mountain on the Eastern hemisphere, and recite French vocabulary words.

The three Mordecai offspring had become accustomed to a carefree plantation life in Raleigh, where their temporary governess, Miss Quincey, stressed art projects and could be persuaded to overlook prolonged childhood games of hide and seek and extended recesses. The children spent their summers planting vegetables, building playhouses from pines and saplings, going strawberry hunting, adopting a goose, and watching goslings hatch from eggs. In the fall the children played in the barn, helping unload wagons filled with corn. Autumn also saw them making traps, excitedly baiting them with meal husk and then waiting patiently until they caged a bird, only to release it to fly away. The Mordecai siblings enjoyed digging potatoes, gathering persimmons, and eating candy made from boiled and pulled molasses. In cold weather, when hog killing time kept adults busy shaping hams, salting shoulders, making lard, and cooking tenderloin and spareribs, the youngsters read or played inside by the fireplace.

In Warrenton, the Mondecai children met situations very different from their former plantation environment. Ellen relates one tragic incident—the death of Joanna Nunnery, one of the boarding school's most intelligent and well-liked students:

During a thunderstorm which came up while most of the girls had gone to dinner, a little girl, who had remained to do her sums, was leaning out of a window just by the chimney and a bright flash came, which killed her instantly. I will never forget that awful scene; the confusion, dismay, and grief.

Ellen did not return to school that day, but she witnessed from her aunt's boarding house, a procession of four men taking the child home. The image of Joanna's dead body, laid on a plank and covered with a sheet, always rushed to Ellen's mind every time she saw lightning.

Pleasant days at Aunt Caroline's, however, outweighed tragedies. Paying guests enjoyed peaches and nectarines from the Plunketts' orchard. Many of Warrenton's "odd characters" also added to the charm of the boarding house. One such regular, Old Nosey Clark, who sold eggs and butter to Mrs. Plunkett, always made a point of staying for breakfast and partaking freely of the very products he had just sold. Another character, nicknamed "Old Smiler" by the boarders, had a laugh that echoed from a mile away. In addition, Old Aunt Betty, a San Domingo native and servant to one of the boarders, talked about her native country and taught everyone how to produce beef jerky by following her special drying process.

Old Aunt Betty's mistress, Mrs. Burdette, a tall, slender French woman with dark eyes, earned a reputation of being rather different because she always walked with a cane and had a blanket wrapped around her flowing linen gown. She also kept her door key pinned in a handkerchief; the knotted wad resembled a rag doll, and Mrs. Burdette hugged this bundle to her, acting as though she cradled a living baby. Aunt Betty obviously understood her mistress' eccentric nature and treated her kindly. The children who boarded with Mrs. Caroline sometimes did not exhibit the same compassion. They loved to spy on Mrs. Burdette, a Catholic, as she fingered her rosary beads and uttered her prayers.

Although each Mordecai child received a superior education at the Warrenton school and kind and gentle care at their aunt's boarding house, they missed their Raleigh home and their step-mother (who, incidentally, was their deceased mother's sister). The big plantation house shaded by black-walnut trees and climbing roses, orchards of apple and peach trees, and gardens with both vegetables and flowers had provided a haven for the Mordecai youngsters to romp and play. Barns and stables, cow pens, and long rows of slave houses beckoned. Woods, branches, springs, and wild flowers transformed their acreage into a fairy land for these youngsters. They would return to Raleigh after only one year because in 1830, their aunt, Caroline Plunkett offered the boarding house and school for sale.

Information for this piece comes from the following sources:
• "Gleanings from Long Ago." The Raleigh Historic Properties Commission, Inc. and The Mordecai Square Historical Society, Inc., 1974.
• Montgomery, Lizzie Wilson. *Sketches of Old Warrenton North Carolina: Traditions and Reminiscences of the Town and People Who Make It."* Raleigh: Edwards & Broughton Printing Company, 1924.

Black-Eyed Pea and Butternut Squash Hash

1 large butternut squash
Salt and pepper, to taste
2 Tablespoons vegetable oil
2 Tablespoons butter
1 small onion (diced)
2 cups fresh or frozen black-eyed peas (boiled until tender)
2 cup cooked greens (your favorite)

After cleaning, peeling, and dicing squash, boil for 5 to 7 minutes in salted water until tender. Strain and cool. Place oil and butter in skillet or saute pan. Add onions and cook over medium high heat until translucent. Add butternut squash and cook approximately 5 minutes, stirring often. Add peas and chopped greens and cook about 5 minutes until heated throughout and tender. Season with salt and pepper to taste. Place in serving bowl or casserole dish. Keep warm until main course is ready. Yields: 4 servings
Cookbook editor's notes: For extra flavor cook greens and peas together with a ham hock or Goya's ham seasoning. Be sure to squeeze excess water from the greens; this will prevent them from being runny or soupy. Other vegetables may also be added, as desired. Corn and boiled (or roasted) peanuts are excellent additions. Recipe from *Lowcountry Delights: Cookbook and Travel Guide.* Third edition. Maxine Pinson and Malyssa Pinson. *www.thefoodscoop.com/Led.html* OR 1-888-717-4040

Pleasant Gardens
(Marion)

Carson House

In the early nineteenth century, stagecoach passengers rarely spoke on the pre-dawn run to Pleasant Gardens. If they did talk, they avoided taboo subjects of politics and religion. Most travelers rode sleeping straight up while being jostled in the swaying buggy because etiquette demanded they not droop their heads onto the shoulders of those seated beside them. They also could not spit on the leeward side or shoot at wild game along the way as it might scare the horses.

Pleasant Gardens, which stood midway between Asheville and Morganton—a forty-mile east to west trip—became a natural stopping place for stagecoaches to rest both horses and passengers. Owners Colonel John and Mary McDowell Carson welcomed travelers and ushered them inside their large home, offering them a hardy breakfast. Prepared and served by slaves, sausages, eggs, and biscuits satisfied the travelers' hunger. Those who stayed the night often slept two and three to a bed. Fully clothed and rolled in blankets to keep from touching another person, they followed a practice called "bundling." Some even preferred to sleep on the floor. Mary, who prided herself on being a gracious hostess to her guests, presided over the boarding house until her death in 1825.

John continued to run Carson House. He kept detailed accounts, as documented by the following entry:

On May 25, 1828, a C. J. and William Polk paid 37 1/2 cents for lodging and provisions, 25 cents for care of their horses, and 12 1/2 cents for the use of servants.

Records indicate that the Colonel's wealth did not come solely from his stagecoach boarding house. He also ran a tavern and involved himself in the affairs of his brothers' mining operations. One early census listed him as owning twelve slaves. Records also show that in 1806 Carson, as a member of the House of Commons, supported a bill "to prevent further importation of slaves and indentured servants, but the bill failed by a wide margin. Carson's support for the measure is likely explained, not by a desire to end the institution of slavery, but to prevent its spread and thereby protect his investment."

In addition to having money and owning servants, Carson possessed a good sense of humor. Various accounts point to his joviality, even in his eighties. Selina Louisa Lenoir recorded some of his antics in her 1832 diary:

Called at Colonel Carsons — looks young for a man of his age — Is a handsome old man. Talks of being lonesome — would like to get married. If every one was of my mind he would stay single I guess. (wicked, wicked Selina Louise).

One of Colonel Carson's friends, Thomas George Walton, praised him for his dignity, common sense, business acumen, sharp wit, and suave manner— all good qualities, and all accompanied with sarcasm. Sometime in the 1830's Carson hosted Walton and a group of friends who were traveling to Asheville for a wedding. "All being very jovial as befitted the occasion," Walton recalled, "a good part of the night was spent in rather boisterous revelry." The next morning Carson entered the room, lifted a violin as if beginning to play, and asked "Did you ever hear me play the violin?" Twice he repeated the question in a loud voice. Then he answered it himself, "Ho, and you never will," wheeled and left the room, savoring his joke.

On another occasion, one of the boarders asked John Carson if he knew that his hogs had gotten out of their pen and into the corn field. Carson replied, "Well, sir, let them ruin it, I don't suppose it will hurt the hogs."

Although tradition has placed John C. Calhoun, David Crockett, Sam Houston, Andrew Jackson, and Nathaniel Macon as boarders at the Carson House, according to historian Michael R. Hill, "evidence as to their visits to the house is sketchy and, in most cases, inconclusive." Possibly because one of Carson's sons, Samuel Price Carson, knew all five of these famous men, normal assumptions might be that they all visited; however, actual visits are unsubstantiated for Calhoun, Houston, and Macon. Because Davy Crockett had

Carson House likely hosted notables such as Davy Crockett.

western North Carolina connections through his father and his second wife hailed from Swannanoa, Crockett's biographer believes Crockett likely visited the Carsons.

Furthermore, Andrew Jackson's early years in western North Carolina, where he practiced law, could have placed him in Pleasant Garden, where he allegedly engaged in horseracing and cockfighting activities. Any trips Jackson made there, though, would have occurred in the late 1790's before Carson House was built.

When John died March 5, 1841, just weeks before his eighty-ninth birthday, the house and farmlands became the property of his son Logan and Logan's wife, Mary Sturdivant Presnell Carson (called Mary S.).

Because Logan had grown up in an environment of strangers at Pleasant Gardens, he felt comfortable inviting travelers into his home. He and Mary S. renovated the house, and in 1843 the residence became the county seat for the newly-formed McDowell County before the construction of a courthouse. Logan and Mary S. doubled previous rates. Now it cost a man and his horse $1.50 per day, $7 per week, and $25 per month to board. According to historian Michael R. Hill, boarders stayed in the house throughout the years it was owned by J.L. (Logan) Carson. In 1850 boarders included a carpenter, a railroad engineer, a blacksmith, a physician, and a mulatto woman and her three children.

In 1856 Logan and Mary S. made more extensive additions to the house. They added eight more rooms surrounded by a wide porch. They planted bulbs and flowers and boxwood, constructed a rock wall, and laid out attractive walking paths. By 1859 Pleasant Gardens earned travel guidebook praise. Logan and Mary S. made Carson House into a well-appointed mountain resort. People

Davy Crockett (left) and Andrew Jackson (right) both may have stayed at Carson House, though evidence to support the claim is inconclusive.

needing healing powers flocked to Pleasant Gardens to enjoy a sulfur spring located two miles from the house and landscaping described in *The North Carolina Standard* as "an earthly Eden."

"We find a stopping-place at Mr. Logan Carson's," the magazine said. "This is a lovely spot. Nature did much, but the hand of art and taste has beautified full well...This house is situated immediately upon the banks of the Buck Creek, one of the prettiest mountain steams to be found anywhere."

Author Henry Colton concurred when he wrote about his stay at the Carson's, saying here is where "the seeker for health may sojourn with comfort and benefit...About two miles up the creek is a fine Sulfur Spring. We have never seen any place which conveyed as good an idea of perfect repose as this."

The Eden concept, however, would be interrupted by the Civil War. After 1861, the war's effects on the economy curtailed business. Patrons did not have the money or desire to travel. Mary and Logan's youngest daughter Margaret was six when the war began.

"I stood in the yard and saw the Buncombe regiment go by our old home," she recalled. "I stood on the porch and waved my little flag. They stopped and took off their caps and waved a salute to my flag. I never forgot it."

At the onset of the war, Logan and Mary turned the stagecoach inn into a private girls' boarding school and hired Emma Lydia Rankin as teacher.

Miss Rankin wrote about the encounters during the winter of 1864-65 between Union soldiers, herself, her students, and the Carson family. The diary entries recount the wartime fears of the residents:

"The invading army in a constantly narrowing circle approached us. We had thought it highly improbable that a blue-coat would ever be seen in our secluded region, but rumors of raids and marauders came thick and fast during the last winter of the war. Kirk's men were plundering in the counties adjoining us, and had come down within ten or even five miles of us. We began to hide our clothes and to arrange our valuables when we retired as to best protect them in

case of a dash in the night. In the early spring of '65 it was confidently reported that the Yankees were coming both from the east and the west."

When the Carson household heard of the impending appearance of Union soldiers, Logan, the head of the household, was sent into hiding. Although he tried to protest, the women believed they and the children—seen as unprotected and at the mercy of the enemy— would be safer. Emma Rankin recorded the events of the day Union soldiers occupied Carson House:

"...the horrid bluecoats were swarming in and through and around the house. We stood in the front door, hoping to keep them out, but when we looked back, they were pouring in the back door, and every other door and window. They rushed past us and up the stairs and in every room. Every office and out house seemed to be full of them, and still they came...The pantry was bare as old Mother Hubbard's cupboard. Most of the meat had been taken out of the smoke- house, and what was left was thrown down on the floor and a barrel of vinegar poured over it and then covered with dust and ashes. It was some consolation that the next set that came along took this same meat and ate it."

After Miss Rankin's death, her brother-in-law released in 1900 her first-hand report of Stoneman's Raid to the *Charlotte Semi-Weekly Observer.*

A number of years after the war, prosperity returned to Carson House. After Logan's death in 1866, Mary S. continued working to re-establish the resort. She ran the popular mountain boarding house until 1874. Harriett Vance, who spent the summer of 1869 with the Carson's, wrote the following to a cousin in Ohio:

"I am boarding and have leisure enough. It is a delightful summer resort. There is a beautiful stream of water running just out side [sic] the yard, so clear that we can see the peebles [sic]. The boys do enjoy the wading, fishing &C there are several families boarding in the house besides much transient customers. We have a nice time. It's very quiet—just enough to suit me...."

Sometime after 1874, Mary S. left Pleasant Gardens and moved in with one of her married daughters. She continued to be listed as a farmer in McDowell County until 1890 and also bought and traded land into the early 1900's. She died in 1908 at the age of 96.

Information for this piece comes from the following sources:
• Hill, Michael R. "Historical Research Report: The Carson House of Marion, North Carolina." Chapel Hill. August 15, 1982.

- Various brochures from Carson House and correspondence with Margaret Fretwell and Anne Swann of McDowell County and Carson House.
- Handwritten account of Emma Rankin, teacher at a girls' boarding school which operated in Carson House during the Civil War. The copy was transcribed from the original book in which the story appears. The book is very old and worn and is the property of The Carson House.

WANT TO GO?

Carson House, located at 1805 Highway 70 W, Marion, N.C., is listed on the National List of Historic Places and is open for tours between May and October. A cane, inscribed "Presented to Col. John Carson by Gen. Andrew Jackson—Growth of the Hermitage," is displayed in the Carson House. Telephone (704) 724-4948. Open: Tuesday-Saturday, 10-4. Nearby attractions include Mountain Gateway Museum, North Carolina Mining Museum, and Old Fort Railroad Museum.

COUNTRY HAM
1 12-20 pound ham
1 cup brown sugar
1 cup apple cider vinegar

Trim and wash a twelve to twenty pound ham and soak overnight. Discard water and add one cup of apple vinegar and one cup of brown sugar. Cover with water. Boil very slowly for 5-6 hours, until bone is loose. Leave ham in water until cool. Skin ham and put in baking pan. Bake until brown. (*Recipe from* North Carolina Plantation & Historic Homes Cookbook, *published and distributed by Aerial Photography Services, Inc., Charlotte, N.C.*)

Raleigh

Haywood Hall

Elizabeth (Eliza) Eagles Asaph Williams Haywood, widow of John Haywood, first North Carolina state treasurer, needed to support herself and her ten living children after the death of her husband, age 72, in 1827, so she opened a boarding house in her 211 New Bern Avenue home built about 1800. A notice in the May 15, 1829, Raleigh *Register* announced her new venture:

Mrs. John Haywood, respectfully announces to the Public, that she is prepared to accommodate Travellers—Gentlemen & their Families—Boarders by the day, week, month or year — School children for any length of time —Her House is situated in the immediate vicinity of the Capitol, the Banks and the several Seminaries of Learning. There is a beautiful and highly cultivated Garden attached to it; her Rooms are spacious and airy. She assures all those who may honor her with their patronage that no exertions shall be wanting on her part to render them comfortable. Mrs. H. has also a good Stable, which shall be well supplied with Provender for Horses, and its careful Order to attend them. Prices as moderate as those of any Boarding house in the city.

Raleigh, May 14.

Two years later, Mrs. Haywood printed special cards—probably distributed privately— cordially inviting members of the legislature to board at Haywood Hall.

John Haywood's portrait hangs over the fireplace in Haywood Hall.

Mrs. John Haywood

IS prepared to accommodate TWENTY FIVE OR THIRTY Members of the Legislature. She assures all those who may honor her with their patronage, that no exertions shall be spared to make them comfortable. Mrs. H. has a number of detached rooms, besides those in the main building.

N. B. The favor of early application is requested.

August, 1831

Mrs. H. continues to receive Travellers and Boarders by the Week, Month or Year.

Apparently these calls for boarders brought paying guests to Haywood Hall. One letter written by David L. Swain to his wife mentions the accommodations of Haywood Hall. "Mrs. Haywood's accommodations, along with E. P. Gion's Hotel...were favorite boarding houses among the legislators," Swain related. Sketchy records in the Ernest Haywood Papers reveal the last names of thirty-six boarders, and the amounts they paid for lodging and food. Prices varied, with "24 @ 80 cts. per day, 2 @ 85 cts. per day, 5 @ 75 Cents, 4@$1, and Stanly's servant @50 cts per day." Haywood also noted that receipts would average "$29.15 a day and 'Mother will make by the session with good luck $1599.25.' " Expenditures included paying "...Toby for Tables $5 — Mrs. Mullen, bed rent 11 — man for white washing 3."

Why did Eliza Haywood, wife of one of the most prestigious men in Raleigh, a gracious hostess and avid gardener during her husband's lifetime, desperately need funds after his death? The answer to that question, though straightforward and simple, also leaves a trail of more unanswered "why's." According to one source, at his death in 1827, John Haywood, "... had embezzled nearly $70,000, (and) deprived the family of most of its wealth." The State sued Haywood's estate to recover the missing funds. How could this have happened?

The answer becomes complicated. According to one historian, "There was not then, nor has there ever been found an explanation for the missing funds," so no one will ever know exactly what happened. Most printed sources, however, agree on the circumstances. After Haywood's death, a committee who examined his accounts found $68,906.80 missing, and the State of North Carolina seized all his land, personal property, and slaves to settle the debt. Records show that Eliza received "one-fourth of the proceeds from the sale of Haywood lands, with which she re-purchased certain slaves as well as the reversionary interest in the house and lot, which cost $1,000.00."

John Haywood, a great statesman and esteemed gentlemen, who had served forty years as State Treasurer, had endeared himself to both politicians and local citizens. As one of the first trustees of the University of North Carolina, he served faithfully on various important committees, helped design the seal for this institution, and pledged and contributed financial support to this school of higher learning.

What had gone wrong? According to one State website, "Haywood's handling of the public funds was so haphazard that long after numerous banks were established, he continued to keep a trunk full of cash in the 'Public Chest' in his office which was used to pay the expenses of government. The accounting of these cash funds was notoriously inadequate by today's procedures."

Thus Eliza, always sickly and extremely dependent upon her slaves for both house and garden work, had to acquire money. The most effective means involved opening her home, Haywood Hall, to boarders. Married to John when she was only seventeen (and he, forty-two) and later the mother of twelve children, Eliza chose boarding house management as a way to support herself and her children because at this time she perceived it to be reputable, safe, and profitable. According to one historian, "The legal status of women in the nineteenth century made widowhood a particularly difficult condition. Unless farseeing arrangements were made for the wife and children in a husband's will, the plight of the widow, rich or poor, was often desperate." Early penciled notes indicate that Eliza first charged her older children for room and board, possibly as a way for them to glean much-needed funds from what remained of their father's estate.

Eliza kept a written record of the people who boarded with her at Haywood Hall, the length of time they stayed, what they ate, and whether they brought servants and/or horses. According to her copious notes, lodging with one or two meals and care of the horses averaged about eighty-five cents daily. Haywood Hall, located about a block and a half from the State Capitol, became a convenient place for statesmen to live. The classical style double front porch, interior wainscoting, beaded weatherboarding, impressive chimneys, and stone foundation made this Federal Period house an impressive home-away-from-home for politicians who traveled to Raleigh on business. A wide entrance hall opened on the right, into a paneled parlor with hand-carved moldings and mantel and, on the left, to a twenty-by-thirty foot great room with large fireplace. The dining room had a double fireplace with foodwarmers, and, interestingly, a screen at one end of the room where "ladies could retire." Carved pineapples and apples in interior woodworking represented symbols of the genteel hospitality extended to all guests. Although servants prepared all food in the detached kitchen of Haywood Hall, two pantries (one with hooks in the ceiling to cure meat) flanked the parlor and hallway of the main house.

A wide paneled staircase led to the second floor and four bedrooms where boarders stayed. The third floor, divided into two parts, served as a dormitory for Eliza and her children. As noted in Eliza's invitation to members of the legislature, a number of attached rooms would also serve as bedrooms for guests. During John Haywood's life, he had constantly remodeled, upgraded, and

Elegance was the word for Raleigh's Haywood Hall, exemplified by the foyer.

enlarged the 211 New Bern Avenue residence, built or moved additional buildings on the property, and decorated the interior of their home.

Apparently John and Eliza favored green dinner plates, green curtains and venetian blinds, and green fabrics, a color that apparently complimented the whitewashed walls and red hearths. Rag rugs and more exquisite Brussels carpets covered the floors. Many of these furnishings, including walnut or mahogany tables, desks, beds, and sideboards—in addition to fine sterling silver and china—had to be sold to repay the State of North Carolina for John Haywood's deficit, so the richness of the furnishings would have already diminished by the time Eliza's first boarders appeared.

During John's tenure as treasurer, the Haywood's lavishly entertained state officials who gathered in Raleigh for annual sessions of the General Assembly. John, himself, recorded in a 1798 letter to his wife (then away visiting her mother), "the Governor and his Council took what is called pot-luck at our House...We gave them Ham, Beef, fried Chickens, Chicken Pie, roast Beef, Peas, Beans, Greens & Lettuce, with a Pudding...some Raisons & some Almonds."

That same year, Eliza wrote to her mother a letter about her busy, and obviously exhausting life as hostess:

"Mr. H. invited, 30, Gentlemen to Dinner. Six and Twenty at the Long Table and four at a side Table—and that has been the Number every other Day since until Saturday last, which finished the first going through with the Assembly Men, but on Sunday following he had a Pick'ed set of Thirty— consisting of Members and Transient People, at an Elegant Dinner...I am almost worn out and Brok [sic] Down with Fatigue...I am up every Night till Twelve or one Oclock at Night...and the Federal Court meets the first of January and I shall have the same Trouble over again..."

In addition to attendance at the General Assembly, people traveled to Raleigh for other activities, including cockfighting and horseracing. One of John Haywood's letters to his wife, indicates that a particular cockfight attracted "from one to two hundred people...where the stakes were as high as $100." Horse races at the Raleigh race ground often lasted as long as three days and presented winners with large sums of money.

Invited guests at Eliza and John's home would probably have conversed about the General Assembly's relief bills following droughts, hurricanes, and severe hail storms plaguing North Carolina from 1807-1820 and their fear that many farmers would head west to avoid more disasters and damages.

Eliza's extensive hostess experience with legislators and state officials prepared her well for subsequent boarding house managerial duties, but after the court-ordered sale of Haywood assets, the interior of the house lacked the elegance of past days. Because of this, Eliza rented beds from neighbors and in a perfectly legal manner, purchased some of her former furnishings from her husband's estate. According to historical reports, Eliza, whose constitution weakened as the days and months passed, always feared losing her home. She received comfort from her brother-in-law, who assured her in a letter, "The law of the land *will* protect you, and the Legislature, even if it was disposed, (which it is not) could not turn you out of your House, or strip you." Though Eliza's health deteriorated even more after John's death, and as her days and her work load became heavier, she liberated three of her slaves, Ned, Sally, and Mozes "for their meritorius services." However, she retained Ned with "a reasonable compensation."

Statesmen who boarded with Eliza at Haywood Hall after John's death would have engaged in heated conversations about their genuine concerns

Rev. John Chavis

surrounding the August 21, 1831, Nat Turner insurrection in Virginia. Although news of the murders did not reach Raleigh for several days, local slave owners began to fear their own servants would rise against them.

Then, when slaves in two North Carolina counties rose against their owners, citizens of Raleigh met on September 13, 1831, and organized a senior group called the Silver Grays to secure the town. These volunteers agreed to ring the bell at the Presbyterian Church in the event of an uprising, so women and children could proceed immediately to the safety of the church. When the Raleigh fire brigade rang this same bell one night to announce a fire in the blacksmith shop, scores of women and children wearing nightshirts scurried to the church.

Topics of dinner conversation at Eliza Haywood's table usually included the General Assembly. Of particular interest was a possible piece of legislation that would prevent African Americans from advocating insurrection from the pulpit. Other topics of conversation most likely included a new fervor in Raleigh for church revivals among Methodist, Baptist, and Presbyterian congregations; local biracial churches with separate sections for slaves; annual Methodist and Baptist camp meetings, when families camped in tents for a week of services and religious experiences; and Reverend John Chavis, a free Negro minister who had opened an integrated school in Raleigh in 1808. As late as 1830 Chavis was praised as "the respectable teacher for the high degree of attainment the students had reached."

Talk of the June 21, 1831 fire that destroyed the statehouse most likely merited the most attention from the statesmen living at Haywood Hall. On Thursday, June 23, The Raleigh *Register* ran the following headline and article:

Guests enjoyed shaded balconies.

**Awful Calamity!
Destruction of the Capitol of North Carolina**
Awful Conflagration!
It is our painful and melancholy duty again to announce to the public, another appalling instance of loss by fire, which will be deeply felt and lamented by every individual in our State. It is nothing less than the total destruction of the Capital of the State, located in this City! Of that noble edifice, now with its splendid decorations, nothing now remains but the blackened walls and smoldering ruins! The State Library is also entirely consumed, and the statue of WASHINGTON, that proud monument of national gratitude, which was our pride and glory, is so mutilated and defaced, that none can behold it but with mournful feelings....

Questions about the future would have consumed statesmen residing in Haywood Hall, and their conversations at dinner most likely focused on that topic: Would the capitol remain in Raleigh and Wake County, or move to another city and county? When would the decision be announced? Did anyone salvage from the fire any important papers and records? Could an expert repair the statue of Washington? Did officials suspect arson? These men and all citizens would have to wait until December of 1832 for answers. However, Eliza Haywood died on July 19, 1832, six months before officials announced definitive plans concerning the State Capitol.

Very soon after Eliza died, her oldest child, Betsey John, now thirty-three years old, took over management of the boarding house and also assumed responsibility for her younger siblings. Betsey John and her gentlemen boarders would read in the December 28, 1832, Raleigh *Register* news which they had so eagerly awaited. The General Assembly had passed a bill that appropriated $50,000 for rebuilding the capitol on its original site. An editorial that same day offered excited optimism.

"This decision will go far to dissipate the cloud which, for more than a year, has hung over the prospects of our community," it read, "and serve to gild the future with the sunshine of hope. Fresh energy will be infused into the breasts of our citizens, who will now set about repairing their heavy losses with promptitude and spirit."

The editorial concluded by inviting members of the Legislature to celebrate this glorious decision to rebuild the capitol building. When the men and their guests arrived at the City Hotel, they were met with huge wall transparencies, designed by artist Alfred S. Waugh, one of which depicted a drawing of a giant eagle above a sketch of the new Capitol building. The Raleigh *Register* of January 4, 1833, reported the gala event. "The assemblage of ladies was brilliant," it said, "the Music good and the Supper splendid."

In the early 1830's, Betsey John began making plans to close the boarding house and open a private girls' day school at Haywood Hall, hoping this new venture would afford more time with her youngest sibling, Edmund Burke, who had been only seven years old when his mother died. By 1835 she had twenty-seven pupils enrolled. But her brother, Fabius, thought that Betsey could earn more money by expanding her day program into a boarding school. Subsequently, in 1841 he purchased Haywood Hall from their mother's estate, and Betsy John made Haywood Hall into a full-time boarding school.

Two grown brothers, William and Thomas, moved out of the house because, according to one relative, "grown young men cannot live with you." The family lived on the second floor and the female students stayed on the third floor. An outbuilding on the property became the schoolhouse. Betsey John supervised the primary grades of the boarding school, and her sister Frances Ann taught the older girls. Accolades abounded because of Betsey John's "well-known intellectual and social abilities, and the prominence and accomplishments of the entire Haywood family, contributed toward making hers one of the more fashionable private schools to which families in many sections of the state sent their daughters."

Betsey John, an intelligent woman interested in writing, music, and current events, had earlier earned a sterling scholarly reputation. In 1858 she received an unusual request from one of her deceased father's friends, former governor Charles Manley. After illness struck Manley, he asked Betsey to write the speech he would give at the University of North Carolina's graduation ceremony. According to one historian, "This was an extraordinary request. Manly believed a woman capable of writing a speech for the commencement ceremony of a school which did not admit women as students until decades later."

Betsey John's response shows her intelligence and tact. "Truly I think sickness has improved you. Your weapons are well kept highly burnished and ready for use. I am resolved to be avenged on you for ridiculing me—you have an inexhaustible mine of red ore which I am determined you shall work without my aid. I may condescend to give you a few hints at a future day but even this is doubtful. Thus you see what you have to expect. I lay my demands on you: haste get well and prepare that speech."

An interesting aside concerns the many family members who participated in various - and often ingenious - plans to save Haywood Hall so Betsey and John could keep her boarding school open and escape the indignities of having to sell the family home. Apparently Betsey John did her best to keep the house repairs up to date, but Haywood Hall obviously faced more repairs than she could handle. Alfred Haywood referred to the house as "nothing but an old Wooden Pile, liable to [be] consumed by Fire at any Time." For many years, Betsey John and her sister lovingly tended to their mother's garden; however, that, too, fell to neglect.

When Frances died in 1883 and left an estate valued at a mere five hundred dollars, Betsey John realized their venture had been one of dedication rather than money-making. She closed the boarding school soon after her sister's death. Her own health declined over the years, and she died in February 1877, having accumulated debts to friends, relatives, and acquaintances totalling thousands of dollars. One of those debts, of over five thousand dollars, resulted in a complex and unpleasant lawsuit. Her baby brother Burke, whom she had reared, remained executor of her will, paid her debts, and saw that Haywood Hall remained in the family.

Following Eliza's death, her brother Burke wrote her obituary: "Miss Eliza Eagles Haywood was born Dec. 8th 1798 at Holly Shelter New Hanover County N.C. Died at Raleigh, N.C. Feby 21st 1877, of compression of the Brain from Serious effusion, in the 79th year of her life, at about 8 ock P.M. Funeral to take place at Raleigh, N.C. at 4 1/2 ock P.M. Feby 23rd 1877. A woman of many sorrows and acquainted with grief."

Information for this piece came from many sources:
• Nickie Doyal's visit to Haywood Hall and conversation with various docents, Resident Manager, Susan D. LeVere, and Mrs. Marshall Haywood.
• Smith, Margaret Supplee and Emily Herring Wilson. *North Carolina Women Making History*. Chapel Hill: University of North Carolina Press, 1999.

• *A Doorway On the Past: Haywood Hall*. Brochure published by The Friends of Haywood Hall, Inc.
• City of Raleigh. *www.raleighnc.gov*
• *"John Haywood-North Carolina Department of State Treasurer."* www.nctreasurer.com
• Stearns, Walter M. "Haywood Hall." Wake County Committee of the North Carolina Society of the Colonial Dames of America. 1948.
• Giggs, Linda Mackie. "Haywood Hall." Volume l: Text and Volume III: Appendices D-T." Chapel Hill: North Carolina Division of Archives and History.
• Murray, Elizabeth Reid. *Wake: Capital* [sic] *County of North Carolina*. Volume I. Raleigh: Capitol County Publishing Company. 1983.

WANT TO GO?

Discover the history in Haywood Hall and the beauty of its gardens. Hours: 10:30-1:30 every Thursday. Haywood Hall is closed at the end of December through February for refurbishing. The gardens are open all year. For more information about special tours and the availability of Haywood Hall for private meetings, weddings and receptions, luncheons and other civic and social events, call (919) 832-8357 or (919) 832-4158, or write The Friends of Haywood Hall, Inc., 211 New Bern Place, Raleigh, N.C. 27601. There is no charge for admission.

Potato Pancakes

4 large Idaho potatoes, peeled • 1 cup heavy cream
1 egg, beaten • 1 Tablespoon garlic, minced
2 Tablespoons fresh chives, finely diced
1 Tablespoon fresh oregano, finely diced
Salt and pepper, to taste
Vegetable oil

Shred potatoes into large shreds; use a box grater and shred directly into bowl, keeping potato juice. Stir in next 6 ingredients. To make cakes a uniform size, hand pack mixture into a ramekin (or use a scoop). Heat vegetable oil in bottom of skillet until sizzling. Add cakes and cook over medium high heat until brown on each side. Drain on paper towels.

Cookbook editor's notes: delicious topped with creme fraiche flavored with freshly chopped chives and a dash of lemon juice. (Recipe from *Lowcountry Delights: Cookbook and Travel Guide*. Third Edition. Maxine Pinson and Malyssa Pinson). *www.thefoodscoop.com/Lcd.html* OR 1-888-717-4040.

Chapel Hill

The Houses of the Hill

The first mention of a Chapel Hill boarding house comes in a May 3, 1795, letter from John and Ebenezer Pettigrew to their father Charles Pettigrew, in which the young men, both students at the University, write about their need to find a new boarding house for the fall term because their present landlords will be moving to "Caintucky" the first of September.

Mr. and Mrs. Kimbel are going from home...his other business is so that he cannot attend to boarder...and will want to settle with you for the bed and bedclothes which he says he will let us have untill that time, and also for our washing which Mrs. Kimbel says she will have done at the rate of three pounds a year, and I supose we shall have to take a room in the College which will amount to 5 dollars a year each.

Two years later, on June 27, 1797, John Pettigrew writes, in a letter to his father, about withdrawing from his geography class and his desire to end his studies and come home. He has recently had a case of mumps and cannot study because of all the inconveniences. John described in detail the bedbugs which plagued him. *"The Chinches [foul-smelling bugs that damage wheat, corn, and other grain] or what we call Sabines have increased & multiplied, & become so numerous, that in the late engagements which they have had with us, they have quite defeated us & obliged us to retreat from our rooms which they hold the entire possession of at night; none of the room-mates have been able to sleep in my room for upwards of three weeks & it is nearly the case with respect to all the rest; as for my part I generally spread the tables in the passage & pour water around their feet, by which means I escape them as they are in general bad swimmers."*

In the same letter John also responds to his father's earlier request concerning student conduct. He writes, *"The Students in general have nothing very criminal in their conduct excep a vile & detestable practice of cursin & swearing, which has become very fashionable here, there can hardly be a sentence spoken without some of those highflown words which sailors commonly*

Early student lodging was far from luxurious.
(Photo: North Carolina Collection, University of North Carolina Library at Chapel Hill)

use to divert each other." He concludes by informing his father that if he and his brother must remain in college, they needed to move to a place where they could get a good night's sleep. He suggests Mr. Puckets, the only place he deems fit.

Ironically, about the time John Pettigrew complained about his accommodations, Pleasant Henderson, steward of the University, sought to remedy on-campus dining experiences. He vowed to accomplish the following goals: *"Breakfast, to furnish each Student...a sufficient quantity of good milk or good Coffee, and Tea, or Chocolate and Tea, together with a warm Roll or loaf of Wheat or Corn Flour...and a sufficient quantity of butter. Dinner, a Dish or Cover of Bacon and Greens, or Beef and Turnips...with fresh Meats or Fowls or Puddings and Tarts; and Supper (served before or after Candle light as the*

Faculty shall direct), a sufficiency of Coffee Tea or Milk...with Bread or Biscuit—And to furnish also Potatoes and all other kinds of vegetable food usually served up in Carolina—And to cause that the Tables be covered every other day with clean Cloths."

Finally on March 24, 1810, Rules on Student Board became official by the decree: "Be it ordained by the Trustees of the University of North Carolina and it is hereby ordained by the authority of the same, that no student shall be permitted to board at any house in the Village without previously obtaining at each session the written approbation of the President of the Institution."

Faculty, who agreed to shop in the village, buy homes, and attend the same church services as the students, helped create ties and ethical behavior, creating the earliest blending of town and gown.

In 1827, University Board of Trustee members appointed a financial superintendent and paid him five hundred dollars annually to make sure students paid their tuition and fees, of which one dollar each month would go back to him for pocket money. The superintendent also assumed responsibility of visiting all rooms at least once a week to check for any damages to the property. If on-campus rooms filled, the superintendent had to pay to board students in various homes in the Village. The Board, who wanted students to wear clothes that looked "decent in appearance and cheap in value," also stipulated exactly what they could and could not wear ("white pantaloons and waistcoat in the summer and coats, pantaloons, and waistcoat during winter months"). Furthermore, officials prohibited students from wearing boots of any type.

An August 6, 1832, letter from Charles L. Pettigrew to his father, Ebenezer Pettigrew, gives a good picture of boarding and academic life at the University:

"I have entered college and am about to recite my first lesson on ancient geography. I have taken up my board at the same place where uncle James boards which is the best place in the village. It is a very good house and I think I shall board as long as I stay here...there is a drought in this part of the country and it is thought there will not be more than half crops made there...I have to study very hard but nevertheless I have adopted the plan of not eating much and taking regular exercise. We recite three lessons every day, one in the morning and another at eleven o'clock."

While letters reveal interesting facts about the Village boarding houses, the real breakthrough came in 1997, when a press release from UNC News Services announced the recent discovery of one of the old boarding houses. Digging in the dirt unearthed remains of a mysterious building on the University of North Carolina at Chapel Hill campus in late June," the report proclaimed,

"...and digging through dusty records in Hillsborough in late July solved the mystery of the building's purpose. The structure housed UNC students between roughly the 1830s and 1850s as a privately owned dormitory. Young residents dubbed their home-away-from-home 'The Poor House.'"

The Poor House

Soon the mystery of Chapel Hill's earliest boarding houses began to unwind. The property, near Franklin Street, was sold by Jones Watson to Abner Roberson in 1847. The deed mentions dilapidated brick offices. In 1845, when the property changed hands again, the new deed referred to the brick buildings as "the Poor House." According to one news service, "Students gave these buildings quaint names such as 'Pandemonium,' 'Bat Hall,' 'Crystal Palace,' 'Opossum Quarter,' and 'The Poor House.'" Archaeologist Dr. Stephen Davis, and graduate student Tricia Samford, involved in the eight-week excavation, became more and more curious about "The Poor House." Their research indicated that these brick buildings next to campus actually consisted of not one house, but a row of buildings, privately constructed by local residents to board students—not indigent people, as the name of the building might suggest—during the housing shortage in the 1840's and 1850's.

While digging, archaeologist Dr. Tom Maher and his students discovered

For much of its existence, Chapel Hill was just a sleepy village, as seen in ths photo by Foster, of Richmond, Virginia.
(*Photo: North Carolina Collection, University of North Carolina Library at Chapel Hill*)

plow scars indicating farmers plowed and planted the land, probably in the early 1800s. Higher up they found many fragments of broken stoneware jugs, clay pipes, dishes and other objects dating as far back as about 1830. A curious copper artifact shaped like a fan and dating before the Civil War appears to have been a ground for a lighting rod attached to a chimney. Closer to the surface, they unearthed horse and mule shoes, nails, window glass, shotgun shells and intact bottles dating to the turn of the century, when the Phi Delta Theta fraternity house stood on the site.

Graduate student Samford continued her research of The Poor House, discovering a letter written by Thomas Brown. As a freshman at the University in 1853, Brown wrote about living "in a quiet brick row building in front of the campus." He probably described one of the earliest boarding houses, which ran east and west from McCorkle Place to the University United Methodist Church and just behind the current Pettigrew Building.

The Village of Chapel Hill

As early as 1795, students lived in boarding houses and accommodations that ranged from homey and comfortable to bug infested and miserable. University trustees attempted to regulate boarding by declaring certain houses off limits and by setting a ceiling on the rates that could be charged. They also attempted to prevent the students from accumulating debts with local merchants. Disorder and vice—especially alcohol—attracted the interest of some students. The trustees battled this on many fronts. Among their methods were limiting the hours students could be off campus, requiring students to deposit their funds with the bursar, lobbying the General Assembly to prohibit the sale of liquor in and near Chapel Hill, and asking parents to encourage their sons to obey regulations designed to preserve them from temptation.

Because train travel did not exist until 1833, students took a stage coach on muddy, rutted roads to Hillsborough and then walked or rode horseback the twelve miles to Chapel Hill. One student, Solomon Lea, rode his horse from Leasburg to Hillsborough, a journey of four-and-one-half hours. Solomon wrote a letter to his brother on September 14, 1832, relating his arrival in Hillsborough, where he met with Mr. Bryant Kittrell, who took in student boarders.

In a May 26, 1837, letter to his sister Emma (back home in Mount Prospect/Edgecomb), Kenelm H. Lewis writes about specific University costs of eleven dollars per month for food, thirty-one dollars for tuition, ten dollars for bed and washing, sixteen dollars for fuel and candles, two dollars to hire a servant to clean his room, ten dollars (sometimes more) for his Philanthropic

Society Literary fee, plus money for stationary, traveling expenses, and pocket money—a grand total of one hundred and twenty-five dollars.

Although Chapel Hill had one livery stable, boarding a horse proved expensive, so students either sold the family horse or arranged for a servant to take the animal home. Once at the University, young men found a boarding house, then met with faculty for examinations in Latin, Greek, and mathematics. In the 1830's a few dormitories existed—Old East, Old West, and South Building—but they filled quickly. Many students lived in boarding houses which "were less noisy than room in the college; the food tended to be better; and boarders were less frequently monitored by faculty members." Faculty members often took in student boarders, but memoirs show that these young men did not enjoy special favors.

Because students could not go to taverns and nearby race tracks, the young men spent their spare time visiting or playing bandy (field hockey), backgammon, and marbles. They attended singings and candy-pulls and occasionally served a 'possum supper to their friends. Early students also wrote many letters. Mail was delivered on Sundays and Thursdays, and the Chapel Hill post office opened for a few hours each day. Other extracurricular actives included camp meetings and religious revivals.

By 1845, the Board of Trustees had set a price limit for boarding houses in the village. "The price...shall not exceed Ten Dollars a month," they declared, "and the Faculty are hereby authorized & instructed to prohibit any student from boarding at any house when this price is exceeded." A memorandum released January 31, 1868, noted rate changes. Then, the maximum charge per month for a boarding house could not exceed fifteen dollars, and faculty were required to be responsible for the enforcement of the resolution.

Students often wrote home about classmates' diseases, such as mumps, tonsillitis, and dysentery. Because no infirmary existed before 1858, men who became ill stayed in their rooms until they recovered. But germs still tended to spread to other students. Occasionally, a student died.

Commencement week began the fourth Monday in June with debates and addresses. Tuesday and Wednesday consisted of orations and debates. Graduation exercises lasted the entire day on Thursday, opening with prayer and followed by the Latin salutatory and each honor graduate delivering a speech. Everyone broke for lunch, and speeches and debates continued throughout the entire afternoon, ending with the valedictory address and the conferring of degrees. The celebration ended with the highlight of the year, a grand ball.

In 1852, student Hector J. McNeill wrote a letter to his parents in Robeson County. After commenting on the "dissipated place...where there is the greatest amount of profanity," he informs his mother and father that he boards at a hotel for ten dollars a month and pays $4.00 for his washing and $1.25 to have his shoes brushed. He comments, also, on the food served by stating, "we have the best table that I ever saw—everything upon it that is good but bacon & collards."

Then, almost ten years later, in a September 27, 1861, letter from Preston H. Sessoms to his sister, Penelope E. White, Sessoms mentions his trip from Coleraine, North Carolina. Sessoms traveled past a soldiers' camp in Weldon to Chapel Hill, where only ninety students had enrolled because most had gone to war. He describes the campus, the town, and his daily routine:

"I went up to see the Professors to be examined to enter college...That day I got my boarding house and room...at a widow woman's house [Mrs. Yancey's], she is very good and nice, I like her very well, my room is up the stairs of her house...At morning sunrise the college bell rings for you to get up and dress. There are here only ninety students, last year there was about four hundred, there is about 300 gone to war. Chapel Hill is very hilly, hills...2 or 3 hundred yards high, and it is very rocky about here. The session ends at the last of november, then there is vacation six weeks I shall come home the first of december."

A year later, on August 28, 1862, Sessoms again writes to his sister and tells of sparse enrollment, expensive board, and little to eat. He elaborates on second calls for conscripts and speculates that if the call does come, "this college will certainly break, it will take all, sweep it clean." He wants to go home but fears the Yankees would cut him off if he should try. He writes, "Yankees or no Yankees, If there was no chance of getting round them, I would go through them. I have written enough."

After the Reconstruction years, new businesses began to dot Franklin Street. In 1881 Hoot Patterson opened a "high-class" general merchandise store between Tom Dunston's Barber Shop and Dr. Thomas Harris' Drugstore at Franklin and Henderson. He catered to wives of faculty members and billed only every three months to coincide with the pay schedule of the University. R.S. MacRae bought Dr. Harris' drugstore in 1885 and added additional stock—artist supplies and stationery—that appealed to students. By 1884 E. P. Boothe operated a dry goods store in Franklin Street's only brick building, and in 1890 Robert Allen Eubanks opened a grocery store that lasted forty-three years. When workmen razed the building in 1934, they found "fingerless ladies' gloves, high white collars, cuffs, white dress bow ties...and a bottle labeled 'Old Nick Corn Whiskey, for family use only.'" An interesting tale is told about the carpenter who found the bottle. Legend has it the man "broke the gold seal, sampled Old Nick slowly, and finding him agreeable drank the entire content, attesting that it was 'mightly mellow' when he next showed up for work, a week later."

The annex built for President Polk's visit at the Eagle Hotel.
(Photo: North Carolina Collection, University of North Carolina Library at Chapel Hill)

The village grew and grew. New boarding houses sprang up, and old boarding houses often changed owners and names. Many new stores and businesses opened, supplying students with necessary clothing and supplies. Various games and sports provided chances for socializing and meeting new people. Professors and their wives invited young students into their homes. Letter writing became a popular pastime. Students had plenty of activities to keep them busy.

The Eagle/Union/Chapel Hill/Pickard Hotel

In 1847 the Eagle Hotel on East Franklin Street, run by Miss Nancy Hilliard, included an annex built for President James K. Polk's (alumnus) return to campus. In 1853 Nancy Hilliard sold the business to Hugh B. Guthrie, who renamed the structure, the Union Hotel. A September 2, 1857, letter from University student Lathan P. Neal to his parents Aaron and Elizabeth Neal, reports on a local stabbing, describes his Sunday schedule, and reveals his battle with bedbugs at what was probably the Union Hotel:

"Our fair at the Hotel is pritty sorry badly cooked and filthy. We have corn pie beef gingercake &c. flies no rarity to be cooked cups and saucer not clean coffe very weak, but I have it very sweet, and get a plenty but not so nice as I like. When I left home I hardly knew what a chinch was but now have become pretty well acquainted with the customers for I sleep with a good many

*and by that means have scraped acquaintances. I
would have the bed scalded but I expect that the
matress is full; if so it would do but little good
they get on me in the day or anytime that I lay
down almost...please excuse blunders and
mistakes as I am in a hurry..."*

Thomas Wolfe

When the name changed again (the norm
for early Chapel Hill boarding houses) and the
hotel became the Chapel Hill Hotel in 1878,
proprietors John H. Watson and his wife Nancy
opened a young women's Normal School in the
building, charging $12.50 a month for "room,
board, and gas lights." Later, in 1892, Watson and
his partner Pickard tore down the original
structure and built a new Chapel Hill Hotel, this
time a ginger-bread yellow house for "drummers"
staying in Chapel Hill to sell their wares. By 1893, boarders staying at the
Chapel Hill Hotel paid $18.00 monthly for board and lodging, well worth the
price to be seated at a table served by master chef Jesse Jones.

In 1907, Horace Williams and George Stephens bought the business and
changed the name to the Pickard Hotel. Later that same year, they sold the
property to the University, and the structure, renamed yet another time, became
the University Inn Annex, a boarding house for students. The tradition continued
when W. W. and Betty Pickard built a second seventy-five room Pickard's Hotel
of hard pine, painted white, across the street from University Inn. On November
30, 1921, the University Inn burned, so the Pickard Hotel "was [now]
unquestionably the social center of Chapel Hill. Harry Houdini stayed there, and
Kay Kyser taught young ladies the Charleston in the ballroom." When Pickard
became seriously ill in 1916, he and Betty sold to William W. and Lulu Uzzell.

As a young scholar at the University of North Carolina in Chapel Hill in
1917, Thomas Wolfe moved constantly from one boarding house to another
either because he had used all of his advance payment or because he had a
dislike for certain people who lived there. After sampling different residences, he
ended up with the Uzzells at the Pickard Hotel. He roomed with J. L. (Nip)
Poston, a student from Statesville, in the attic room facing Franklin Street.

The main level of the hotel contained a parlor with piano and card
tables where students gathered after supper each evening. Legend records
Thomas Wolfe entertaining everyone who lived at the Pickard and making the
following comment about the armistice of World War I: "What we felt was that
the war was glorious and magnificent, and that it offered us a thousand chances
for glory, adventure, and joy."

Old Soldiers Club

An unpublished autobiography in the files of the Chapel Hill Historical Society, *The Life and Times of George McKie, professor of English at the University of North Carolina, 1894-1941,* recalls a boarding house dubbed The Old Soldiers Club, founded in 1921. Mrs. Blanche Pickard, a widow, presided as hostess to the young men who lived there. Tales of camaraderie among Mrs. Pickard's boarders have survived to this day, especially the young men's teasing each other about a special piece of furniture called "the marriage chair." Anyone who sat in it soon got married.

Mrs. Barbee's Boarding House

Nell Battle Lewis wrote a column for Raleigh's *News and Observer* about Mrs. Seton Barbee's student boarding house of yore. The young men at Mrs. Barbee's, who liked to create parodies of UNC athletes' shout songs, came up with the following ditty:

> *Ham and eggs for breakfast,*
> *Ham and eggs for tea,*
> *Cornbread, beefsteak—*
> *Sete Bar-BEE*

Chapel Hill native Louis Graves recalled that Sete Barbee stanza. He related, "The boarding house used to be a kind of club, and one year (maybe more than one year) it was a form of student humor for those clubs to make up yells, based, of course, on the yells that had been first composed for athletes." Mary served boarders until her death in the early 1930's.

Julia Charlotte Hooper Graves
(Photo: North Carolina Collection, University of North Carolina Library at Chapel Hill)

Mrs. Graves' Boarding House

Julia Graves began taking in boarders in the old Pannill house (on the Carolina Inn corner) after her husband Ralph, a mathematics professor, died in 1889. To support her four children, Mrs. Graves charged thirteen dollars a month for lodging and three meals a day, which consisted of a breakfast of batter-cakes with molasses, sausage or steak, hominy, and hot biscuits.

Julia Charlotte Hooper Graves' ancestors and her early experiences probably provided this young woman with the stamina to persevere and succeed in times of adversity. Her family roots included William Hooper of Hillsborough and Wilmington, one of the three North Carolina signers of the Declaration of Independence. Julia's association with the University began at an early age, according to a recent newspaper article. It related, "A later William Hooper (1792-1876)...Julia's grandfather, moved his family to Chapel Hill in the early 1900s and built the house at 504 E. Franklin Street, now one of the town's two oldest surviving residences. Hooper Lane was later carved from the rear of his large property. Hooper's widow married Joseph Caldwell, UNC's first president, and Hooper was raised as his stepson...Julia's father, John deBerniere Hooper, was on the UNC faculty before the Civil War but left to work in Fayetteville."

While living in Fayetteville, young Julia witnessed General William T. Shermon and his victorious Union troops march through North Carolina. When the University (which had been closed for four years) reopened, Julia's family moved back to Chapel Hill, where her father taught Greek and French. According to historical notes, "Julia's parents found the pleasant village that they remembered reduced to a wasteland of dilapidated houses and stores, many unoccupied campus building in disrepair, a Franklin Street overgrown with weeds and most of the prewar faculty long gone to more promising places."

Julia stayed in Chapel Hill and married Ralph Henry Graves. They moved into a house built by famed professor Elisha Mitchell, and they had four children, Ernest, Ralph, Louis, and Mary. After Graves' death, Julia opened her boarding house to support her children, and her reputation as a wonderful cook spread over the entire village. Mrs. Graves' monthly charge included just about everything: "the cost of food, labor, laundry, damage to crockery, and miscellaneous wear and tear."

Louis Graves, one of Julia's sons, recalled a special supper his mother served. "Farmers used to trap partridges and would bring 'em in and sell 'em at five cents each dressed and ready for cooking," he said. "I remember that once my mother bought about thirty and served a broiled partridge to each boarder. That was extravagant even with the cost only five cents each, but she couldn't resist that splurge."

Mrs. Graves' beaten biscuits, which she made daily from scratch, won, hands-down, the prize for the best homemade bread. She literally placed her flour, lard, and buttermilk mixture on a sturdy tree stump and beat the ingredients with a stick. Later, when the beaten biscuits came from the oven, they resembled a thick cracker, which kept indefinitely in a tin box. She swore that the secret came from the stick beating!

After approximately thirteen years of managing her boarding house, Julia Graves and her daughter Mary moved north so that Mary could study art. When they returned to Chapel Hill, Mary painted portraits of famous men such

Mrs. A.A. "Queenie" Kluttz
(Photo: North Carolina Collection, University of North Carolina Library at Chapel Hill)

as Frank Porter Graham and Paul Green. At Julia's death in 1944 at age 88, "she was the only survivor among the faculty families who had reopened UNC in 1875. She had become highly honored as an icon of the village past as well as the mother of Chapel Hill luminaries Louis Graves and Mary Rees, and of her other two sons who had also later achieved success."

The Central Hotel, Which Became Mrs. "Queenie" Kluttz's Boarding House

Across from the Chapel Hill Hotel stood the James Hogg house, which later became the Central Hotel. Jones Watson, mayor of Chapel Hill in 1881 and 1883, ran this business until his death. Dr. A. B. Roberson purchased the hotel, opened a drug store there, but then leased the building for $25 per month to Mr. and Mrs. N. G. L. "Bunn" Patterson. After Dr. Roberson's death in 1897, "Dr." and Mrs. A. A. Kluttz took over management of the establishment, boarded only females, and changed the name of the establishment to Mrs. "Queenie" Kluttz's Boarding House.

Cornelia Spencer Love recalls her boarding days, from 1918 to 1929 at the Kluttzes' big yellow house, after moving there from Mrs. Bain's Boarding House. "Kinder people and a pleasanter home could not be found," Love remembers. "They lived in a large house surrounded by ample grounds, in the center of town, across from the President's home...I was given the large front upstairs bedroom, which I said was the best in town, and it was. The meals were the best in town, too, presided over by Mrs. Kluttz, with fresh vegetables from Doctor's garden and an excellent cook. Both the Kluttzes were 'characters,' in the sense that they had very definite personalities...Mrs. Kluttz was the spokesman for the couple, but...Doc's quiet word was the final one. If Doc was asked to do something for which he was disinclined, he 'had to ask Mrs. Kluttz,' while she, in turn, would have to consult the Doctor."

"Doctor" or "Doc" Kluttz, as friends called him, had not completed his M.D. and ran a general store. Mrs. Ora Crawford Kluttz, who remained childless, nevertheless nurtured her female boarders and provided cots for $3.00 a night for bed and breakfast to those females attending the traditional University two-day balls. She also made herself responsible for calling curfews and insisting male visitors leave at a designated time. By all accounts, Mrs. Kluttz adjusted to Doc's eccentric habits, such as driving his Cadillac up and down Franklin Street with his milk cow tied to the back of the car or always eating a huge corn pone as his dinner appetizer.

A wonderful cook, especially with hot sizzling fried steak strips she prepared on an old wood-burning stove, Mrs. Kluttz welcomed visitors to her table. After a hearty meal, she issued a cordial invitation to sit and talk in front of her parlor's open fireplace. Nothing could keep her from her philosophy that she had to stay on schedule. Once, when she fell and hurt her ankle, she allowed, without making a sound, her medical doctor neighbor to forcefully put the bones in their proper place. Something as minor as a dislocated ankle bone would not discommode her! She had to prepare dinner for her boarders. In addition to her other chores and duties, she appointed herself Doc's "back seat driver," striving to prevent serious accidents like the one Doc had when he ran into and seriously damaged nine out of ten parked wagons.

The Kluttzes had a vegetable garden that produced summer radishes, corn, beans, and tomatoes. They generously contributed to campaigns to help the soldiers abroad in 1918 and 1919. Regular attendants at the Presbyterian Church, Mrs. Kluttz always supplied the altar flowers. Wearing a small sixteenth-century plumed velvet French look-alike cap, she led her husband down the aisle to the very front row, and when he started to fall asleep, she removed a long and lethal pin from her hat and edged it slowly down the pew towards Mr. Kluttz—never taking her eyes off the minister in the pulpit.

Mr. Kluttz, a good-natured man, probably considered the hatpin incidents funny. A favorite merchant among Chapel Hill students (who nicknamed him "Adam Applejack), Mr. Kluttz owned a store across Franklin Street from the Methodist Church. A.A. made a great deal of money after he opened his business, and according to legend, also lost money by giving children free candy and extending credit and loans to students who never bothered to repay him. Accounts receivable never seemed to bother Mr. Kluttz, who thought of his store as a social club rather than a business. University of North Carolina students, who loved to make up rhymes about people they liked, noted in this ditty their understanding of Mr. Kluttz, who delighted in playing back-room checkers, and his black manager, Ernest Thompson, who did most of the clerking:

> *Ernest runs the business*
> *Doc chews sig-ar butts*
> *Everybody works in this old town.*

Between 1918 and 1929, Chapel Hill residents and students played golf on a primitive nine-hole course located to the right of Franklin Street. Most people enjoyed dancing to the name bands of Benny Goodman and Paul Whiteman. The few UNC-CH coeds and town girls joined young women transported from Woman's College and St. Mary's to provide dance partners for male students. Faculty couples chaperoned these affairs. Bridge playing, afternoon teas, and women's study clubs kept faculty wives busy while their husbands pursued on-going academic studies in departmental libraries. The little town grew.

Interestingly, one lasting description of the Village came as a result of Doc Kluttz's final question before dying. Doc asked his minister what heaven would be like. Pastor W. D. Moss responded, "I believe heaven must be a lot like Chapel Hill in the spring." This description still lives in literature that has survived throughout the years. Mrs. Kluttz lived twenty years after her husband's death. She died in 1947 and left an estate worth $162,655.

During her time, boarding houses became more the norm than the exception. When Mrs. Kluttz closed her boarding house, Cornelia Love moved across the street to Mrs. Thomas' Boarding House. The table conversation proved interesting, but Miss Love found the food deplorable. "Brains and eggs was a favorite luncheon dish," Love said, "but Dr. Mangum would come in from his classroom and say he had been teaching brains all the morning, and just could not eat them too. The best dish was molded corn sticks. One of the boarders, Mrs. Turlington was a brilliant woman but so highly keyed that she told me any alcoholic drink would be poison for her, that even a glass of water could make her high."

Chapel Hill began to see many changes during the second decade of the twentieth century. Women served on jury duty, even though they could be excused simply by asking. Alma Holland, an assistant in the Botany Department, was the first young woman in the village to buy a house. The Chapel Hill boarding house experiences, dating back as early as 1797, began its demise in the late 1960's. After 150 years, however, most of the houses had earned the highest praise for clean lodging, delicious meals, and social interaction.

Bill Prouty, a Chapel Hill historian and writer, explains the uniqueness of meals in each and every boarding house, and he asks his readers, "How long has it been since you bellied up to a table groaning under the weight of steaming food transfixed by eager eaters, alertly ready to contest you for the choicest victuals? Boarding house dining was a fascinating game, wherein the meek either changed their ways or became emaciated, and the bold, hardened to none-too-subtle censure, found great bounty." By the early 1970's most boarding houses had closed in Chapel Hill. Only the memories remained, and according to Prouty, those old, lovable landmarks came tumbling down. He recalls one vivid scene that stuck in his memory:

"...I saw a skeleton of a house, its bared frames sticking up to the gray winter sky like last year's crops stripped and blackened corn stalks standing in a fallow field, where only a few days before had stood a familiar landmark. Here, up until only a few years, ago, Mrs. P.B. 'Ma' Burks operated the last of our Town's long list of boardinghouses, dating back to the opening of the University."

Many factors contributed to their closings. The growing price of groceries, the availability of more restaurants, the inability to find good help, and a job market offering more and better positions to women all played a part in their disappearance. As long-time boarding house resident Cornelia Spencer Love points out, the food could not have been better:

"Other specialty dishes...were persimmon pudding, sweet potato biscuits, barbecued chicken, Sally Lunn bread, lemon chess pie, chicken spaghetti...and Brunswick stew, which could vary greatly in ingredients, from a chopped up meat of rabbit to chicken, pork, or a mixture of these, with a melange of corn, beans, tomatoes, sometimes mashed potatoes, if you wanted it thickened."

In addition, times changed and, according to Bill Prouty, so did attitudes about eating. He believes boarders began to worry about being analyzed when they sat down to eat, and he compares eating at a boarding house table to being fed in a fish bowl.

"Boardinghouse eating is personal, almost as family eating," he explains. "It's a three-times-a-day contact with the same folks week after week, not like in cafes and cafeterias where you can choose your fellow diners or eat alone. And if you can't read a person's character from across a boardinghouse table, then you just can't read. And if you can, then so can others, too."

Prouty laments the closing of Chapel Hill boarding houses and the "sociable...way of taking on nourishment...sitting down with friends and having the food brought out steaming hot and placed in front of you, without worrying about finding a seat...and without somebody breathing down your neck..."

The era had ended.

Information for this piece comes from many sources:
- Love, Cornelia Spencer. *When Chapel Hill Was a Village*. Chapel Hill 1976
- Vickers, James, Thomas Scism, Dixon Qualls. "Chapel Hill: An Illustrated History." Chapel Hill, Carclay Publishers, 1985.
- Prouty, William W. *Bill Prouty's Chapel Hill*. Chapel Hill: Creative Printers, Inc., 1979.
- Zogry, Kenneth Joel. "The University's Living Room: A History of the Carolina Inn." Chapel Hill: University of North Carolina at Chapel Hill, 1999.

- Walser, Richard. *Thomas Wolfe Undergraduate*. Durham: Duke University Press, 1977.
- Lewis, Nell Battle. "Incidentally." *The News and Observer.* July 8, 1956. Section 2-III.
- Stolpen, Steven. *A Pictorial History*. Norfolk: Donning Company Publishers, 1978.
- "The Poor House." News Services. Chapel Hill, NC. Aug. 14, 1997.

The following sources are all from *Documenting the American South* found at *www.docsouth.unc.edu:*

- "Graves Family Had Ties to Chapel Hill Luminaries." *Chapel Hill News.* Taken from *www. chapelhillnews.com:*

    "The First Century of the First State University"

    "Letter from Kenelm H. Lewis to Emma Lewis," May 26, 1837

    "Letter from Kenelm H. Lewis to Emma Lewis," February 28, 1836

    "Letter fro Solomon Lea to William Lea," September 14, 1832

    "The School Day and the School Year" by Erika Lindemann

    "Letter from Charles L. Pettigrew to Ebenezer Pettigrew," August 6, 1832

    "Letter from Preston H. Sessoms to Penelope E. White," August 28, 1862

    "Letter from Preston H. Sessoms to Penelope E. White," September 27, 1861

    "Letter from Nathan P. Neal to Aaron and Elizabeth Neal," September 2, 1857

    "Letter from Hector J. McNeill to Daniel C. and Ann M. McNeill," August 18, 1852

    "Student Boarding Houses," Board of Trustees Minutes, January 31, 1868

    "Price of Boarding Houses," Board of Trustees Minutes, December 26, 1845

    "Student Bursar Accounts," Board of Trustees Minutes, June 27, 1827

    "Rules on Student Board," Board of Trustees Minutes, March 24, 1810

    "Letter from John Pettigrew to Charles Pettigrew, June 17, 1797

    "Letter from John and Ebenezer Pettigrew to Charles Pettigrew," May 4, 1795

    "Letter from Thomas I. Lenoir to Thomas Lenoir," May 30, 1839

APPLE, SAGE, AND SAUSAGE BREAKFAST GRAVY

3 ounces butter	3 ounces flour
1/2 apple, diced	2 cups whole milk
2 springs fresh thyme	2 leaves fresh sage
1-1/2 pounds ground sausage	Biscuits

Make a roux with butter and flour. Set aside. In a medium saucepan, sweat the apple about 5 minutes; add milk, thyme, and sage and bring to a boil and thicken with the roux. Simmer for 15 to 20 minutes. Meanwhile, brown the sausage in another medium saucepan. Once browned, drain excess fat. Strain the milk mixture into the saucepan with the browned sausage. Return to a simmer and adjust seasoning. Serve over split hot biscuits. Yield: 4 servings

Cookbook editor's notes: To "sweat" the apple, cook it in a small amount of butter over low heat with a piece of foil (or parchment paper) placed directly on top of it. Then cover the pot tightly. The apple will soften, without browning, while cooking in its own juices. This classic recipe is definitely worth the trouble, and it is always a hit. Recipe from *Lowcountry Delights: Cookbook and Travel Guide, Third Edition* by Maxine Pinson and Malyssa Pinson. *www.thefoodscoop.com/Led.html* OR 1-888-717-4040.

STUFFED CAROLINA QUAIL

1 cup spinach, wilted in butter
4 ounces smoked Gouda cheese
6 oven-roasted shallots
4 semi-boneless quail
2 Tablespoons extra virgin olive oil
11/2 teaspoon seasoned flour

Combine first 3 ingredients. Divide mixture into 4 portions and stuff into body cavity of quail. Brush each bird, liberally, with extra virgin olive oil and lightly dredge in flour. In a hot pan, sear quail on both sides to achieve a golden crust. Transfer to a 425-degree oven and roast approximately 8 to 10 minutes or until firm to touch. Yield: 2 servings

Cookbook editor's notes: Quail can often be found in frozen meat section of most supermarkets.

Recipe from *Lowcountry Delights: Cookbook and Travel Guide, Third Edition,* by Maxine Pinson and Malyssa Pinson. *www.thefoodscoop.com/Lcd.html* OR 1-888-717-4040.

Kate Stuart in later years.

— *Southport* —

Smithville's Stuart House

Born in 1844, Kate Stuart had celebrated only seventeen birthdays when the Civil War began. She assisted her mother, Mrs. Mary, providing top-quality boarding house hospitality to Confederate officers. The dining table at Stuart House became a popular gathering place where pilots of blockade-runners (vessels that kept the Confederacy supplied with guns and ammunition) exchanged tales and adventures. Kate often sat with them, listening quietly as soldiers swapped stories.

Georgia-born poet Sidney Lanier, stationed in the area as a signalman, became good friends with Kate. He recited his poetry and played his flute for her while the two of them sat in the moonlight on the banks of the Cape Fear River. Kate especially valued the autographed copy of Lanier's famous poem, "The Marshes of Glynn," that he presented to her. Stories abound that young and beautiful Kate fell in love with Lanier and was devastated when Union soldiers imprisoned him.

James Sprunt, author and historian of Wilmington, dedicated the following poem to Miss Kate Stuart. It was printed in one of the Wilmington newspapers but the surviving typed poem does not show a date or the name of the paper:

FRYING PAN LIGHT-SHIP
We drew together in the sheltered room,
    Awed by the storm and breakers sullen roar,

And talked of shipwrecks, in the gathering gloom,
    And of the surf complaining to the shore.
Against the deadly Cape Fear Shoals,
    Which stretch far out to sea,
There rides, while anchors firmly hold,
    A light-ship on their lee.
Beyond the treacherous Middle Ground,
    For twenty miles and more,
A thousand gallant ships went down,
    Almost in sight of shore.
In war, in peace, the strangled groan,
    Of drowning victims' breath,
Was mingled with the ocean's moan,
    As they went down to death.
Its shallow depths can scarce conceal
    Its many woeful wars,
Whose tragedies, in mute appeal,
    Still show a thousand scars.
For many weary, stormy years,
    No friendly light was shed,
Upon this gulf of human tears,
    This charnel of the dead.
But now the light-ship's glowing beams,
    And warning signal bells,
Send o'er the waves a steadfast gleam,
    And echoes of "all's well!"

After the Civil War, Mrs. Mary and Kate continued as cordial hostesses at the Stuart House. They served sumptuous meals of vegetables they had grown in their swamp gardens, game they killed, and fish they caught. By this time, Mrs. Mary, who had been 48 when she gave birth to Kate, decided to turn a great deal of her more strenuous inn-keeping responsibilities over to her daughter.

Stuart House, originally a one-story brick home, may have been a store house for explosives for nearby Fort Johnston during the Revolutionary War, because the first floor walls measured one foot thick. Eventually the Stuarts added a second floor for guests and a third floor reserved for lawyers. Apparently, this proved to be the ultimate in lodging accommodations. Legend indicates Mrs. Mary always told attorneys they could never become judges unless they slept in the upper room of her boarding house. Staying at Stuart House would be on par with registering at a five-star hotel today. Prestige and importance surrounded the premises and the Stuarts' bountiful tables.

Many important guests signed the register at Stuart House. The father of the late President Woodrow Wilson, a Presbyterian minister in Wilmington,

Kate Stuart was a fixture of Smithville and the Lower Cape Fear.

boarded there — often accompanied by young Woodrow. North Carolina Governor Elias Carr and several members of his council enjoyed Kate's Southern hospitality. Former Governor Daniel Lindsey Russell and his wife stayed for several weeks. Col. Hamilton C. Jones, dean of the Charlotte (N. C.) bar and one of the foremost lawyers in North Carolina, spent three weeks at the Stuart House. Robert E. Lee, then a young Colonel, also enjoyed the gentility of the old boarding house.

In addition to providing upscale room and board, Kate Stuart, an honor graduate of Glen Anna Female Seminary in Thomasville, acted on her progressive ideas regarding education. She believed young people should have proper schooling. Because public education did not exist after the Civil War, she and her friend, Miss Anne Drew, chartered their own school, Smithville Academy, in a private home. Kate served as both principal and teacher. Enrollment grew until eventually the school and its more than eighty students moved to the Masonic Building on Nash Street.

Kate took all her responsibilities seriously and exhibited bravery when a young friend, Mary Hunter, was visiting from Philadelphia. Mary's father, Captain Alexander Hunter of the Clyde Line Freighter *Fairbanks,* had returned to Southport to take his daughter home. Little Mary became so excited and anxious to welcome him that she ran swiftly out on the Stuart House wharf. Falling off the dock and unable to swim, the child sank deep into the eighteen feet of water in the Cape Fear River. Kate, who had been watching from the piazza of the Stuart House, ran out on the dock. Fully clothed in long skirt and petticoats, she plunged in, grabbed the child, and swam to the dock's pilings. With one hand, Kate grabbed the wood; with the other, she held the child securely until assistance arrived.

To show his appreciation, Captain Hunter presented Kate with a gold watch inscribed: "For your deed of heroism from the Hunter family of Philadelphia." Captain Hunter also decreed that whenever the *Fairbanks* passed the Stuart House, the ship's horn would toot and a flag would fly in Kate's honor. In time, other Clyde Line vessels gave the salute. Vessels from other shipping lines also adopted the custom. Eventually almost every boat that passed acknowledged Miss Kate Stuart.

One newspaper article (unidentified and undated) reveals: "On another occasion, Miss Kate is credited with saving the life of a small Negro child who had fallen into the river. In this case, as with that of the Captain's daughter, she jumped into the river, fully dressed, and dragged the drowning child to safety."

Apparently bravery ran strong in the Stuart women's blood. Mrs. Mary and Kate once delighted in catching a six-foot-man-eating shark from their wharf. Mrs. Mary also reacted in emergency situations. In 1869 a terrible fire struck Smithville, spreading from house to house and store to store. Records shows that during the fire, "Mrs. Stuart...found some looting going on and chased the culprits away."

Robert E. Lee stayed at Stuart House.

When her mother died, Kate continued to run the boarding house as charming hostess and famous cook. Kate kept in her scrapbook the following newspaper article which extolled the virtues of consuming rice and explained how this starch enhanced battercakes, waffles, and muffins:

The Southern Railway has inaugurated a campaign to encourage the consumption of rice. A day is set apart on buffet cars for serving dainty and substantial dishes made of the great Southern cereal. People who do not know what rice battercakes, waffles and muffins are surely are to be pitied. Rice is cooked and served in a great variety of ways, but we feel sorry for anybody whose opportunity in life has been so limited that they are in total ignorance of the superb Brunswick County dinner featured with steamed rice and stewed

"Stuart House," Southport, N. C.

The Stuart House graced the Southport riverfront.

chicken and dumplings, with plenty of rich gravy. A real Brunswick County dinner consists also of a great variety of other things, and it reminds us to say that we have often wondered why Miss Kate Stuart, of the Stuart House, at Southport, did not start a correspondence school to teach the uninitiated what a crackerjack dinner is.

News of Kate's gardening talents also often appeared in the local newspaper: "Miss Kate Stuart, of Southport, was exhibiting an orange grown and ripened in the open air in her yard at Southport. The tree was on the north side of the house and received no attention or protection by way of sheltering it from the weather." Obviously Kate exhibited great pride in her homegrown fruits. In 1904, the local newspaper wrote, "Thieves were shot at who were stealing grapes from the extensive vines of Miss Kate Stuart, who had a swamp garden near her residence."

A proficient writer herself, Kate occasionally contributed pieces for the newspaper. In an essay entitled "In the Cemetery at Southport," she takes the reader to a quaint old burying ground and describes the oak trees, whose leaves whisper the secrets of the centuries. She moves to the granite stones, recalling the past. "Here is the Pilot's monument with its tall shaft like some marble finger pointing mutely to the sky," she wrote, "and telling of brave men who went forth to their perilous duties and never returned—and deeply graven on the marble sides are these words: *The winds and the sea sing their requiem and shall forever more.*"

Shaded porches caught the ocean breeze to cool guests at Kate's house.
(Photo: NCMM at Southport)

Always involved in civic affairs, Kate strongly advocated getting a railroad for the town, and she succeeded. In November 1911, Kate—the only female in the local Chamber of Commerce—participated in what was called "The Glorious Celebration" by riding into town on a hand car ahead of the first passenger car. Sixty-seven years old at the time, she celebrated the occasion by writing a poem entitled "The Railroad's Come to Town."

> On old Rhett Street each one you meet
> Just shakes hands all around,
> For don't you see, they say with glee,
> The railroad's come to town.
>
> From far Supply to Calabash,
> See how they cover ground,
> They've come to help us celebrate,
> The railroad's come to town.
>
> Good farmer Pyke, just from the "Pole",
> Who often used to frown,
> Now wears a vast substantial smile,
> The railroad's come to town.

Bring out your flags, let's all hurrah!
And do the thing up brown,
It's been coming forty years,
By Jinks, its got to town!

Kate's progressive spirit reigned in various ways. In September 1900, she exhibited a collection of "High Art" at the Stuart House. Drapery, flags, palms, and pictures handsomely mounted and numbered decorated the upstairs hallways. She embraced and implemented aesthetic improvements.

In October 1909, Kate Stuart became the first president of a Civic Improvement Society. Two years later, as a representative of the North Carolina Society of Colonial Dames of America, she assisted in unveiling at Fort Johnston a tablet commemorating the stirring incidents which marked the downfall of the royal government in North Carolina. In 1917, at age seventy-three, she participated in a patriotic rally held to analyze the United States' involvement in World War I.

As a good businesswoman, Miss Kate continued to renovate and improve Stuart House, often after tropical storms struck the area. The piazza of the boarding house, wildly wind blown across the street, had to be replaced. She added a new bath house for guests. Once a bolt of lightning tore through the entire house. Although structural damage resulted, everyone escaped injury. Kate also had a breakwater built on the waterfront and her yard filled in and converted into a flower garden.

Kate ran the boarding house until her death in 1929. She was eighty-two. The structure remained standing until Hurricane Hazel destroyed it in 1954. D. W. Manson sums up Miss Kate and The Stuart House in the following February 19, 1920 accolade in the Wilmington *Dispatch*:

But first, let us go to our boarding house. This large square frame house with the 20-foot wide porches upstairs and down and all around the house was built 135 years ago and many of the country's foremost statesmen have registered and enjoyed the home hospitalities afforded here, among them our President Wilson who penned his name on the house register in the youthful days of his life. This is Miss Kate Stuart, owner of the Stuart House. She was born in this room over 75 years ago, and while her hair is silvery white yet she is quick of step, clear of eye and keen of intellect, and during the days you will spend in her presence you will be impressed with her utmost, kindly desire to please, be called upon to follow promptness at meal times, and you will feel yourself grow into the religious atmosphere which constantly pervades her presence, and if you are alert, you will come nearer than ever before to the real love of God if you try to emulate her spirit as she succeeds in the attainments of a most lovable hostess, and thus you have an example of the fine hospitality of the largest percentage of Southport people.

Information for this piece came from the following sources:

• Lathrop, Elise. *Early American Inns and Taverns.* New York: Robert M. McBride & Company, MCMXXVI.

• Carson, Susan S. *Joshua's Dream.* Southport Historical Society, 1992.

    ---. "Miss Kate Stuart, Heroine of Smithviille."

    ---. "Hub of Activity Needed Rooms for Summer Visitors." Wilmington *Morning Star.* March 15, 2002.

    ---. "Stuart House Was Popular Destination for Lawyers." Wilmington *Morning Star.* March 22, 2002.

    ---. "Colorful 'Miss Kate' a Southport Legend." Wilmington *Morning Star.* May 20, 1999.

    ---. "Our Miss Kate-Heroine of Old Smithville." *Pelican Post,* October 1997.

• Preik, Brooks Newton. "Kate Stuart." The author of this article is a native of Southport and the great-granddaughter of Joseph Bensel, Kate Stuart's half-brother.

• "Pretty Tribute to a Brave Woman." Wilmington *Evening Dispatch.* November 9, 1914.

• Keziah, Bill. "Heroine of 1869 Still Gets Salute." Raleigh *News and Observer.* March 26, 1950.

OYSTER DRESSING

1-1/2 cup chopped celery
1 (16 oz.) package seasoned bread crumbs
1-1/2 cup chopped onion
3 cups turkey broth or canned chicken broth
1/4 cup better (melted)
2-1/2 pints oysters
2 eggs

Preheat oven to 350 degrees. Sauté onion and celery and 1/2 cup butter until tender. Place in mixing bowl and add rest of ingredients, mixing well. Melt 1/2 cup margarine in 9 x 13-inch pan; place dressing in pan and bake for 30-35 minutes. (From *North Carolina Plantation & Historic Homes* Cookbook).

PICKLED SHRIMP

3 pounds fresh shrimp (cooked, peeled, deveined)
2 Tablespoons Worcestershire
1 clove garlic, crushed
1-1/2 cups vegetable oil
8 ounces capers
2-1/2 cups vinegar
4 medium onions, sliced
2 Tablespoons lemon juice
1 teaspoon Tabasco
1/4 cup sugar
1 teaspoon white pepper
1 Tablespoon salt
1 Tablespoon thyme

Combine shrimp, capers and onions. Mix all other ingredients and pour over shrimp. Marinate at least 24 hours. (From *North Carolina Plantation & Historic Homes Cookbook,* published and distributed by Aerial Photogrpahy Services, Inc., Charlotte, N.C.).

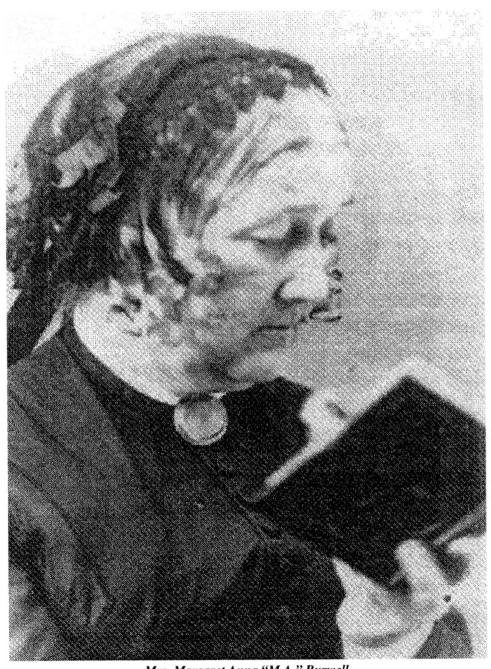

Mrs. Margaret Anna "M.A." Burwell.

(Photo: Historic Hillsborough Commission, Elvan Cobb, Executive Director)

Hillsborough

Mrs. Margaret Anna Burwell's Boarding School

She wanted people to call her "M. A." instead of Margaret Anna or Anna. Nearly six feet tall and a member of Virginia's old, proud Spotswood family, M. A., at age twenty-five, moved in 1835 with her husband Robert and their two small children from her home state to Hillsborough, North Carolina. Robert had accepted the call as pastor of the Presbyterian church. Because his congregation rarely met their promise to pay the yearly salary of four hundred dollars, the Burwells had a difficult time, often unable to purchase even essential food staples or firewood to heat the manse.

To supplement Dr. Burwell's pastorate income, M. A. opened a boarding school in her home. Although she had no formal education and eventually gave birth to ten more children, she upheld her responsibilities as a minister's wife and head mistress. Burwell School for Young Ladies became a tremendous success. Females between the ages of eight and eighteen arrived by stagecoach from all areas of the state to live and study and "to become absorbed in the pleasant, well-structured home life of the Burwells and to learn...reading, spelling, grammar, and neat, acceptable handwriting" in addition to courses in "music, oil painting, and needlework. Good manners, good grooming, impeccable behavior, and a firm self-improvement schedule were expected of each Burwell girl." Interestingly, many of Mrs. Burwell's graduates started their own private schools in Reidsville, Statesville, and other towns.

The manse at 319 North Churton Street, built by architect John Berry in 1837, contained seven high-ceilinged rooms with a straight up-and-down hall staircase. It became home to the fourteen Burwells and as many as eight live-in students. One Burwell researcher believes the "little box room at the top of the stairs traditionally called 'The Prayer Room'...possibly was [M. A.'s] refuge."

Apparently M. A.'s personality, described as "young and girlish...and delighting in friendly and amusing gossip (an inclination against which she forever did battle)...affectionate and warm-hearted, industrious, frugal and clever with money; and, a social lioness at the tea-tables of Hillsborough," fortified M. A. with the necessary survival tools to succeed as a minister's wife, homemaker, mother, and teacher.

All of these glowing accolades for Mrs. Margaret Anna Burwell contrast considerably with the memoirs of a Burwell former slave. Elizabeth Hobbs Keckly relates her horrible mistreatment by her owners. As paraphasing cannot do justice to Elizabeth's experiences with the Burwells, excerpts from her diary follow:

When I was about fourteen years old I went to live with my master's eldest son, a Presbyterian minister. His salary was small, and he was burdened with a helpless wife, a girl that he had married in the humble walks of life...I was their only servant, and...from the very first I did the work of three servants, and I was scolded and regarded with distrust...I was nearly eighteen when we removed from Virginia to Hillsboro, North Carolina, where young Mr. Burwell took charge of a church. Mr. Bingham, a hard cruel man, the village schoolmaster, was a member of my young master's church, and he was a frequent visitor to the parsonage...

The events that follow indicate Lizzy Keckley's sense of self and her refusal to lower herself to the white man, Mr. Bingham. The diary entry continues:

It was Saturday evening, and while I was bending over the bed, watching the baby that I had just hushed into slumber, Mr. Bingham came to the door...and in his blunt way remarked: "Lizzie, I am going to flog you."

I was thunderstruck, and tried to think if I had been remiss in anything...and with surprise exclaimed: "Whip me, Mr. Bingham! What for?"

"No matter," he replied, "I am going to whip you, so take down your dress this instant."

Recollect, I was eighteen years of age, was a woman fully developed and yet this man coolly bade me take down my dress. I drew myself up proudly, firmly, and said, "No, Mr. Bingham, I shall not take down my dress before you. Moreover, you shall not whip me unless you prove the stronger...

Lizzie's perseverance did not prevent Mr. Bingham from beating her with both rope and rawhide, cutting her skin, raising welts, and causing blood to flow. But she suffered her beating without uttering a sound. When Lizzy went to her master, Robert Burwell to ask why she had received such a savage beating, he struck her with a chair, knocking her to the floor. After spending that night wondering why such unjust treatment had besieged her, she determined the cause of her torture—Mrs. Anna Burwell! Lizzy writes, "It seems that Mr. Bingham had pledged himself to Mrs. Burwell to subdue what he called my 'stubborn pride.'" After several more unsuccessful beatings by Mr. Bingham to teach Lizzy a lesson, he promised he would never attempt to beat her again. However, all did not end peacefully. When Mr. Bingham refused to whip Lizzie any more, Dr. Burwell "was urged by his wife to punish me himself." That punishment soon came:

One morning he went to the wood-pile, took an oak broom, cut the handle off, and with this heavy handle attempted to conquer me. I fought him but he proved the strongest. At the sight of my bleeding form, his wife fell upon her knees and begged him to desist. My distress even touched her cold, jealous heart...The Rev. Mr. Burwell was not yet satisfied...He made the attempt and again failed...he told me, with an air of penitence, that he should never strike me another blow; and faithfully he kept his word.

The Burwell's slave Lizzie suffered other mistreatments. She admits, "The savage efforts to subdue my pride were not the only things that brought me suffering and deep mortification during my residence at Hillsboro...for four years a white man—I spare the world his name—had base designs upon me...and I became a mother."

Whether masters considered beatings justifiable and fair or whether they needed to exercise power, or whether they used them as an excuse to vent their own faults mirrored in slaves' eyes, no one knows. Lizzie's beatings did not resume, and in a diary entry, she noted, "My troubles in North Carolina were brought to an end by my unexpected return to Virginia, where I lived with Mr. Garland, who had married Miss Ann Burwell, one of my old master's daughters." Elizabeth Hobbs Keckly later became a successful businesswoman, author, activist, educator, and confidante of Mary Todd Lincoln.

In 1857, M. A. and Robert moved to Charlotte to open the Charlotte Female Institute, which is now Queens College. In 1859, their son John joined them as teacher, and in 1871, all three moved to Raleigh, where they accepted jobs at Peace Institute, now Peace College. Mrs. Burwell died on June 21, 1871. Her husband and son John continued teaching at the school.

M. A.'s superb educational endeavors earned her a memorial at Charlotte Female Institute. The inscription of the tablet, placed in Burwell Hall, reads:

This Hall is Erected to the Glory of God
It is Dedicated to the Memory of Margaret Anna Burwell
Wife, Mother, Educator
The better part of her life was devoted to the building up of a school upon this spot from which her pupils went forth to bless many homes. This institution will perpetuate her work and that of her successors in the cause of the Education of Women

Information for this piece came from the following sources:
• Keckley, Elizabeth, *Behind the Scenes.* N.Y.G.W. Carleton & Co., Publishers. MDCCC LXVIII.
• Engstrom, Mary Claire. "The Legend of M. A. Burwell." *The State Magazine.* September 1976.
• *www.campus.queens.edu/library/history/annaburwell.htm*
• *www.chovb.org/catalog.php?mode*

WANT TO GO?
The Burwell School for Young Ladies (1837-1857) at 319 N. Church Street in downtown Hillsborough. Restored and dedicated to Margaret Anna Burwell's service, the old school is under the supervision of the North Carolina Department of Cultural Resources Division of Archives and History. The site offers free docent-led and self-guided tours, a variety of cultural events, and engaging and innovative programs for children and young adults. Parking. Open Wednesday-Saturday, 11 am-4 pm and Sunday 1-4; closed mid-December to mid-January and major holidays. Call (919) 732-7451, or email to info@burwellschool.org.

One of the original railroad "Company Shops" (left) and employee homes.

Ann "Miss Nancy" Segur Hilliard's
Boarding House

As manager of Chapel Hill's Eagle Hotel, Mrs. Nancy Hilliard had gained experience, finesse, and managerial skills needed to run the boarding house at Company Shops. In the mid-1850's, she arrived at the growing town to take control.

Yes, Company Shops, actually the name of a town, has a rich and unique history. By January 29, 1856, the railroad route between Goldsboro and Charlotte transported passengers and also farm products, lumber, coal, and machinery. North Carolina Railroad president, Charles Frederick Fisher, needed a central location to build facilities to handle railroad-related repairs. When Fisher found the perfect place in Alamance County, a couple of miles northwest of Graham, the company purchased approximately 632 acres of land for $6,748.37. Private citizens then pledged $3,168.50 to construct needed buildings. The next step consisted of furnishing each of the buildings with equipment and hiring workers. By July 1, 1857, fifty-two employees (30 white, 12 slaves) from ten different states had moved to the community, now unofficially named Company Shops.

New arrivals found limited dwellings for themselves and their family members. In 1857 only three houses had been built and designated for company officials. Some six wooden and brick houses (called Brick Row) accommodated newly-arrived families. The Railroad Hotel, a brick and wood structure—actually a boarding house located on the south side of the main track near the passenger shed—provided food and lodging for passengers and for train crews and employees. "Miss Nancy" Hilliard, who had years of previous managerial experience, gleaned Company Shop's glowing accolades as gracious hostess and diligent worker. Praise for her many skills was widespread.

"Miss Hilliard's previous experience proved invaluable to her at the Shops," said one admirer. "A major effort was required to keep the hotel clean, as the linen was easily soiled by the oily clothing of the railroad workmen, and soot-laden smoke drifted frequently through the windows from passing locomotives. Yet the innkeeper was equal to the task. Even more appreciated by the hotel guests, however, was the bountiful, expertly prepared food served in the dining room. An impressive variety of meats, vegetables, condiments, cakes, and pies always graced the tables and were served at reasonable prices. The Railroad Hotel soon became well known for its superior cuisine. Satiated by their sumptuous meals, diners were unanimous in their praise of 'Miss Nancy's' establishment."

The Railroad Hotel, a large and architecturally attractive building, had a ground-level wrap-around porch behind columns which supported a verandah on the second floor. Inside, thirty high-ceilinged rooms provided spaces for a lobby, a dining room, and many bedrooms (all with basin, towels, and water pitcher). Of course, no indoor plumbing existed during these earlier years, so a row of outhouses stretched across the back yard of the property. No one knows the exact cost of the hotel boarding house, but estimates have been as low as $15,000 and as high as $30,000. Although some early critics referred to this elegant structure as "ornamental" and "extravagant," the boarding house served as a comfortable accommodation for guests.

Nancy Hilliard's management made that comfort possible for transients and locals who enjoyed the amenities.

"The trains stopped for twenty minutes to allow time for passengers and crew to dine," one account relates. "After the telegraph was installed, conductors wired ahead to inform the innkeeper how many wished a meal when the trains arrived, a practice that improved the efficiency of the hotel's service. Traveling salesmen frequently stayed overnight and toured the countryside in rented horse-drawn buggies during the day to call on area merchants. Numerous railroad employees became permanent boarders, and the hotel usually had few, if any, vacant rooms. It obviously filled a pressing need at Company Shops, and it is difficult to visualize what the situation would have been without it."

Company Shops trains played an interesting role in North Carolina's Civil War history, according to Durward T. Stokes. In the spring of 1865, the North Carolina Railroad "offered the only escape route from the military net closing around the state in the east. Bales of cotton were shipped out on freight

An early photo of Main Street in Company Shops.

cars as fast as possible to prevent their destruction by the invaders. Banks and commercial institutions followed suit by packing what gold and other specie they had into kegs and consigning them to trains, while terrified individuals filled the passenger cars in their frenzied flight to the west."

Because Company Shops, located at the middle of the railroad line, received many bales of cotton that were consigned to no one, local citizens unloaded the goods and hauled them away for their personal use. Unlike the cotton, shipments of gold ended up at destinations that remain a mystery. Greensboro railroad agent J. S. Scott received a large gold supply on one train that stopped at his station. According to Stokes, he "was terrified at the responsibility of guarding such a treasure in the face of two converging armies. He placed the gold aboard the next train that stopped, without regard for the direction in which it was headed. The fate of that money remains unknown." Perhaps some Company Shops residents benefited from this shipment. No one will ever know.

After the Civil War ended, Company Shops, still under military occupation, experienced even more activity. Soldiers fleeing from the Confederate capital arrived with gold, rumored to be several million dollars. Actual reports indicated that the soldiers probably arrived with only $500,000. Of course, the mystery centered around the question, "Where is the rest of the money?" No one knows, but, of course, rumors still circulate. One story indicated that Jefferson Davis received the treasure and used it to bribe General Sherman to guarantee Confederate officials a safe retreat. Another report said that the gold, originally buried in boxes and sacks, found its way as disbursement to officers. Still another speculation involved Company Shops directly. On May 7, 1865, Union Army Captain Henry Brown sent a notice to the Chief of Police at Greensboro, which stated:

Sir:

*On the 4th of May, 1865, companies B and K, of the Tenth Ohio
Volunteer Cavalry, at the railroad company's shops of the North Carolina
Railroad, between Hillsborough and Geensborough, N.C., found between
$80,000 and $100,000 in gold buried in boxes and sacks, and marked
Commercial Bank of New Bern, N.C. The money had been divided amongst the
finders and officers of the command...I understand some of the officers
concerned are about resigning [sic] with their booty in their pockets...If any
action is taken in the matter it should be at once.*

Many letters and official reports followed, and apparently the two or
three men who had taken and buried most of the gold returned the booty to
proper officials. Of course, because no one knows the amount buried, no
accurate accounting exists. Stories and rumors continue to this day. One farmer,
plowing near the tracks, says he uncovered gold coins. Strangers appear with
shovels from time to time to seek the tresure, but the mystery continues.

"To this day no one knows how much money was buried or how much
was recovered," Stokes writes. "The roadbed of the line, now a part of the
Southern Railway, is virtually where it has always been, and in many places the
right-of-way is still an undisturbed strip on both sides of the rails. We know that
treasure was once buried beneath its surface; after the passage of more than a
century, some may still be hidden there. No one can say for sure. At any rate,
Company Shops was the center of the furor over buried treasure in 1865, and it
was quite a while before the town again became remote from 'disturbing
influences,' if it ever did."

In 1869, other events helped mold the history of Company Shops. Ku
Klux Klansman Thomas Gray set fire to the schoolhouse because the
schoolmaster used the building to teach "darkies at night." Because Alamance
County citizens opposed the Klan's violent acts, Senator T. M. Shoffner
introduced the "Force Bill" in the 1869 legislature which "empowered the
governor to use military force to preserve law and order." As a result of
Shoffner's intervention, the Klan issued a death sentence on the Senator, and he
left Company Shops and North Carolina in a hurry.

Before long, Company Shops regained some sense of peace and balance.
Businesses sprang up and the railroad flourished. William Wesley Staley, early
president of Elon College, recalls his life in the community.

"In 1869 I taught [at] the Graham Public School and in the spring I
entered the store of Col. A. C. McAlister in Company Shops as a clerk," said
Staley. "In addition to my store duties, and with the consent of my employer, I
attended to the morning express train and sale of tickets at four o'clock. My pay
as clerk was board, laundry, and $10.00 per month; and I received $10.00 per
month for attending to the early morning express train."

The community grew. By 1875 merchants began advertising in the Graham *Alamance Gleaner.* In 1876, when Dr. J. S. Murphy established the Company Shops Drug Store, he placed this ad in the newspaper: *"Go to Company Shops Drug Store and buy Mrs. Person's Cure for Scrofula and be relieved...Dr. Pierce's Golden medical Discovery, and Hop Bitters are highly recommended for purifying the Blood and renovating the System."*

More new businesses appeared in Company Shops, including a jewelry store, an emporium, general stores, manufacturers, mills, and specialty shops. Also, in 1870, forty-four-year-old Mrs. Anna E. Troy and her seventeen-year-old son Thaddeus took over management of the boarding house. Accounts indicate that service and cuisine at the Hotel had deteriorated after Nancy Hilliard returned to Chapel Hill in 1865 to open the Crystal Palace Boarding House for university students. Conditions immediately improved under Mrs. Troy's supervision, and the hotel once again became a popular place to board. Tributes flowed in newspaper articles:

Recently, this house has become the supper house on the N.C.R.R. for the trains going west. We find the table an excellent one with every thing to reward the traveller for his long fast. It is a great improvement on any thing at the Shops since the days of Miss Nancy Hilliard, and we can cordially recommend the house to the public.

A 1879 compliment appeared in the paper:

Mrs. Troy for some years has been in charge of the hotel at Co. Shops— we find no table better supplied—and we don't wish to; hers is good enough.

Because Mrs. Anna E. Troy and Thaddeus provided such great service to their guests, the Railroad Hotel received a new name, the Troy Hotel. After Thaddeus obtained a position with the railroad and moved away from Company Shops, he and his family often visited their old hometown. An 1881 *Gleaner* snippet refers to the Troy Hotel as "the center of the community's social life" and continues with praise for Mrs. Troy: *"...the drummers say [she] has more good things to eat than any other place they stop."*

By 1881 Company Shops had its own newspaper, the *North Carolina National*, a journal strongly supporting the Greenbackers political party, but also printing both national and local news. The reporting resembled announcements, rather than articles or editorials. For example, the execution on June 30, 1882, of Charles Julius Guiteau, who had assassinated President James Garfield, merited only one line: *"Charles J. Guiteau was undoubtedly hung by the neck, Friday, June 30th, until dead, and that's all there is of it."*

Social activities at Company Shop at the close of the nineteenth-century centered around school and church events, such as recitals, commencements, and Sunday school picnics. Baseball and Tilting Tournaments became the favored sports in the little town. Residents worked and played in peace—for a while.

Then in 1875, the final blow came in a short *Gleaner* announcement: *"Everything is moving...The offices of the R & D R.R.N.C have all been moved from Company Shops."* Thus began the slow exodus that would increase each year. Most people left, but some citizens stayed, determined they would recover. And recover, they did, but under a different name. On February 1, 1887, the town name changed to Burlington, and was incorporated on February 14, 1893.

Information for this piece came from the following sources:
• *www.burlington-area-nc.org*
• Hilliard, Ann "Nancy" Segur. UNC University Library. On-line: "Documenting the American South."
• Stokes, Durward T. *Company Shops: The Town Built by a Railroad.* Winston-Salem: John F. Blair, Publisher

---

Waldorf Astoria Chocolate Cake

1/2 cup butter
2 cups sifted cake flour
2 teaspoons baking powder
2 teaspoons vanilla
4 squares chocolate
1-1/2 cups milk
2 eggs
2 cups sugar
1 cup nuts (optional)

Cream butter and sugar. Add melted chocolate and eggs well beaten. Sift dry ingredients together and add alternately with milk. Add vanilla and nuts. Bake in loaf pan at 350 degrees for about 1 hour. (Batter will be very thin, but this is the way it is supposed to be)

Icing for cake: 1/2 cup butter
1 egg, well beaten
1 teaspoon vanilla
1/2 cup nuts (optional)
2 squares chocolate
1-1/2 cups powdered sugar
1 teaspoon lemon juice

Melt butter and add chocolate; add egg; stir in sugar. Add vanilla, lemon juice and nuts and beat until smooth. From Alice Sink's family recipe file. This recipe belonged to her Grandmother Jenny Alice Wood Evans, who originally passed it down to her three daughters. Alice still has the recipe typed on her aunt's old Underwood typewriter on a piece of notepad paper from The Ohio Salt Company in Wadsworth, Ohio.

Mary Jane Connor

New Bern

Mary Jane Conner's Boarding House

Thanks to old letters, we know about Mary Jane Conner's boarding house in New Bern, North Carolina, during the Civil War. Private Henry Clapp, a Union soldier from Massachusetts stationed in New Bern from the fall of 1862 until the summer of 1863, wrote to his family about Mary Jane, a former slave. These memories are preserved in the book *Letters to the Home Circle: The North Carolina Service of Pvt. Henry A. Clapp, Company 3, Forty-Fourth Massachusetts Volunteer Militia, 1862-1863.*

On December 26, 1862, Private Clapp wrote to his mother about his Christmas Day experience:

"...I got our party together and wandered down to the abode of Mary Ann, a famous cook, who had arranged to provide our great dinner. A party from Company G had dined before us and the preparations were so much delayed in consequence that we did not begin our dinner till 4 1/2 P. M. The bill of fare consisted of oysters for soup—roast ducks and chickens, with turkey for entrees, and for vegetables (prepare to be astonished!) potatoes, squash, cabbages, onion and beets. Cranberry sauce also—one plate and apple-sauce (and finally nuts, shellbarks, almonds, pecans, and filberts) and raisins [sic]...The boys all said they had a fine home-flavor and were very nice in themselves—I told them who furnished and cracked the same."

In a letter dated April 19, 1863, Private Clapp wrote to his brother Willie, and after encouraging Willie to make the most of his high school days

Private Henry A. Clapp

and relating snippets of war news, recounts events connected with the boarding house where he has lived for approximately one month.

"*I want you to tell mother about the seamstress whom we employ to mend our clothes,*" Clapp wrote. "*She is a sister-in-law of our famous boarding house keeper, Mary Jane, and glories in the classical name of 'Sylvia.' She was formerly the slave of one of the richest men in New Berne [sic] who owned the house Gen. Foster now lives in, and was the family seamstress I should judge. She is about forty, and though very dark of very pleasant appearance. Her address and manner are remarkably agreeable and really of unusual refinement. I've seen the wives of millionaires who were much her inferiors in urbanity and polish of manner. She is a superb seamstress, as my dress-coat just rescued from many rents will bear happy witness. She seems also to be a woman of very good sense & well developed reflective facilities and her conversation is often very good and well worth listening to. We often wait in the house while they are putting the finishing touches on the dinner and spend the time in talking with her and Mary Jane. The lovely Eunice who waits on our table does not seem over and above intelligent, but her beauty makes ample amends for her stupidity—if I may use so harsh a word. You see that Mary Jane's house contains many remarkable inmates.*"

Apparently Private Clapp's mother sent him a box of books and clothes for Mary, Sylvia, and Eunice because in a letter dated May 18, 1863, he acknowledges to his father the receipt of these gifts:

"*The pieces of clothing and the presents for Mary, Sylvia, and Eunice were sent with admirable judgment, as mother's always is. The three ladies I am sure are bound to me forever. I thought it best to give the clothing to Mary Conner and tell her to use her own best judgment as to the disposition of it. She has a sister inn-law [sic] named Lewis, a very nice decent woman indeed, whose little girl will be only too glad for the frock, and for the other things Mary will distribute them judiciously, I am sure. She showed the fullest appreciation of everything. I did up the little packages for the ladies themselves with the clothing and carried them down to their house two days before I saw Mary. She had not been well and had gone out a little way into the country to visit one of her relatives. I left the bundle at the time however with Eunice, and told her to put it away in a place of safety and not to open it till I came again...This course had, unwittingly, the effect of exciting Mary's curiosity in the highest degree. The bundle was opened in the presence of Mary and the elegant Sylvia...and it was very interesting to watch the faces of the spectators as I passed them their separate packages with a few appropriate remarks in each case, and information, as to who the giver was. I think—indeed know—that they were very much pleased indeed. It was really delightful to look at Mary's countenance. No face can beam like a darkie's, it seems as if they shot forth light, clear clear black and yet shining. They are however no common colored people and they did not go into fits of delight but showed their satisfaction very much as cultivated people do in the*

Sylvia, the seamstress of New Bern
(Photo: Tryon Palace Historic Sites and Gardens, New Bern, N.C.)

North. Sylvia remarked that mother 'seemed to have guessed her taste exactly' and Mary reechoed the sentiments. Sylvia commented two or three times on its being so 'thoughtful' in [sic] Mrs. Clapp and I think they were really very much touched at the attention."

Clapp goes on to inform his family that all three women asked him to write in their [memory] books. In Mary's, he wrote, "Henry A. Clapp. Boarder & Friend. True love has an eye for the dinner." In Sylvia's, he inscribed, "Friend & Patron" with the motto, "A stitch in time saves nine." Eunice received the words, "Friend & Admirer" with a motto from Virgil's Ecologue's [sic] *Nimium ne crede colori :* " Do not put too much confidence in your beauty."

Private Clapp sent a total of 44 letters to family and friends. In the final three, he does not refer again to the three women or to the boarding house. Photographs of Mary Jane Conner and Sylvia, wearing their clothes sent from Massachusetts, were made on June 5, 1863.

Mary Jane Conner's boarding house does not stand today. It may have been torn down, or perhaps destroyed by New Bern's Great Fire of 1922.

Information for this piece comes from:
• *Letters to the Home Circle: The North Carolina Service of Pvt. Henry A. Clapp, Company 3, Forty-Fourth Massachusetts Volunteer Militia, 1862-1863.*

Edited by John R. Barden and published in Raleigh: Division of Archives and History, North Carolina Department of Cultural Resources, 1998.

WANT TO VISIT THE AREA?

Contact Tryron Palace Historic Sites and Gardens, P. O. Box 1007, New Bern, North Carolina 28563, Telephone: (252) 514-4937. Also enjoy A Walk Through New Bern's African-American Heritage. This walking tour begins downtown in the business district, where civil rights marches and sit-ins in the early 1960s integrated the segregated white businesses.

Hot Springs

Jane Hicks Gentry's Boarding House Legacy

Jane Hicks, born in Watauga County, on December 18, 1863, married Jasper Newton Gentry, a neighbor boy, shortly before her sixteenth birthday. Jane and Newt had nine children when they decided in 1898 to move their family to the town of Hot Springs, a town located on the French Broad River, six miles east of the Tennessee boarder. They wanted their offspring to attend Hot Spring's Dorland Institute, a Presbyterian mission school. Jane could read and write even though she had no formal schooling, but she and Newt wanted more education for their children.

Newt built a house on Meadow Fork next door to Dorland Institute, and Jane paid for her children's tuition by boarding teachers, scrubbing floors and doing laundry at the school. Even with all this hard work, Jane did not believe in all work and no play. She graciously shared mountain stories and songs for classes and special chapel programs.

Jane Hicks Gentry also ran a boarding house for tourists who made pilgrimages to Hot Spring's famous mineral pools and the more than 100-degree mineral water that bubbled along the banks of the French Broad River. These therapeutic springs reportedly cured gout, rheumatism, dyspepsia, torpid liver, paralysis, neuralgia, and other diseases and afflictions. People seeking cures for their health problems had begun visiting the waters as early as 1778, but it took another hundred years before the Buncombe Turnpike made travel more

The Hot Springs Hotel as it looked in the 1890's.
(Photo: North Carolina Collection, University of North Carolina Library at Chapel Hill)

accessible. By 1837, James Patton had completed his 350-room Warm Springs Hotel . Shortly after that, the railroad brought wealthy visitors for extended stays to what was then called Warm Springs, North Carolina (the name changed in 1886) and to the hotel's sixteen marble pools, lush lawns, and croquet and tennis courts. Those who could not afford the luxuries of the hotel boarded with Jane Gentry. While she cooked, cleaned, farmed, sewed, and nursed the ill, Jane told mountain tales and sang ballads. Her stories and songs still survive today. And rumors indicate that Grandma Gentry's ghost still roams her old boarding house.

Winters in the mountains brought blizzards and frozen rivers, so the Gentrys prepared early for this bitter season. After all, everyone—including the boarders—needed enough provisions to endure and survive the harsh months ahead. Jane, Newt, and their children sawed and gathered firewood, stored potatoes they had dug earlier, harvested pumpkins, gathered nuts, dried fruit, made apple butter, killed hogs for hams and shoulders, smoked and stuffed sausage, and canned souse meat and liver mush. After Jane and Newt put the children to bed, they sometimes hoed corn and repaired their barn roof by moonlight.

Jane confessed that a horseback ride to the mill provided a little precious time for herself. She recalled, "When we needed hit, I'd leave the babies with pappy, an' go off to the mill with half a bushel o' corn two an' a half miles an' back. Kindly enjoyed hit on a purty day—hit were so still an' nice in the woods."

The Gentrys raised their own sheep, and Jane spun, wove, dyed, knitted, and sewed their clothes and household linens. A talented weaver and spinner, she used her gnarled hands to make coverlets, tat, knit, and make pulled lace, which she often sold for additional income. While she worked, she sang. Popular titles (and often first lines) included the favorites, "My Mother She Bid Me," "There's Nothing to Be Gained by Roving," and "If I Had As Many Wives." Her repertoire of traditional ballads included "False Knight in the Road," "The Wife of Usher's Well," and "Gypsy Laddie." For the children, she combined songs and played party games, including "Eh, Lor! Miss Molly," "Baby's Ball," and "We're Marching Round and Round." She also entertained with tales, a favorite being "The Baby in the Briarpatch." This story and others, told and enhanced by Jane's amazing sense of humor and perpetuated through oral tradition, survive today.

Jane's talents as singer and story teller fascinated author Irving Bacheller, a famous writer of the day. Bacheller, who came to Hot Springs for a vacation, made Jane Gentry the subject of a novel, short stories, and magazine articles. He admired her, not only for her tales and ballads, but for the happiness she exuded. In 1914, the Bachellers invited Jane to their home in New York. Daughter Maud ran the boarding house in her mother's absence. While in New York, Jane reportedly received a standing ovation at the Metropolitan Opera House for her rendition of "The Cherry Tree Carol."

Irving Bacheller

As if her daily chores were not enough to keep her busy, Jane traveled throughout western North Carolina's Appalachian Trail as a spiritual leader and nurse. In an interview before her death, she said, "Sometimes the neighbors would send for me to get the blues tuk off 'em, an' I'd go an' pray with 'em, nurse the sick an' tell 'em stories an' cheer 'em up." Jane Gentry recalls her nursing duties: "I'd find 'em crowded into a little room, around some un burnin' up with fever, moanin' and wringin' their hands and skeerin' the sick un, and breathin' up the air. I'd drive 'em all out the house, an' open the door an' windows an' when the sick were half dead I've pulled 'em up the slant, with just air an' nourishment an' cheerful talk." She bathed their foreheads, administered sponge baths, changed the bedsheets, fed them homemade broth, and treated their afflictions with herbs—ginger, peppermint, sassafras, and ginseng—and also with various plants, bark, and roots growing wild in the mountains.

P 24

HOT SPRINGS
Health resort since 1800. Name changed from Warm Springs, 1886. Internment camp for Germans in World War I was here.

Hot Springs changed its name to Warm Springs, and held German POWs in WWI.

If something worried Jane, she took action. Once she heard about a moonshine still that was "spilin' up the boys," so "she set out...to take care of the problem." Stories vary as to her methods of closing the still, but it was shut down. That is how Jane Gentry became known as the 'Revenoor Lady.' Although Newt was a staunch Republican in a town of Democrats, Jane refused to become involved in arguments over politics. Reports indicate she "just grinned and enjoyed the discussions and continued with whatever handwork she had in her lap."

Woodrow Wilson honored the women of the Appalachian mountains in 1913 by decorating the Blue Mountain Room in the White House with their hand-woven rugs, curtains, and bedspreads. Although no definitive records have surfaced, historians believe Jane helped weave the draperies.

In May of 1917, the Mountain Park Hotel changed from an upscale vacation spa to an internment camp of approximately two thousand Germans from two ships detained by the United States government. Because these men—many of them German officers—had been captured in U. S. harbors at the onset of World War I, they could not leave to go back home. The United States government leased the Mountain Park as a place for their internment and allowed forty-five cents daily for each man's diet of rice, curry, apples, black or wheat bread, butter, tea, and coffee.

Forty families had arrived with the German officers. Women and children, who spoke no English, lived in nearby homes. Jane Gentry boarded some of the wives and admired their sewing skills and expertise in making sauerkraut. The women could visit with their husbands, under guards' supervision, only one hour each Sunday. One of the women who boarded with Jane regularly sent notes, tucked in a collie dog's collar, to her German husband. The townspeople treated the internees and their families with respect, and after the war, the Germans went back to their homeland. Some returned to Hot Springs for visits.

In 1919 Jane and Newt bought a bigger house, and Jane named it Sunnybank, probably from an old English carol. By this time, Jane was experiencing extreme back pain. A short, stout woman, she walked stooped, probably a combination of a congenital condition and an injury she sustained as a youngster when she fell from a horse. Nevertheless, she continued to smile, sing, tell mountain stories, and provide room and board for her paying guests.

As the years passed after World War I, Jane's daughter Maud stayed at Sunnybank to assist her mother with their boarders. After supper, both women entertained guests with tales and ballads. Jane died on May 28, 1925, and Maud continued to run the boarding house. Years later, one of her granddaughters, Bobbie Shuping, visited Maud at Sunnybank and experienced a strange incident.

"Sometime that night, I can't tell you what hour, someone came into the room from the room next to us, walked by the baby crib...checked the baby," she said. "The person, silhouetted in the light, walked back by the baby crib and walked out. At that time there was nobody in the house but us and Aunt Maud and Aunt Nola, and they were downstairs. We thought maybe someone had come in for a room in the night and lost their way. In the morning I told Aunt Maud about it. I said, 'Someone came in our room during the night.' And she said, 'Oh, yes, dear, I understand. That was Grandma Gentry. She always comes and checks the babies who stay in this house.'"

So, according to legend, Jane Hicks Gentry continues to care for others, probably singing ballads and telling stories, even to this day.

Information for this story came from the following sources:
• Smith, Betty N. *Jane Hicks Gentry: A Singer Among Singers* . KY: The University Press of Kentucky, 1998
• Bacheller, Irving. *My Lost Novel*,N.Y.: Farrar & Rinehard, 1938.
• Moore, Della Hazel. *Hot Springs of North Carolina*. Biltimore Press, 1992.

• Weir, Sally Royce. "Hot Springs, Past and Present." Tenn: S.B. Newman & Co.,   1906.
• Hot Springs, North Carolina. www.hotspringsnc.org/-History

WANT TO GO?

Hot Springs is a town in Madison County, North Carolina. Today the springs are privately owned as a spa. Water is piped to outdoor tubs beside the river and Spring Creek. The town itself is becoming ever more popular as a modern tourist destination, for aside from the springs, outdoor recreation is abundant in the area. The Appalachian Trail runs along downtown's Bridge Street and climbs the mountains on either side of the river. Rafting and kayaking are popular on the French Broad River itself. There are numerous other hiking, mountain biking, backpacking, and sightseeing opportunities in the nearby Pisgah National Forest.

SWEET POTATO BISCUITS
2 cups cooked, mashed sweet potatoes
4 cups self-rising flour
1 stick butter, melted • pinch baking soda
1-1/4 cups milk • 3 Tablespoons sugar

Mix together the sweet potatoes, butter, and milk until well blended. Stir in the flour, baking soda, and sugar. Shape the dough into a ball and knead about 9 to 10 times on a well-floured board. Roll the dough out 1 inch thick and cut with a 2-inch biscuit cutter. Bake in a greased baking pan in a 400 degree oven for 15 to 20 minutes or until brown. Makes about 15. *(From* Mama Dip's Kitchen *by Mildred Council, copyright 1999. Used by permission the University of North Carolina Press, www.uncpress.unc.edu.)*

Growing Up in a Boarding House:
Lillie Meyers' Diary

I*was born in 1882, December 14."* reads Lillie Meyers' first diary entry, dated August 22, 1898. *"I remember one time...my mother (Sarah Susan Meyers) kept an [sic] hotel, and one day a lady and a little girl stoped [sic] at our house. I ate at the big table, and ate so much pumpkin pie that my mother had to take me away from the table, and then I would not let the little girl sit in my chair."*

Actually, beginning in the early 1880's, Mrs. Meyers ran a boarding house, not a hotel, in her home at 313 Rankin Street in High Point, North Carolina. According to daughter Lillie's diary entries, the young girl considered herself more of a guest than a hostess. This behavior proved to be the exception rather than the rule, because most children whose mothers ran a boarding house during this era worked as diligently as their parent. They usually had chores which began early in the morning and extended to bedtime. Not Lillie.

In 1898, at sixteen years of age, she and her neighborhood girlfriends - Lena, Olive, and Annette - invented plays with their dolls acting, singing, and dancing. *"I think childhood days are the happiest days of one's life. Oh, for mine to come again,"* Lillie records.

Young Lillie admits she and her sister Ada would rather play than work. On August 22, 1898, she writes: *"I did not get up very early this morning because it is our wash day and I did not care much about work. After dinner I made a doll hat for my oldest doll, her name is Mabel, she is going on a visit to Baltimore to see Lizzie Crutchfield. Lizzie is one of Nannie Aldridge's dolls, and Lizzie and Mabel are great friends."*

Innocent experiences fill those summer days of 1898: *"I was eating an apple and some cake this evening and Ada was sewing on the machine making her a white waist and she turned around and sneezed all over my apple and cake and I cried because it was all that I had. Lena gave me one of her cakes and another apple and that had a worm in it."*

While Lillie casually reminisces about gathering pears, helping "get supper," going to a neighbors to get a sack of beans, and picking apples and berries, she writes excitedly about attending prayer meetings, going to lawn parties, visiting friends, playing ball, and hunting hickory nuts. She and her friends also obviously delight in collecting long-handled gourds hanging from trees. These probably become unique doll-house decorations. Lillie takes great pleasure in reading, talking and visiting with her girlfriends, and going regularly to Sunday school and church.

Instead of changing linens or peeling potatoes, Lillie prefers creative endeavors. When she is seventeen years old, she writes her first story called "Under the Black Berry Briers," and recalls *"it is so simple I don't think any one will give it a word of praise. Although Ada said it was as good as some she had read. I always think every thing she says is right."* High school days include library days, Latin lessons, and drawing: *"I drew George Washington's picture and Grace took it to look at and Mr. Lane saw it and asked me to let him see it. I guess he thought I was trying to draw him. He said, 'I don't mind your drawing but couldn't you find something better to do.' Grace showed it to Miss Roberson, one of her favorite boarders, and she said, 'Lillie you ought to make an artist.' I shall try to keep the picture for ever."*

Lillie spends most of her summer days between her seventeenth and eighteenth birthdays decorating her play house. When her mother insists Lillie engage in boarding house chores, they are simple ones: gathering vegetables from the garden, helping her mother prepare meals, and shucking popcorn. That's more than enough for her! At one point, she records: *"I have worked all day as hard as I could and am going to bed soon and rest. I haven't been outside of the yard today."*

By September 15, 1899, the boarding house is apparently filled to near-capacity. Lillie writes: *"To day [sic]...we took two [more] boarders."* For the remainder of that month, Lillie's dairy entries include a large dose of school and church activities, along with only a few boarding house duties, such as *"I baked a cake and helped get dinner."* Only a week later, on September 22, 1899, potential trouble rears its ugly head: *"A new boarder came in to day and he is as wild as a wild cat,"* Lillie writes, but she does not elaborate how or why. Obviously, her interests lie elsewhere.

In 1900, at the age of eighteen, Lilly receives an invitation to a doll's wedding. This is probably a pretend event where one of her friend's dolls gets married. Lillie's diary entry records her inability to attend because *"Mama did not get my waist [blouse] done in time and I didn't have anything fit to wear."* This same summer Lilly, lonesome and bored, vows: *"I am going to try to read the bible through this summer by just reading the books—skipping about. I am reading the Psalms now, my favorite verse in my reading to night is 'But I am poor and needy: yet the Lord shineth upon me: thou art my help and my deliverer: Make no tarrying, O my God. Psalms 40-17."* She is sad because one of her favorite former boarders, Miss Donnelly, has gone elsewhere to teach and has not sent her a promised letter.

About the only diversion from work and play during the summer of 1900 comes on May 28: *"I got up sooner than usual to see the eclipse of the sun. It came on about sixteen minutes after eight, but was not much darker than twilight. We were all looking through smoked glass and Julia said they said there was to be another eclipse in 1918, then we all began to wonder where we would be by that time. I will be about thirty five years old then."*

On May 30, 1900, Lillie reveals that warm weather has arrived. *"I just pulled off my undershirt last night."* her diary records. *"We all went down to the branch to wade this evening. I wrote Miss Donnelly a long letter."* Only once that spring of 1900 does Lillie record helping her mother cook for the boarders *"I got dinner today and forgot to salt anything."* Instead of helping with chores, she reads a book called *Red Rock*, attends prayer meeting, quilts, writes letters to relatives, has dental work done, and grieves over losing another favorite boarder, Mrs. Evans.

"Today was the longest day in the year but not to me for it is the last day that Mrs. Evans will ever board with us," Lilly wrote. *"I am so lonesome I could have cried all day but did not let myself. I went to the depot with her and got back with out crying I don't see how I did it, for I love her so much we were together and told each other everything. She says she will send for me when she gets money enough."*

Summer 1900 finds Lillie still wishing for that promised letter from Miss Donnelly, receiving mail from Mrs. Evans, and recording on July 3, 1900, *"When I look at that 'mush pot' of a looking Mrs. Davis who boards here and then think of Mrs. Evans I could cry all night for I love Mrs. Evans so much."* Lillie is the product of her times when young women students were often filled with adoration, complete respect, and heroine worship for their female teachers.

From Mrs. Evans, who has moved to Charlotte, North Carolina, Lillie receives a letter, an invitation to visit, and "an order for $2.75." Lillie graciously accepts Mrs. Evans' kind offer because the end of July, Lillie's diary reveals, *"To-night I am 78 miles away from home."* While on vacation, Lillie pays an August 5, 1900, visit to *"the Jail [for] prayer meeting. As soon as we started up stairs I began to wish that I hadn't come. There were seventeen prisoners, four white men, two Negro girls and the rest Negro men — it was a very sad sight and it was all I could do to keep from crying. It seemed so bad to hear the heavy door close us up in that out of the way place where we couldn't see anything of the bright world about us."*

Also, while visiting in Charlotte, Lillie walks past the boarding house where a friend from High Point had formerly lived. *"Poor child, for I am sure she was never use to such a place as that,"* she recorded in shock, *"for it is a house that was used for the fire engine dep't and looks like an old store room on a kind of back street."*

Lillie has a frightening experience: *"August 19th, 1900—Just about the time I finished writing in my diary my window blind rattled and when I went over there to fix it I saw a man a standing at the window and I went and called Mr. Evans and about that time he was comming [sic] in at the back door and asked me if I had gone to bed he said just as he was comming [sic] in the lightning flashed and he saw a man running away from my window of course I was scared and made them leave their door open."*

Back home in High Point, Lillie learns sad news about another former school teacher who used to board at the Cartland home. Lillie records, *"I hear this evening that my Miss Gertrude has the consumption and that people don't think she can live long. Oh! Must I let her die and never [see her again]? I cannot...What kind of a person am I anyway? Does [sic] other girls think as I do? No I am sure they do not, for they only think they love the foolish boys and I don't care anything for anybody except dear sweet pretty women and very few of them."*

That autumn, however, Lillie delights in the boarding house setup: *"We have had a cook all the week and to-day I haven't done any work at all."*

Escaping chores, Lillie does what she most enjoys. She plays. First on her agenda is a Young Women's Christian Temperance Union Social on Thanksgiving night. *"Almost every body was dressed tacky,"* Lillie confides to her diary. *"I wore an old-time costume, Quaker bonnet, white stockings and such—I carried an umbrella and walked up to Mr. Moyer, while he was talking to Miss Ethel, and punched him on the arm with my umbrella and said, Ain't me, then looked at Miss Ethel and then walked off. I didn't know he was so bashful and so easy hacked [disturbed]."*

While December 1900 brings telephone service to the Cartland boarding house, March 26, 1901, delivers a dreaded disease, scarlet fever, to High Point. *"We all went to school yesterday morning as usual,"* Lillie writes, *"but had not* been there more than an hour until ever so many men came after their children and the phone bell kept ringing and Mr. Crowell came in and told us that Mr. Johnson would ring the bell and we would be dismissed for the people were all scared to death about the scarlet fever being in town."

On Wednesday morning, May 15, 1901, nineteen-year-old Lillie, graduates from high school. "I...do feel very sorry that this is my last year to go to school there and more than likely I will never go to school any where again— Ah! The dear Days that are no more." After a couple of summer trips, Lillie goes to work as a clerk in Sapps Racket Store. She continues to live with her mother at the boarding house and grieves when favorite boarders leave.

"I am feeling very lonely and blue to-night," Lillie writes on August 19, 1901. "I suppose it is all due to Mrs. Beard's going away. She and the baby and Junius have been boarding with us for over three month and it is so hard to part with them...I can't keep from liking almost any woman that I am with any time and then I do hate to have to part with them and especially do I hate to part with the children."

On Saturday, April 20, 1902, Lillie learns that her dear Miss Gertrude has died. "As I was going to the store Saturday morning I met Lena Best and she said, '...I feel sorry for you, you have lost Miss Gertrude.' Well it almost knocked me down—I don't know just what I did but I believe that I hit her and just said, Lena, then turned and went right on to the store with out saying another word. I thought that I would stay in the store just the same and keep all to myself but it was too much. I couldn't stay, so I wrote Crissie a little note and got her to ask Mr. Sapp if it would be alright [sic] for me to go home."

By July of 1902, Lillie was corresponding regularly with her beloved Miss Donnelly, and had purchased a new suit of furniture for her bedroom at the boarding house. "It is my first suit of furniture and I am planning to have my room very nice...I am going to try to be nice and clean from this on for I should feel ashamed to look careless now, and then besides I am going to put out my pictures of Miss Gertrude and Miss Donnelly and of course I would never think of letting them stay in a dirty room."

The last of Lillie's diary entries in March 1903 finds her welcoming back home her sister Ada and Ada's baby. Lillie still attends Sunday school and church and prayer meeting. She occasionally assists her mother at the boarding house, she writes regularly to Miss Donnelly, and she holds Miss Gertrude's memory dear. Lilly writes a poem for her final diary entry:

There is not in this life of ours
One bliss unmixed with fears;
The hope that wakens our deepest powers
A face of sadness wears
And the dew that showers our dearest flowers
Is the bitter dew of tears.

Lillie lived in her mother's boarding house until she married in 1913 at the age of 31. She had four children. Lillie died in 1927 when she was 45 years old.

Information for this piece comes from copious dairy entires made by Lillie Meyers while she was growning up in her mother's boarding house. Thanks to Kay Snow who provided these diaries for this book.

Lillian Frye's Boarding House

Randolph House Country Inn in Bryson City has a long and interesting history and a few name changes along the way. Lillian and Amos Frye first built a huge private home. Years later they constructed an inn within walking distance of their house. Each structure boarded both friends and strangers who came to this mountain town. Neither the versatility of the residence nor the inn, however, can match Lillian Rowe Frye's eclectic nature, varied interests, and notable accomplishments.

At a time when hostile Indians still resided in the area, Lillian and Amos Frye moved to Charleston (later named Bryson City), North Carolina, after their marriage in 1895. Lillian wanted Richard Morris Hunt, Biltmore Mansion's key architect, to design her new home. She scheduled an appointment and traveled for a day and a half by horse and buggy to Asheville to meet with him. They both agreed that French doors and many windows would give the residence that light and airy look that Lillian so desired. Early on, she first named her estate "Eden of the Smokies," but then changed the name to "The Peaceful Lodge."

Ten bedrooms and six bathrooms provided ample space for family members, special visitors, and boarders. Built from the finest maple, oak, and chestnut, the exterior of the house was covered with rustic poplar tree bark. The first building in the area to have electricity, a telephone, and indoor plumbing, the finest workmanship went into the residence. Hand-forged hinges adorned cabinets, while bathroom fixtures bore the cobalt blue logos of early

Vanderbilt's Biltmore House, in Asheville, N.C.

infantrymen. Lillian used to remark, "Biltmore Mansion likes to brag that they were the first to have working toilets in a house, but we flushed long before they did." Then she would qualify that statement with, "Only because Biltmore took longer to build!" From time to time, various religious denominations held their services in the living room. The Baptist, Methodist, Presbyterian, and Catholic congregations would rotate, meeting different Saturdays and Sundays. Also, children attended school in the house until a schoolhouse was built. The Fryes believed in community involvement.

Although Captain Amos sanctioned Lillian's desire to have a house like the Biltmore Mansion, he did not agree with some of Mr. Vanderbilt's philosophies. For example, according to distant relative Stephen Adams, "It seems they had different viewpoints on business and local people. It was the Captain's mode of operation to help local people prosper through jobs and education. It was Vanderbilt's to bring in outside people to do his work." Adams shares an interesting story to illustrate the different values of the two men. "Captain Amos would hire people who would pick him up at the depot and take him up to his house. Vanderbilt would save his money and walk to the outer gate of his house and ring for a servant to come to the gate and fetch him."

Lillian, an early environmentalist and naturalist, invited traveling artists and educators to her home and held social gatherings. She liked earthy primitive objects and had a kiln in the basement to fire her handmade pottery. She stored looms in the attic to weave cloth. Using natural stains such as pokeberry, Lillian stained the walls of her new home herself. She also dabbled in blacksmithing. A watercolor of Lillian as a young woman, dressed in a pioneer-type dress and bonnet, in a field of flowers portrays her love of nature and gardening. Also an excellent cook, Lillian had a basement kitchen with open hearth, where she roasted quail, duck, pheasant, and venison.

From 1895 to 1923, the twelve-gabled residence—built when no town or other amenities existed— had a two-fold purpose. The Fryes visualized a city springing up in this isolated mountain region, so they enticed professional people, writers, and educators to come see the area and stay with them as non-paying guests. The house also served as a boarding house for travelers and traveling salesmen. Because no paved roads existed, a horse and buggy would go to the railroad station to pick up these paying guests, who enjoyed the same gracious amenities as family and friends.

Lillian's devoted servant Emma prepared food on a wood stove in a separate basement area called "the summer kitchen." She used a dumbwaiter to send dishes upstairs to the thirty-foot-long dining room, referred to as "the banquet room," where Emma's husband Grover and other servants assisted in formal serving. Grover passed a twenty-eight-inch turkey platter and then served vegetables from large bowls. Starched white linens, freshly cut flowers, and Haviland china with delicate tiny roses graced the table.

Captain Amos Frye, a legal attorney for Whittier Lumber Company in California, had by this time accumulated over 650,000 acres of land, acquired from the Cherokee Indians and as land grants from the government. When the government began claiming some of the Frye's property for a Great Smoky Mountains National Park, Amos and Lillian anticipated the profitable tourism that such an attraction would bring because people would need a place to stay. Taking advantage of their three-years' timber rights, they collected the finest building materials the mountain trees could offer and built an inn next door to their house. Before the inn's opening in 1923, the Fryes hired John Randolph, a local man with a reputation for laying hearthstones, to install fireboxes in the many fireplaces. Randolph became enamored with Lois, the Frye's daughter, and they eventually married.

Now both the house and the inn—named Fryemont Inn—boarded visitors who came to the mountains. Captain Amos had a fleet of colorful buses that went back and forth from the inn to the train depot, transporting guests. Paying guests usually stayed in the inn and ate at the public table. "It was swanky," Stephen Adams recalls. "I remember getting up very, very early and my parents driving to the Inn in order to get there in time for breakfast. It was New York style in the mountains."

One family member describes Lillian as "trim, slender, and wiry. She stood about five feet, five inches tall—never heavy." She enjoyed hiking, building stone steps and a lily pond, and cultivating her flower gardens. Described as a "working tornado," Lillian Frye had interests outside her home. She and Amos owned gift shops in Bryson City, Miami, Washington, and New York.

The first woman accepted to the law school of the University of North Carolina, Lillian completed her studies (a law degree was not required) in 1911 and became the second woman to pass the North Carolina Bar examination. Having earned the distinction of being the first female member of the North Carolina Bar Association, she practiced law in partnership with her husband and her son-in-law, John Randolph, whom she had earlier persuaded to attend law school. After John earned his law degree, he went to Washington as a congressman.

Instrumental in the establishment of the Girl Scouts in western North Carolina, Lillian also used her strong personality to support women's rights. According to distant relative Ruth Adams, "She went to Raleigh to serve on the Governor's Commission many times and also to Washington D.C. to attend women's rights meetings. She stood her ground and was a strong personality."

When her husband died in 1936, Lillian gave up her law practice to resume the role of hostess at Fryemont Inn. Her daughter and son-in-law, Lois and John Randolph, assisted Lillian in this full-time endeavor. According to Emily Colin and Lynn P. Roundtree in their book, *A Look at the Fist 100 Women Attorneys in North Carolina,* Lillian and Lois "hosted prominent figures of the day, including President Franklin D. Roosevelt (who attended the dedication of the Great Smoky Mountains National Park), Senator Richard B. Russell, sportscaster Mel Allen, and Ochs Adolph, editor of the *New York Times."*

When Lillian died in 1957, daughter Lois and her husband John Randolph inherited the two properties. Lois and John had no children, so after Lois' death in 1962, John asked his niece, Ruth Randolph Adams, if she wanted The Peaceful Lodge and The Fryemont. "I didn't," she recalled. "I said, 'Uncle John, thank you so much, but no thank you.' Uncle John said, 'Honey, you just take the old house and do your thing.'" John continued to live at the inn until his death in 1978.

Ruth marvels that present-day guests remember Lillian Frye. "About five years ago, an attorney from Raleigh was here, having dinner with a group of people," Ruth relates. "We talked for a while, and he told me, 'If Lillian Frye had been alive when Sandra Day O'Connor was admitted to the Supreme Court, Mrs. Frye would have been there. That would have been her.' And I thought, wow, she really must have been something...She was a terrific attorney who never wanted to lose a case. From all of the people I have ever met who knew of her, she was really something else...Mrs. Frye was quite an influential woman."

Ruth and Bill Adams renamed the inn The Frye-Randolph House in 1970.

Information for this piece comes from the following sources:
- Nickie Doyal's telephone interviews with Stephen Randolph Adams on Lillian Frye, who was his great-uncle's mother-in-law. November 10, 2003 and April 28, 2006.
- Nickie Doyal's telephone interview with Ruth Randolph Adams, mother of Stephen Randolph Adams and niece of John Randolph. November 17, 2003.
- "The History of Bryson City's Randolph House" at *www.randolphhouse.com/History.html*
- Colin, Emily and Lynn P. Roundtree. *The Changing Face of Justice.*
- "Lillian Rowe Frye: Licensed 1911." North Carolina Bar Association Publication.

WANT TO GO?

Innkeepers at Randolph House Country Inn in Bryson City, North Carolina, a nostalgic Country Inn where mountain hospitality is a tradition, welcome you to enjoy the finest of gourmet food and good old-fashioned true hospitality. The Inn is centrally located to many local attractions, including the Great Smoky Mountains National Park, hiking, fishing, whitewater rafting, and is only a short drive to the casino in Cherokee. Contact them at: 223 Fryemont Road, Post Office Box 816, Bryson City, N.C. 28713. (828) 488-3472, (770) 938-2268, or (800) 480-3472.

STUFFED TROUT
Sauté 1/2 cup onion, 1/4 cup bell pepper, 1/2 cup mushrooms and garlic for 3-5 minutes (salt and pepper to taste). Stuff 2 trout cavities with mixture. Place in sprayed baking pan. Pour 1/2 to 2/3 cup of Marsala wine over trout. Cover with foil and bake for 15-20 minutes.

SQUASH CASSEROLE
3 cups of cooked squash, 1/2 cup of sautéed onion, 1/4 cup of bell peppers, 2 eggs, 1/2 cup mayonnaise. Salt and pepper to taste. Mix and bake 325-350 degrees until set. Serve.

ARMARETTO PARFAIT
In parfait glass, put 2 pear halves, 1 jigger of amaretto, 1 scoop of vanilla ice cream, and top with whipped cream.

(Recipes courtesy of William L. and Ruth Randolph Adams, innkeepers for 35 years.)

Salisbury, N. C., June 21, 1913

To Whom It May Concern:

The waters of Healing Springs have long been noted for their health giving qualities. The place should be made a great resort and have the very best accommodations for guests and visitors every day in the year. The climate is excellent and the Springs only need to be known and the waters to be used to become one of the most famous watering places in America.

Very truly yours
JOHN S. HENDERSON

Hundreds of others who have visited the Springs could be named, but we give the above list of well known North Carolinians to show that Healing Springs is not something new, just being sprung on the people.

THE WATERS

The water from both developed springs especially affects the stomach and kidneys, and is said by eminent physicians, to be a splendid remedy for all stomach and kidney diseases. Both springs are principally calcic waters but contain several other minerals. Following is the analysis:

Analysis of Healing Springs Waters.

No. 9222, Sept. 27th, 1895.

Total Mineral Matter on evaporation—10.80 grain U. S. Gallon.
Consisting largely of Calcium Carbonate with small quantities of
Magnesium Carbonate
Oxide of Iron
Aluminia
Silica

(A CALCIC WATER)

12

Healing Springs

**At Healing Springs, Nature, in
capricious mood, made a turn-key job.
She planted her forests, she fashioned
her hills, she gave natural drainage;
she threw up minature [sic]
mountains, restful to the eye; she
made her vegetation grow in tropical
profusion, and then to crown this
work, her glory, she furnished some
four or five strong ever flowing springs
of mineral waters—waters acting like
magic and a charm on the person who is ill.**

From *Nature's Turn Key Job*, a
promotional booklet about Healing
Springs, circa 1915.

Legend has it that Native Americans first discovered this cluster of springs and believed the miracle water could heal. In 1798 William Moore and Thomas Carson received a grant for 3,988 acres of land, which included the Healing Springs Mountains. Interestingly, the mountains— with the highest elevation in Davidson County (over a thousand feet above sea level)—covered about one-fifth of the township. During the mid-1800s, residents and visitors "drank, bathed and bottled the spring water which was said to cure any type of stomach or kidney ailment." Word spread from generation to generation, and for more than a hundred years, people swore by the water's health-giving qualities.

Where is this place that touts miracle cures? Healing Springs, surrounded by mountains, is located on North Carolina Highway 8, one mile south of where it crosses Flat Swamp Creek, and approximately fifteen miles southeast of Lexington. According to one newspaper reporter, "From the Gay Nineties until 1915 or so, Healing Springs was *the* place to be in Davidson County. That idyllic period has been called the age of innocence in America, after the Civil War and before 'world wars' were numbered."

As people began to spend extended periods of time at Healing Springs, they needed a place to board. A large log structure built prior to 1900—through the years called a hotel, a resort, and a rooming house—actually met the criteria of a turn-of-the-twentieth-century boarding house. Wealthy citizens stayed entire summers to enjoy lodging, meals, social activities, and the benefits of the healing water. Guests enjoyed picnics and Fourth of July celebrations. Gurgling streams provided the backdrop for summer games, greased pig races, porch rocking, ice cream socials, greased-pole contests, and Sunday afternoon bands with sing-a-longs. People traveled in horse and buggy to spend a summer with relatives and friends.

Once the Winston-Salem Southbound Railroad delivered guests within a mile of the springs, native Lewis Rogers transported them from the train to the boarding house in a horse-drawn buggy. Lewis and his son, Fred, also delivered vegetables, eggs, and chickens from their family farm to the dining room of the resort. "People would come from Lexington, Winston-Salem, Greensboro, High Point, just all over," Rogers said. "We even had a lot of people from Virginia. Some would come down for six weeks at a time in the summer."

Another native, George Franks, recalls the bands, shows and games, such as "knocking down the nine pins," and greased pig races. "Oh, there'd be all kinds of contests. They'd have contests for the ugliest man and the prettiest woman. They'd have greased-pole climbing contests. I remember the bigger boys got together and just got on each other's shoulders to win that one...It was just a lot of plain-old fun. They sold ice cream and candy. I spent several nickels down there. During election years, politicians mingled with the crowd and debated each other."

Locke Craig campaigned on the grounds for the North Carolina governorship in 1912. Healing Springs, according to *Homespun,* "was the mustering grounds for the entire lower district of the county." It also served as the local polling place.

Mrs. Ellen Beck, whose grandfather, James Manly Daniel, was also one of the founders of Denton, told about his starting the Healing Springs Hotel.

"It was nothing for 400 to 500 people to come on the weekends," she said. "People who would stay there would carve their names in the logs on the front porch, which went all the way across the hotel, and the hallways. When we were children we used to sneak upstairs to watch the people dancing in the ballroom. All the old prominent people...would come and stay for weeks—some the whole summer...this was before people could get in a car and go to the beach."

Some guests came with ulterior motives according to Denton resident Gilbert Futrell. "One family would bring a daughter they wanted to marry off, and one family would bring a son they wanted to marry off, and they would try to hook them up," he said. This matching game worked for Miss Margaret McNulty. In the summer of 1924 she traveled to Healing Springs from Columbus, South Carolina, and met her future husband, Don Walser, then a lieutenant general stationed at Fort Bragg. They married in 1925. They obviously had not gone to Healing Springs solely for mineral water.

Others, however, made the trip for that very reason, "drinking the mystical mineral water or wading in the small pool, basking in the rejuvenating liquid." In April 1839 William Harris announced an expansion and improvements to the popular resort. "He intends to open his house on the first of July, and will spare no pains to render his customers easy and comfortable," proclaimed the advertisement in the *Western Carolinian*.

An early recommendation for this area as a spa came in the form of a letter to the editor of a regional newspaper, the *Lexington and Yadkin Flag*. In 1855, an anonymous visitor asserted, "The springs do in reality possess valuable healing properties, and...are a fit place of resort for dyspeptic patients." A first-person account describes the resort's rustic living conditions and beautiful scenery:

"There were at the same cabin with myself, two married and five single ladies, and unfortunately for me, there were but two rooms in said cabin; consequently, I had to roost in the passage, and my bed was made of carriage cushions, placed on a large pine table, which served also as a dining table. I should doubtless have done fine here, had it not been that a complete army of winged insects came buzzing their martial music above my head, and would you believe all these audacious little creatures actually claimed to be relations of mine, for they would fly close to my ears, whispering softly Cousin-Cousin-Cousin; and then dropping down upon my cheeks, they imprinted kisses that were not at all agreeable to the better feelings of my nature. Nevertheless, I maintained my position manfully until they called for the bedstead to place our breakfast upon. Late in the afternoon of the same day, I set out with three bonnie blue-eyed beauties, for the purpose of exploring the mountain, and from its top, we gained the summit of Chalk Mountain. Need I tell you that we were all delighted at the broad expanse of our scenery, laid open to our view, from this

elevated point. We viewed with pleasure the bold, beautiful Yadkin flowing rapidly downward in its deeply washed channel, from four miles above, to four miles below where we stood, then turning our eyes northward we beheld with wonder and admiration, the grim majestic looking pinnacle of Pilot Mountain, towering in all its native grandeur and suitability, high above nature below; but I believe we gazed with most pleasure upon the curling smoke, as it ascended from the quiet farm houses, which were scattered here and there over the face of the surrounding verdant plains, and was wafted by gentle zephyrs gracefully heavenward..."

In 1895, twenty years after the anonymous visitor's testimonial, government testing of the water showed it contained calcium carbonate, magnesium carbonate, oxide of iron, alumina and silica. James Manley Daniel III, in an August 19, 1996 *News and Record* interview, said that he believed the water to be rich in lithium and, thus, an effective treatment for depression. H. B. Varner, editor of the Lexington *Dispatch* wrote, "If you are sick and drink this water, it will make you well; if you are weak, it makes you strong; if you are tired and run down, it builds you up."

In a promotional booklet about Healing Springs published circa 1915, Dr. J.W. Austin testified to the water's benefit. "It gives me a pleasure to recommend this water," he wrote, "to patients with torpid kidneys, associated with gouty or rheumatic tendencies. It is of benefit to 'flush' the kidneys when the system becomes laden with impurities through imperfect elimination of tissue-waste. I also recommend it to patients who are suffering from so-called uric-acid diathesis."

When he was interviewed at age eighty-three, area native Fred Rogers remembered a great deal of the hype surrounding Healing Springs and admitted his belief that much of the medicinal value ascribed to was mere superstition. "There was iron water in one [spring]," said. "You could taste the iron. I guess that was good for you to have in your system. The other one was a sulfur spring. It just tasted like old sulfur—you could smell it, too. Then there was a small spring rock that was supposed to be good for sore eyes."

Conversely, George Franks believed the waters did have curative powers. "I used to go get five-gallon wood kegs of it," he said in a 1983 interview. "It'd make you sweat, though. But it made you feel good. I know I did, and that was 60 years ago. When I go past there I still get it...It'll clear your kidneys really good."

According to most sources, the popularity of the springs reversed when medical advances disputed the springs' therapeutic value. The crowds left, the log boarding house decayed, and the Daniel family gave up their dream of building a grand hotel and establishing a first-class health resort. Weeds, beer bottles and trash litter the grounds now. The rocks contain the spray-painted names of teenagers who have ventured on the property. Occasionally visitors stop and sip the sulfuric-smelling water flowing from a small pipeline. The popular gathering place now resembles a true ghost town. Only a rock formation and a couple of ramshackle buildings remain. Horse and buggies no longer rattle down the road, relatives and friends do not gather for reunions, politicians do not hold Sunday afternoon rallies. As one reporter aptly described the scene, "If you listen closely you can hear the trickle of water at a nearby stream, a bird chirping, and the occasional passing car at the old healing springs...History has been written. If the mountains could only talk."

Information for this piece comes from the following sources:
- An unpublished essay entitled "Healing Springs" by Alice E. Sink.
- Holeman, Jeff. "Water's Power Drew Hundreds Seeking Relief." High Point *Enterprise.* January 21, 1944.
- Tovart, Paul Baker. "Building the Back Country." The Davidson County Historical Association, 1987.
- "Springs Outlasted Area Resort." Piedmont/Focus. The Lexington *Dispatch.* April 7, 1983.
- "Healing Springs Township." *Homespun.* Vol. 3, No. 2.
- Sink, Jewell and Mary Green Matthews. *Pathfinders Past and Present: A History of Davidson County, North Carolina.* High Point: Hall Printing Co., 1972.
- Snipe, Michele D. "Heal Thyself: Spring's Fame Trickles." *News and Record.* August 19, 1996.
- "Nature's Turn Key Job: Healing Springs, North Carolina." The Concord Job Printery. 1916.

WANT TO GO?

Healing Springs is located off an unmarked dirt and gravel drive about a mile past Flat Swamp Creek Bridge on Highway 8. Today the only visible remains are two arched rock shelters on the west side of the highway. If you look closely, you will see brick chimney remains and stone and slate steps which led to the front porch of the old boarding house, long ago decayed and fallen. Plastic milk jugs and six-pack rings once covered the grounds, but members of the Healing Springs Volunteer Fire Department have adopted the area for Project Clean-Up. Today visitors can stop to picnic under the sweet gums and maples, and with a little pretending, listen to the legendary healing waters flowing from holes at the bottom of cobblestone arches. Or they might—if they have vivid imaginations— hear the old strains of "In the Good 'Ol Summertime" or "Down by the Old Mill Stream" coming from where the old boarding house used to stand. Of course, all guests must sip the rusty-tasting water flowing from a pipeline...just in case.

Rufus and Ora Moore

Greensboro

Mrs. Moore's Boarding Houses

Beginning in 1913, Mrs. Ora Moore's house at 218 Ashe Street, provided a convenient and comfortable home-away-from-home for Greensboro lawyers and clerks. Ashe Street began at the back of the County Courthouse, and number 218—a stately residence with two imposing columns— stood just four houses down on the right. Mrs. Moore earned such a good reputation for the delicious food she served that her establishment soon filled to capacity.

Ora's kitchen had a large wood stove with an oven, cabinets to warm sweet potatoes, and places to heat irons for pressing clothes. Her pantry supplied home-canned vegetables and fruits. A large sink contained both washing and rinsing sections. The washing bowl had moveable racks, operated by a handle, that moved back and forth in the soapy water. Strong lye soap, which Ora made, proved so potent it could kill poison ivy. She did not own an electric refrigerator, but had several ice boxes on the back porch. Every day a local company delivered huge blocks of ice. Mrs. Moore had a unique and inexpensive pest-control system. Her fox terrier, trained to go into the kitchen at night to kill rats, kept the area free of rodents.

Money was always short, but Ora did not let that bother her. In fact, an old cliché, "Hand to mouth" would sum up her circumstances. Only after she had collected twenty-five cents from those who came from nearby offices to eat their noon meal did she have enough money to buy food for that evening. In the afternoon, she sent her grandchildren to the store to purchase the groceries she would need for supper. Grandson Bob Moore says he remembers Ora, who was of German descent (Huffine), making kraut in a big crock in the basement. "It would make your eyes water," he relates. "It was strong."

The Ashe Street dining room had eight large tables, seating eight people at each, for a total of 64. Bowls of vegetables and platters of meat crowned the center of each table. Diners would then reach for the dishes they wanted—thus the term "boarding house reach." Mrs. Moore served breakfast, dinner, and supper seven days a week (except Sunday night). The standard fare for every meal included homemade biscuits sopped with molasses or Karo syrup.

According to Bob Moore, "The cooks were colored, and my grandmother was the supervisor. The bus boys were A&T College students, and we grandchildren filled water glasses. My grandmother insisted that everyone say, 'Yes, sir' and 'yes ma'am' to older people."

If the dining room became filled to capacity for the first noon seating, businessmen and secretaries from downtown offices waited on the front porch for a vacancy in summer, or in the living room during bad weather—where granddaughter Violet played the piano. "Discussions included tall tales, jokes, teasing, and occasional lying," Bob Moore relates. "Lawyers discussed tough cases while waiting for their meals." Election time, in particular, brought forth all kinds of arguments between the attorneys.

Topics of conversation probably concerned on-going litigation involving child labor laws and slander, murder, and libel suits—just a few cases on the

Mrs. Moore's boarding house.

busy Guilford County Court House docket heard by the Honorable W.P. Bynum. No doubt, Guilford jailhouse stories surfaced, the most famous concerning Judge Archibald D. Murphey's incarceration in 1829 after his liberal theory that no one should be imprisoned for debt.

Lyndon Swaim's article in an 1883 issue of the *Greensboro Patriot* recalls Murphey's imprisonment:

"His honor was unspotted. He was the victim of a law inflicting torture as exquisite to the sensitive soul, if not to the body, as the rack or thumb screw of the Middle Ages. I heard good old Sheriff Doak say that no occurrence of his life, official or otherwise, was so painful to him as the [sentence] upon the venerable judge, the meekness and dignity of whose bearing was so impressive, and his resignation to the inevitable so touching. When he was conducted to the prison and surveyed the surroundings...he remarked that the room was not...sufficiently lighted or ventilated. He requested the sheriff to leave the door open! And the sheriff went off and left the door open!"

Lawyers on Mrs. Moore's porch or in her living room would have loved that long-ago true story, marveling that Judge Murphey never tried to leave the jail. It seems that when a friend and colleague, Judge Camero, confronted the sheriff about leaving the jail door unlocked, the sheriff replied, "I would risk life and sacred honor with Judge Murphey. You don't think he would go away?"

Judge Camero countered, "I do not mean that. I mean that it might be considered in law an escape, and you might yourself become involved to your hurt." The sheriff replied, "Murphey knows the law, let us go back and consult him." And when they did, Judge Murphey responded with these words: "Mr. Sheriff, my friend, it will be safest for you to lock the door upon me."

Lawyers at Mrs. Moore Boarding House would have reminisced about another celebrated prisoner in the Guilford County Jail, the Reverend Daniel Worth. A Wesleyan Methodist minister, Worth received a jail sentence in 1859 for "teaching Negroes to read and write and circulating subversive literature." While incarcerated during a particularly harsh winter, his feet froze and his general health deteriorated. Finally tried, found guilty, and asked to leave North Carolina, Worth quickly went north.

Entertainment in the Ashe Street parlor while lawyers waited for their home-cooked meals did not focus entirely on court cases and law suits. A piano, radio, newspapers, magazines, a sofa and chairs filled the huge room. At Christmas, a decorated tree made the men feel at home. When warm weather arrived, boarders gathered on Mrs. Moore's porch after supper to listen to the music of the black jazz bands that roamed the neighborhood.

After Mrs. Moore and the servants washed the dishes, cleaned the kitchen, and began soaking a big pot of pinto beans for the next day's dinner, the work day had ended. Bob Moore remembers his father, John Craven Moore, tucking him into bed at night and reciting the following to him as a bedtime story:

"When on Columbia's eastern plain still roamed the forest child (Indians), the new homes of the European friends (Quakers) were rising in the wild. Upon a clearing in the woods, Amos built his cot, tilled his farm, and lived contented with his lot. A just, peace loving man was he, kind to all, and well the wandering Indian knew, an ever open door. One morning a neighbor passed in haste, 'Indians they say are nigh, so Amos bar your door tonight and keep your powder dry.'

"'Nay friend,' he said, 'My God commands me not to kill, and sooner would I yield my life than disobey His will.'

"'Well,' said the other as he went, 'My faith is not so clear, if the wretches come to take my life, I mean to sell it dear.'

"That night his wife urged her husband sore until at last he barred the cottage door. Soon the wife was wrapped in slumber deep, but Amos turned and tossed about and vainly tried to sleep. A voice within him spoke, with mild rebuke it bore, 'Amos, why hath thy barred thy cottage door?'

"Then softly from his bed he 'rose and slowly trod the floor, and noiselessly unbarred the cottage door. He looked forth into the night, starlit and still it was, and slowly rose the wavering moon behind the free-fringed hills.

"Then back to his forsaken bed he slowly groped his way and slept the slumber of the just until the dawn of day.

"That night a great, painted warrior band, through the dark forest sped, with steps as light upon the leaves, as panthers steadily tread. They came to Amos' house. 'Here dwells the son of Penn. How shall we surely know? We will go and gently try the door, if it opens it proves as it was before.'

"It yielded, and they entered in, across the room they crept, and came to where Amos and his wife calm and unconscious slept. With Tomahawks and scalping knives they stood beside the pair, but angels' guard was there.

"Quietly, they left the room and closed the door behind..."

Bob Moore says, "At this point, I always went to sleep. I know what happened. The Indians went on to kill [other] people and burn houses, but I don't remember the words."

After little Bob fell asleep, the extended family gathered in Ora's room, talking while she darned socks, sewed on her sewing machine, or rocked in her wicker chair. In addition to her immediate family's needs, she generously volunteered to darn or sew for anyone who needed a torn seam mended or a rip repaired.

Chores and routines became the norm at 218 Ashe Street. Rufus Moore, Ora's husband had only one task: he stoked the coal-furnace in the basement. According to grandson, Bob, "Grandmother made all the decisions. She handled

Ora Moore's Ashe Street dining room.

the money, paid the bills, and was very patient. Nothing bothered her. Grandmother never disciplined anyone."

Servants, who lived in a small house at the back of the property, reported for duty each morning and worked throughout the entire day. The Moore family and their servants got along well. Nanny, the cook, taught young Bob how to tie his shoes, and he helped her shell peas. Outside, also in the back yard, chickens scratched in the dirt until it was time for them to become Sunday dinner. One of the servants would dip the chickens in boiling water to take the feathers off. Bob also recalls his grandmother caging 'possums, grain feeding them, and then serving them for supper. "I ate what she put in front of me rather than get a lecture on people who didn't have anything," he confesses.

Boarders slept upstairs in the seven bedrooms. They shared one bathroom with a large shower, bathtub, sink, and toilet. Mrs. Moore and her grandchildren changed bed linens on Saturday and sent them out to the laundry on Monday. They removed only the bottom sheets (which were laundered); the top sheets became the new bottom ones.

All went well until the stock market crash. The bank repossessed the 218 Ashe Street house in 1932. Ora Moore relocated at 211 West Sycamore Street, across from Piedmont Memorial Hospital. Although Mrs. Edward's Boarding House next door and Mrs. Flemming's Boarding House down the street made for fierce competition, Ora Huffines Moore would not give up. For the next four years, her life consisted of hard work, little money, and many hungry people at her back door.

The Sycamore Street address became a haven for a multitude of poor people. They came in droves to Ora's house because they knew they would find a kind soul and a hot home-cooked meal. Ora never refused to provide them with food. No one left hungry. Some ate outside, and during cold weather, a few came into the kitchen and sat around the stove. The men did odd jobs, like cutting wood and mopping floors to pay for their food, but no one went away without something to eat. At one point, transients would mark her house with chalk, showing others down on their luck where they could get a good free meal. When this escalated out of control and Ora ran out of food, she had no choice but to send her grandchildren outside to erase the chalk marks.

Times got better, and in 1936 Ora returned to her beloved 218 Ashe Street address and reopened her boarding house. This time her clientele included schoolteachers, single working people, and occasionally a family recently moved to Greensboro and waiting for living quarters. Once, after an ice storm, an influx of tree surgeons arrived to repair trees in Sunset Hills and Irving Park. These men doubled up by sleeping in the same bed, a common practice to save money, especially after the Depression.

This time around at 218 Ashe Street, boarders listened to Greensboro's first radio station, WBIG, affiliated with the Columbia Broadcasting System, that operated from the eighth floor of the Jefferson Standard Building. Music and sports entertained listeners while public service announcements, agriculture and soil conservation programs enlightened them. Boarders also attended movies at The Carolina Theater. Its 167 x 400 foot auditorium quickly earned the reputation of being the largest theater "South of New York City."

Women boarders could shop at Meyers or Ellis Stone Department Stores for yard goods, millinery, and shoes. In addition, Montgomery Ward, Belk's Department Store, and Sears, Roebuck and Company opened retail branches in Greensboro and advertised a variety of merchandise. Wills Book and Stationary Company and Straughan's Bookshop offered books, stationery items, and magazines. S.H. Kress and Company had anything and everything from Evening in Paris perfume, lipstick and face powder, to dry goods, costume jewelry, and dress patterns.

The different periods surrounding Mrs. Moore's boarding house management specifically reflect the changing times in downtown Greensboro and—in a more universal way—the country's economic history. Although Ora Moore never made a great deal of money during her many years of hard work, she instilled in her grandchildren a work ethic they will never forget. In 1936, Ora's life changed from being the operator of a boarding house to being a resident in one. She moved from her beloved 218 Ashe Street to the house next door and lived there until her death in February 1938 at Piedmont Memorial Hospital.

Information for this piece comes from the following sources:
- Nickie Doyal's personal Interview with Robert A. Moore on September 21, 2002.
- Arnett, Ethel Stephen. *Greensboro North Carolina: The County Seat of Guilford.* Chapel Hill: The University of North Carolina Press. 1955.

Phillip Branan's Black-Eyed Pea Soup
3/4 pound dried black-eyed peas
1/4 pound bacon, diced
1 cup white onion, chopped
1 cup celery, chopped
1 cup carrot, chopped
2 cloves garlic, minced
3/4 cup tomatoes, diced, with juice
1-1/2 quarts rich chicken stock
1 cup fresh collards, rinsed, stems removed, diced
1 smoked ham hock
1/2 teaspoon kosher salt
1/4 teaspoon dried oregano
1/8 teaspoon dried thyme
1/8 teaspoon ground white pepper
1/2 cup cooked ham, diced
1-1/2 teaspoon chopped fresh cilantro
1 ounce sherry

Soak peas overnight in cold water. Melt down bacon's fat, over medium heat, in a large, heavy-bottom soup-pot. Add onion, celery, and carrot and cover. Cook until onions are soft, about 10 minutes. Add garlic and cook about 10 seconds. Drain peas and add to the pot, along with tomato and collards. Cover with stock and add ham hock; season with salt, oregano, thyme, and white pepper. Bring to a boil. Reduce heat to low and simmer, covered, for about 1-1/2 hours. Remove ham hock and dice any meat left on bone. Return ham hock to pot, along with diced ham and cilantro. Finish with sherry and adjust seasonings, if necessary. Yield: 8 cups. *(Recipe from Lowcountry Delights: Cookbook and Travel Guide. Third Edition. Maxine Pinson and Malyssa Pinson. 1-888-717-4040.)*

The Boarding House on Johnson Farm.

Sallie Johnson's Boarding House

Sallie Liverett Johnson, a forty-seven-year-old widow who opened her farm house to boarders in 1913, earned a reputation as the feisty landlady who never hesitated to wallop rule breakers with her broom. People desiring permission to board at Johnson Farm first had to present a reference to Sallie. If she did not like their looks, she would say, "I don't think you'd like it here."

Before her husband's death, the Johnsons lived about five miles from her parents' home and farm. When Mr. Johnson died in 1896 from a gangrenous infection, their boys were five and one. Sallie lived on her own with her sons for many years until a 1913 family tragedy, when Sallie's father, seventy-seven-year-old Robert Liverett, argued with his son John Liverett and shot and killed him. Then Robert took his own life. After that, Sallie and her boys moved to the four-hundred-acre farm to tend to her elderly mother and her sister Bettie. Eventually, Sallie bought out her sister's and brothers' share of the estate. Eventually, Sallie bought out her sister's and brothers' share of the estate, thus beginning an enterprising business that prospered for forty-five years. Until her death in 1918, Sallie's sister Bettie stayed at the farm to help with the boarding house.

Sallie's two sons, Vernon and Leander, never married. Except for their college years at N.C. Agricultural and Mechanical College (now N.C. State University), they lived with their mother and helped her run her Hendersonville boarding house. According to locals, "Mamma never approved of the girls they courted. Once she traveled to Virginia when Vernon announced his engagement. Sallie brought him back home." When Vernon and Leander thought the five bedrooms in the farmhouse too crowded, they built an annex with eleven bedrooms and two baths on two floors. When these rooms reached maximum capacity, the boys usually slept in the chicken house or in the barn.

Vernon and Leander got up at four o'clock every morning to milk the cows, and boarders—called only one time to get up—often accompanied them. For entertainment Vernon played the fiddle, and he enjoyed woodworking. When someone gave Vernon a fine piece of walnut, he decided to make his own coffin, but his plan changed when he discovered his workshop too small. So he made a cradle. Leander, interested in nature, invited boarders to witness beautiful mountain sunrises. He would identify all the area plants, give both the common and Latin names, and explain their use.

Boarders, mostly Floridians who stayed the entire summer, received three meals a day—except on Sunday, when supper consisted of homemade ice cream and leftovers from the bountiful Sunday fried chicken dinner. Guests sat at the big table—one Sallie's father had made—in the dining room, and others ate at tables in the adjoining room, referred to as the "settin' room," which also served as a winter bedroom for Sallie. Children liked to eat on the screened-in porch with Vernon and Leander. Meals included smoked ham, fried chicken, fresh vegetables, biscuits, home-churned butter, jellies, eggs, grits, and more—all served family style.

Sallie's boys hired Etta Pressley to help their mother in the kitchen and expressed their profound relief that finally here was someone Mamma could get along with. After electricity became available in Hendersonville, Vernon and Leander surprised their mother with a new electric stove. She didn't like this new contraption and refused to use it except to boil water. Claiming the range did not cook right and she couldn't control the temperature, she chose to prepare all her food on her old wood-burning cookstove that, according to Sallie, "made everything taste good."

In addition to her regulars, Sallie fed noon meals to German prisoners of war who resided in a camp just down the road during World War II. After the War Department rescued German sailors from U-boat 352, which sank May 9, 1942, the United States government began setting up a number of branch camps—this particular one in Hendersonville— for POWs. These quarters offered safety and provided "living quarters and rations...equal that of the captor country's...[in hopes that] the Axis governments would reciprocate by treating American soldiers fairly."

In Hendersonville, POWs worked in the fields at Johnson Farm to alleviate the labor shortage caused by locals serving their country in other parts of the world. In addition to harvesting crops, they also built roads, cut timber,

The original house on Johnson Farm.

repaired barns, and replaced roofs. The Geneva Convention ensured that these men could be employed if they received good care and did not work in any job associated with the war. Although the POWs earned the same pay as regular employees, they also received, for their personal allowance, about eighty cents a day, which went into a special account. The prisoners could then draw on that account when they wanted items such as cigarettes, soap, and snacks. The rest of their pay reverted back to the United States government to provide base camp amenities like equipment for their recreational enjoyment and a library.

According to one historian, the Germans "found that life in an American POW camp was much more luxurious than life in the German army. During their free time, they formed music bands, worked on art projects, grew flower and vegetable gardens, and played their favorite sport from back home—soccer." According to the website TRACES, the POWs "underwent considerable changes as individuals and as a group—thus fundamentally influencing post-war German values and institutions, as well as American-German relations."

The POWs found plenty of good food, respect, and comfort at Sallie Johnson's table after a morning of working in the fields at Johnson Farm. Obviously, Sallie's broom knew no favorites. Although the guards overseeing the POWs expected to eat first, Sallie guarded the doorway with her broom and made them wait until the prisoners had finished.

After the Allied victory in 1945, the War Department returned German POWs to Europe. Many sent to Siberia died from the extremes of forced labor; others went to France or England to rebuild those counties. Those who survived finally arrived back in Germany by 1947, but many returned to the United States because they had "formed significant...friendships with 'the enemy.'"

Sallie Johnson may not have formed friendships with the prisoners, but she and her vicious broom always stood up for their rights as human beings. Maybe Sallie's red hair precipitated her fiery temper. People remember her as a feisty women who always wore a long dress, high-top boots, and an apron pinned to the front of her dress. She strictly prohibited alcohol on the premises, but boarders living in the annex often disobeyed that rule and kept a hidden bottle. When they ventured to the icebox located in the main house, Sallie suspected they wanted ice for their Happy Hour drink. She grabbed her broom and headed to the annex shouting, "You know I don't allow alcohol here." Often men climbed from the bedroom windows to escape her wrath.

Pastimes at the Farm included rocking on the porch, sightseeing drives on the Blue Ridge Parkway, trips to Sliding Rock, Saturday night square dances, and visits in town. Children enjoyed helping with the chores, playing in the barn, and presenting original plays on the porch.

Even with stooped shoulders due to osteoporosis, Sallie remained determined, feisty, and firm. She refused to let boarders use her sewing machine because they might break the needle. In her later years she slept in the kitchen, in a wooden beach chair with a sling fabric seat.

She ran her farm and boarding house until her death in 1958. Her sons kept the farm going as a bed and breakfast. Leander did the cooking, but long-time boarders at Johnson Farm, who had become like family, always helped with kitchen and farm chores.

An old friend and neighbor, Becky Varnadore, recalls Vernon's and Leander's last years. "After the death of their mother in 1958, Vernon and Leander were lost," she said. "They developed a unique and special friendship with students at West Henderson High School."

Becky Varnadore remembers when she and her husband Tony and their daughter Julie moved to the Farm after Vernon's passing.

"We did not have farm chores," she said. "Tony mowed the grass. Leander had just planted some white pines, rows of them, and Tony mowed between the pines to keep the weeds from choking them. He and Leander would make a trip to the grocery store every three or so months. Leander was healthy and very independent. He made it clear he did not want us waiting on him. We did a lot of things together—walks in the woods, picnics, visits. Leander very much respected our privacy. Our second daughter, Sallie Leana, was born in September 1981. She is named after his mother and him."

Becky Vanadore described Leander as stocky, well built, about 5' 7" with a slight stoop towards the end of his life. He had deep-set gray eyes and large hands, his fingers somewhat gnarled with arthritis. Although mostly bald, he did have a little white hair around the edges. He wore khaki work pants and shirts, and a sailor's cap—except when he wore his wide-brimmed straw hat in the hot sun. In cool weather he wore a red plaid wool shirt and in winter, a heavy coat and cap with ear flaps so he stayed warm while outside feeding the birds and squirrels.

Leander, according to Vanadore, "was so gentle birds would land on him as he sat still on a bench outside. Chipmunks would come up to him and eat out of his hand. He was very clever, intuitive, and observant. He was the most giving person I have ever known. He had a wonderful sense of humor. At times, he showed great emotion and would cry when speaking about certain things or people, but he also had a temper that, when ignited, could be fierce." Vandaore says she saw him mad only a few times—not at her or her family, but at situations.

In his older years, Leander liked to talk about past square dances on the boarding house porch, the meals Sallie cooked, his garden, animal projects, favorite old recipes, and the way his mother made gravy, biscuits, or a certain pie. When Vanadore made biscuits, Leander told her they reminded him of his momma's because they had a little cream of tartar in them.

Leander maintained a lifetime estate at the Farm until he passed away in January 1987. His final gift to the school children he loved so much consisted of bequeathing the beautiful farm to the school system. Today the property serves as a heritage education center and farm museum. Students and adults make field trips to Hendersonville to learn about life on a family farm and participate in activities such as making homemade ice cream, quilts, and home-churned butter, or learning about plants and animals. They also hear about Vernon and Leander and their love of learning and nature, and about how Sallie ran her boarding house and cooked for all those people.

Information for this piece comes from the following sources:
- Nickie Doyal's informal interviews with Ingrid McNair and Lisa Whitfield, Executive Director of the Historic Johnson Farm. Lisa also supplied a narrative of Sallie Johnson and recipes via email attachment.
- Feller, Steve and Michael Luick-Thrams, "The Legacy" TRACES: WE BRING HISTORY TO LIFE. *www.traces.org/germanpows*
- Belton, Tom. "North Carolina at Home and in Battle in World War II" *www.ncmuseumofhistory.org*
- Giles, Jennie Jones. "Historic Farm's Restoration About to Start Thanks to Grant, Fund-Raisers." Hendersonville *Times-News.* August 14, 2005.

• E-mail Interview with Mrs. Tony (Becky) Varnadore on June 12, 2006.

WANT TO GO?
Located four miles north of Hendersonville, across from Rugby Middle School (Hwy. 191). Address: 3346 Haywood Road, Hendersonville, NC 28791. For more information, call (828)891-6585 or go to *www.johnsonfarm.org* **or** *www.henderson.k12.nc.us,* and click on Johnson Farm. Operating Hours are Tuesday-Friday, 9:00 a.m. - 2:30 p.m.

Listed on the National Register of Historic Places, the Johnson Farm was a late 19th-Century tobacco farm that became a popular summer tourist retreat. The farm features an 1870's boarding house, a barn loft museum, ten historic buildings, two nature trails, and fifteen acres of fields, forests and streams. Guided tours are available year-round at 10:30 a.m. and 1:30 p.m. Admission is charged for adults and children over 5 years old. Group rates are available on request. No concessions are available; however, picnicking is

Although Aunt Sallie Johnson was widely known for the tasty meals she prepared, no recipes have survived in her own handwriting. She did share a few seasonal favorites with her longtime friend and neighbor, Lucy Tate Reese, who has kindly made them available to friends of the Historic Johnson Farm.

MRS. JOHNSON'S LIVER MUSH
Boil a pork liver and a small amount of fat pork in clear water until tender. Cool liver. Save the stock. Put liver through meat grinder. Add an amount of corn meal equal to (or a little more) than the liver. Skim fat off top of stock and add it to a small amount of clear water; bring to a boil. Add onion, a small amount of sage, red pepper, salt, and pepper. Add liver and corn meal and cook for some time. Liver mush should be thin enough to spread itself when poured into a pan. Cool. Spread lard over top of edges to keep liver mush from drying out.

LEANDER'S CAKE
(Scottish short bread)
1/2 cup butter • 1/2 cup sugar
3/4 cup flour • 1 egg
rind of 1/2 lemon or 1/2 teaspoon lemon extract
pinch of salt
Mix, spread in greased pan and bake at 375 degrees for about 20 minutes.

Winston-Salem

Reynolds Inn
Early Boarding House for R. J. Reynolds Tobacco Company's Women Employees

In 1918, wage increases at the R. J. Reynolds Tobacco Company brought many young women to Winston-Salem. Cigarette production had increased rapidly, and the manufacture of Prince Albert pipe tobacco had doubled at the tobacco plants. Females flocked into Winston-Salem to seek employment. Many had lived on their family farms all their lives, and now they wanted to earn money in the city's cigarette plants. But, where could these women live in a pleasing, comfortable, and safe environment?

Katharine Smith Reynolds (widow of tobacco king R. J. Reynolds), her sister-in-law Kate Bitting Reynolds (wife of Will Reynolds), and social reformer Lenora H. Sill spearheaded the opening of a suitable boarding house exclusively for women working in Reynolds Tobacco Factory #1. Before R. J. Reynolds died, he had negotiated, through his tobacco business, the purchase of the Plaza Hotel at the corner of Chestnut and Third Streets, opposite the railroad station and across from Factory #1 in Winston-Salem. On August 2, 1918, less than a month after Mr. Reynolds' death, buyers and sellers agreed on a final purchase price of $35,000. The old Plaza would soon become a boarding house.

After extensive repairs throughout, the boarding house received the official name, Reynolds Inn, and young women began moving in as early as September 21, 1918. Katharine, Kate, and Lenora made sure Reynolds Inn would provide proper accommodations and competent managers to ensure the welfare of all boarders. One of the earliest feminists in Winston-Salem, Katharine spared no time or energy in her efforts to provide comfort and safety, and to prevent young women from exploitation while they worked in the burgeoning tobacco business.

Boarders at Reynolds Inn enjoyed running water and bathrooms, as well as a community dining room, lobby, and access to the kitchen on the main floor. Their cost for all of this totaled a mere $4.00 or $4.25 per week. For this amount, they received a comfortable room with two meals for six days a week and three meals on Sundays. Patrons ate their noon meal, called "dinner" during this era in the South, in the lunchroom at the tobacco plant. The cafeteria, seating approximately 400 and managed by an expert cook, provided low-cost meals. At this time, women workers made about thirteen cents per hour. They could purchase cafeteria tokens for two and a half cents each and receive a meal of beans, corn bread, and a pickle—for one token. If they were still hungry, they could buy, for another token, a bowl of soup with bread and crackers. Half a large Moravian sugar cake took yet another token. For seven-and-a-half cents (about one-half of their hourly wages), they satisfied their appetites until suppertime back at Reynolds Inn.

While Mr. and Mrs. Charles C. Bodenheimer officiated as general managers of the boarding house, Ruth Hopkins served as matron, a position insisted upon by Katharine Reynolds to ensure the welfare of these young workers and keep them safe. As matron—a position similar to that of a long-ago dormitory housemother—Ruth Hopkins made sure everyone observed curfew, gentlemen callers visited only in the lobby, and morals and ethics remained uncompromised.

Wholesome weekend activities included attendance at parades and circuses, a cultural program in Elks Auditorium, or a moving picture show at either the Amuzu or Liberty Theaters. The Carnegie Public Library at the corner of Cherry and Third Streets, with its circulation of thousands of books, provided a pleasant change of pace from the hustle and bustle of the tobacco factory. Winston-Salem's downtown area boasted businesses such as Nichol's Hat Shop and Efird's Department Store, which sold millinery and ladies' ready-to-wear. Saturday excursions from Winston-Salem to High Point on one of the city's buses, equipped with 35 horsepower Model T. Ford engines, gave boarders a unique day trip. Church services on Sunday morning provided spiritual refreshment.

Only during tobacco markets did the women traditionally refrain from frequenting downtown Winston-Salem. Once a year farmers made their annual pilgrimage to town. The opening of the tobacco sales warehouses flooded the downtown area with prospective buyers and sellers. Farmers used circular baskets to haul their hands (a "hand" equaled the number of leaves the farmer could hold in one hand while another man tied or knotted the ends of the stem with another leaf) of tobacco to various warehouses. Workers weighed the hands of bright leaf tobacco, inspected and graded them, and then auctioned them to the highest bidder. The chant of an auctioneer, the pungent aroma of cured tobacco, and the eagerness of farmers lent an air of festivity to the scene—definitely a male-dominated event where women did not belong.

Katharine Smith Reynolds

If the tobacco farmer did not accept a particular bid for his product, he would "turn the ticket" or refuse the bid, pack up his tobacco, hoist his leaves onto his hip, and leave the warehouse, waiting until the next day when prices might be better. When he felt he had received the price that compensated for his back-breaking days in the fields, the farmer sold his crop, went to the payoff office, and collected the money that would feed and clothe his family for the next year.

Once out on the street, he encountered merchants selling everything from shoes, overalls, and dress suits to fresh produce in open-air markets. Under signs which advertised, "Drink Royal Crown Cola," farmers pressed against each other as they purchased goods they needed. Occasionally, they stopped for a shoeshine on Trade Street or listened to barkers hawking their wares or watched an Indian war dance. Buying and selling continued late into the night, and if farmers became bored with merchants, they could view some of the world's wonders, such as the smallest mule or figures from a portable wax museum. When they tired, they prepared a late supper by the light of lanterns and then slept either on warehouse floors or camped in their covered wagons. Obviously, women needed to stay away from the downtown area during this time, and the matron at the boarding house made sure her charges understood.

Thus, the comfortable lobby of Reynolds Inn became a favorite gathering place for women to socialize. Conversations concerning the events of each day in various areas of the factory created a great deal of interest. For example, the male foremen of the leaf department often cursed female employees who stayed in the bathroom too long. Some of the more obnoxious men even entered the women's private domain, yelling at the females inside to get back to work. Why these male foremen thought that women would want to hide in a filthy, crude, dark, non-ventilated toilet escaped the female workers' comprehension and most certainly became part of nightly talks in the boarding house lobby.

The famous story of Cora Robertson Brewer likely became the topic of conversation among these young women in 1919. Historian Nannie M. Tilly records this saga:

"Cora, who had been with Reynolds since 1897, became a worker on the untying line before learning to pick and class leaf. In 1919 the foreman advised Cora to come to his factory but by that time the company had adopted a rule that no employee could quit at any time and go to another foreman for a job. She left for a job with Mengel Box Company before returning as a stamper to Number 256 under her favorite foreman. Again he was transferred, this time to Number 97, and a foreman prejudiced against her took his place. He gave her untrained cappers, seven in all, who, as they became adept, were transferred to other machines. The other stamp girl quit because she could not afford to work with green cappers. In great anger Cora decided to quit but instead she was transferred to No. 12. Going to work the following morning, she obtained her stamps, folded them for easy tearing, and stood ready to work at the rate of forty-four cents for each one thousand packages she stamped. But she found that the prejudiced foreman had been transferred with her and that she had green cappers. This proved too much and she turned in her stamps to the stamp clerk, went downstairs, and told the entire story to John Whitaker (probably a plant supervisor). Whitaker called in the offending foreman and accused him of favoritism. She was taken back and given an experienced capper. But the foreman continued to ignore her in many small ways. One morning she came in to work, took a number of Camel packages made by the night force, reported her action to the busy record keeper, and began work. Evidently, in the rush of the early morning stir, the record keeper had failed to note her action and soon the foreman accused her of having stolen several packages of Camels. Leaving her machine, she started to get her coat but found the dressing room locked. Edgar E. Bumgardner, then in training to be a foreman, approached and persuaded her to remain. He arranged for her transfer to Number 97."

Of course, in 1918, women residing at Reynolds Inn would not have known the ending of the story that they discussed so openly. Cora Robertson Brewer worked happily at Number 97 with her favored foreman and ultimately completed forty-eight years of employment with R. J. Reynolds Tobacco Company.

In addition to their immediate fear of being exploited like Cora Brewer, the boarders at Reynolds Inn met another obstacle in the autumn of 1918. A hard-hitting Spanish influenza epidemic struck Winston-Salem, and the germ surely claimed some of the women tobacco workers who resided in the boarding

R.J. Reynolds Factory #1, adjoining Reynolds Inn.
(Photo: North Carolina Collection. University of North Carolina Library at Chapel Hill.)

house. Medical personnel in the city warned all citizens to be extremely careful and take every precaution to stay well. Health workers advised all to wash their hands in alcohol and to wear aprons and masks.

During this epidemic, the Winston-Salem Chapter of the American Red Cross recruited nurses from other parts of the United States to assist overworked local doctors and nurses, some of whom worked twenty-four-hour shifts. Often medical caregivers would collapse from exhaustion or from having contracted the highly contagious disease themselves. Eventually the influenza germ affected so many people, hospitals could not accommodate the multitude of patients. Churches, schools, and residents of Winston-Salem offered spaces for make-shift hospitals. The prominent John W. Hanes family volunteered their home, accommodating as many as 67 patients in one day.

November 1918 brought the end of World War I, but less than a week later, Winston-Salem experienced another catastrophe—a race riot. On November 17, 1918, the women residing at Reynolds Inn would surely have discussed, in hushed tones, the reports circulating throughout the plant. Jim and Cora Childress, a white couple, were walking from their home to a neighborhood store. When they got to Inverness Street, a man came out of nowhere and pointed a gun in their faces. The stranger shot Mr. Childress and raped his wife. Police later arrested Russell High, an African-American who had recently moved to Winston-Salem from Durham. High was jailed even though Mrs. Childress said he wasn't the man responsible for hurting her and her husband.

White men swarmed City Hall amid rumors of a lynching. Talk among the women at Reynolds Inn probably focused on speculation. What had happened? Some ventured that the trouble sprang from an unwillingness on the part of African-Americans to leave jobs they had filled in the whites' absence during the war. Others noted recent marches through East Winston by the Ku Klux Klan and wondered if they might be at the root of the discord. Theories abounded.

By early evening, the irate mob had rushed Russell High's cellblock and fired random gun shots. Firemen, called to the scene, hosed the crowd. In all the confusion, a stray bullet injured a fireman. When the force of water coming from fire hoses quickly repelled the mob, the men fled, only to break into downtown stores to steal guns. Armed, they tore off into African-American neighborhoods, shooting aimlessly, wounding many and reportedly killing twenty-three people.

Subsequently, Federal troops arrived and stationed a huge armored tank at the town square. While many soldiers patrolled the streets, others escorted Russell High safely to the Raleigh jail. One can imagine the concern of Reynolds Inn's matron, responsbile for her female charges, who in all likelihood immediately issued two important rules: "Don't go downtown; there is still trouble brewing there. And don't discuss any of this, because speculation might somehow get you in trouble."

The women who lived at Reynolds Inn had, no doubt, listened to report after report in the plant lunchroom. They knew many African-Americans had been killed. They probably heard that the slain were hauled out of Winston-Salem in boxcars and shipped out of town, or dumped in big holes outside the city limits. Apparently the boarders did heed their matron's warnings, because reports show no indication that harm came to any of the women.

After the panic following the riot, Winston-Salem returned to normal. Once again women began to venture out to shop, to go to special programs or movies. The boarding house, never intended as a profit-making venture and generally operating at a slight loss, remained in operation until 1929.

Information for this story comes from the following sources:
• *The R.J. Reynolds Tobacco Company* by Nannie M. Tilley. UNC Press (Chapel Hill) 1985.
• Information about Winston-Salem comes from research culled from various archival files at Reynolda House, later incorporated into an unpublished manuscript entitled *Katharine Smith Reynolds: A Story of Her Life* by Alice E. Sink.

High Point

Mrs. Nannie Phenix Kilby:
The Kilby Hotel

Nannie Kilby, born in 1877, moved from Alamance County to High Point in the 1890's with her husband John. During this time in the South, women of color usually worked as maids for wealthy families. Not Nannie. Her creative business transactions made her famous in the city now known as the Furniture Marketing Capital of the World.

This ambitious African-American woman earned money as a practical nurse, serving her neighborhood on East Washington Street as a mid-wife, delivering babies. In return, she would receive a couple of dollars if the family could pay her, or maybe "a few eggs, a mess of fish, or simply a verbal thanks" if they couldn't. For other sick neighbors, she would mix herbs for common ailments and dress wounds. Traveling from house to house, she also peddled fire wood from her horse-drawn wagon and freshly-caught fish from a wheelbarrow. Just where she got her fish, nobody seems to know, but her great grandson, Joe McElrath, who calls her "a workaholic," thinks she may have gone to nearby Swearing Creek and caught them herself.

As if Nannie did not have enough jobs, she also became a hairdresser, setting up a make-shift shop in her kitchen or basement. Because she had no training in hair treatment or access to black hair care products in the earliest part of the twentieth century, she resorted to homemade methods. She probably

Nannie Kilby

followed directions handed down by word of mouth from more experienced women in this field. Shampoo for African-American women's hair consisted of dishwater or turpentine mixed with lard. If a customer needed a dry shampoo, then grits, powdered charcoal, or coarse corn meal filled that need. To soften the hair, hairdressers mixed together cooked apple leaves and chicken fat to produce a homemade conditioner. Warm grease softened too-tightly plaited braids, kitchen forks became combs, and hot knives produced curls. Heating a coarse material such as burlap and pressing the hot strips against the hair straightened a black woman's locks.

Saving most of her profit from these ventures and from her husband's pay at the railroad, Nannie and John bought a parcel of land from Lone and Rosa Sechrest. In 1910, with the help of their brothers—and no other outside assistance—the couple began building a three-story hotel at the corner of Hobson Street and East Washington Drive in High Point. The twenty-one room brick structure, completed in 1913, originally housed only the extended family. But soon it opened for business to board African-American men seeking work in High Point's furniture factories.

By 1914 every Southern state had laws that created two very different societies—one white and one black. Hotels were segregated, as well as schools, hospitals, and restaurants. Separate bathroom facilities and water fountains appeared in public places. Under this system, known as "jim crow," African-Americans did not have full and equal rights.

This did not deter Nannie Kilby. In fact, segregation probably provided an impetous for Nannie's entrepreneurship and creativity. The twenty-one room

Kilby Hotel, built in the Romanesque style of architecture, boasted decorative brickwork, ornate arched windows, spacious hallways with high ceilings, and wide stairwells. Local preservationist Benjamin Briggs has described the hotel as "looming over the black downtown of East Washington Drive in those days." Nannie rented shops on the ground floor where African-Americans opened various businesses.

Kilby's 21-room hotel on East Washington Street.

Oral history indicates that a barber shop opened in one of those spaces and provided not only haircuts, shaves, and shoe shines, but also a place for black men to congregate and engage in conversation. This social function allowed men to share the news of the day, express their opinions on current events, and even engage in community gossip. The black barber earned a sense of pride by his self employment, economic gain, and social status. The 1919 *High Point City Directory* names two tenants at 513-1/2 Washington Drive, Eurnice Baldwin, hair dresser, and C.J.H. Gaylord, a physician.

While thriving street-front businesses catered to residents of Washington Street, the second floor of the hotel became living quarters for the Kilby clan, and the upper level provided clean, well-ventilated bedrooms—furnished with brass double beds—for Nannie Kilby's boarders. A wide hallway with generous skylights led to a common bathroom on each level. Wood and coal stoves heated the rooms. Family members chopped and stacked wood in the back yard, and a delivery man brought coal to the basement. No one was exempt from toting wood and coal to stoves installed on all three floors. While John continued his Southern Railroad job, his wife ran the Kilby Hotel as a boarding house.

According to Joe McElrath, he had always heard that his great-grandmother Nannie cooked substantial meals of meat and potatoes in her second-floor kitchen and served her family and boarders in an adjoining dining room. No one ever went hungry. In fact, Joe speculates, "Knowing the kind of person my grandmother was, there were probably people who stayed here for nothing. I'm sure she wouldn't have turned anyone away."

Various newspaper files and museum records identify Nannie as "the hardest working woman in the city during this period." This cannot be disputed. Her labors and talent for saving money enabled her to eventually acquire thirty rental houses in the East Washington Street area. It seemes that everything she touched turned to gold.

Although Nannie used much of her resources to buy real estate, she unselfishly showered her generosity on others. As a loyal member, she supported First Baptist Church, built in 1907 at 701 East Washington Street. A small brick building measuring 50x70 feet served the congregation until 1916, when members led by Rev. O. S. Bullock built an attached Sunday school annex facing Hobson Street. Nannie's donations most likely helped pay for the church's center altar, elevated choir loft, baptismal pool, biblical painting, new altar furniture, oak pews, and carpeted floors. Although she belonged to and generously supported First Baptist Church, Nannie also pledged a large cash gift for the building of High Point's First A.M.E. Church on the corner of Washington and Gilmer Streets.

By 1919, East Washington Drive hummed with a shoemaker, tailor, undertaker, wood dealer and also with clergymen, grocers, barbers, and hair dressers. The Hinton Hotel also catered to African-American guests while the Odd Fellows Hall provided a meeting place for neighborhood men. Ramsey Drug Company filled prescriptions issued by neighborhood physicians C.J.H. Gaylord and G.A. Gerran.

A hair dresser was just one of many businesses that operated at the Kilby Hotel.

Nannie Kilby, who barely lived long enough to see the surge of vital energy on Washington Drive, died in 1920, at the age of forty-three. Joe McErath can only speculate about the cause of her death. "My great-grandmother was someone who just worked hard and it went to a point that she just died. I haven't heard of any stories that she got sick. She was a workaholic...she worked hard all her life."

After Nannie's death, her only child, Mrs. Ora Kilby Martin, wife of prominent High Point physician Dr. Joseph Alfred Martin, took over the business affairs of Kilby Hotel. She removed the second-floor porch facing Hobson Street and made the entrance smaller. In 1927, Mrs. Martin built a two-story building attached to the existing three-story hotel. Dr. Martin's medical office and a barber shop occupied the ground floor spaces of the older structure. The 1927 addition became a lively entertainment center called Club Kilby. How celebrities such as Nat King Cole, Billy Eckstein, Ella Fitzgerald, and Duke Ellington came to play at Club Kilby in High Point, North Carolina, provides an interesting dimension to the history of the family. How could Nannie Kilby have guessed that famous jazz musicians would perform on the very property she worked so hard to buy?

As a young girl, Nannie's granddaughter Marion Martin (daughter of Dr. Joseph and Ora Kilby Martin) had attended Palmer Institute, an exclusive boarding school for black females founded in 1902 by Dr. Charlotte Hawkins Brown. Located in Sedalia, a small town near Greensboro, the Institute originally promoted industrial training, but in the 1930's changed to a respected preparatory school, stressing academic and cultural education for young African-Americans girls. The story goes that Marion and one of her classmates, Maria

Hawkins, the niece of Palmer's founder, and, interestingly, the future second wife of Nat King Cole, bonded in a lasting friendship. The two young women stayed in touch after graduation and ultimately Marion, who now managed Club Kilby, invited Maria's husband Nat King Cole to perform there.

This African American night spot soon became a favorite Saturday night hangout for adults. Patrons visited the downstairs bar before going up the wooden steps to dance and enjoy musical magic. Imagine Nat King Cole, who played only in clubs welcoming black people, crooning "Mona Lisa" or "When I Fall in Love" for the eager crowd. Club Kilby rafters probably shook as Ella Fitzgerald, dubbed "The First Lady of Song," sang ballads or jazz in her flexible and wide-ranging voice. "Love and Kisses" would have brought clubbers to their feet. To add to the famous list of entertainers, Edward "Duke" Ellington and his top-notch band offered favorites such as "Choo Choo Gotta Hurry Home" and "Rainy Nights Rainy Days." Billy Eckstine also added his magic to the entertainment line-up. In 1940, the Furniture City Elks Lodge Ball spotlighted "Hartley Toots" and his orchestra. Club Kilby closed in the early 1960's. "When alcohol is involved, it can lead to problems," says Joe McElrath.

Singers Nat King Cole (above)
and Ella Fitzgerald (below) both
performed at the Kilby.

Joe McElrath, who with his sister inherited the hotel at their mother's death, presently resides on the top floor of the two-story addition which was once Club Kilby. Joe remembers, as a kid, having to haul coal from the basement to his mother's beauty parlor, located in the same space where he now lives. "That's why I know this building has strong steps," he says. After Joe graduated from Western Carolina as a football star, he went to Seattle and worked there until 1988, when he learned that his twin brother had been killed. Knowing that his mother was ill, Joe McElrath returned to High Point, only to find prostitution and drugs rampant in the hotel. Wearing guns for his protection, he evicted everyone and set about cleaning up the place. Modern electric heating replaced old wood and coal stoves. Tile now covered the old heart pine wooden floors. Because the occupancy rate never really increased enough to pay all the bills and make a profit, McElrath accepted public employment and rented only a few of the eighteen available rooms. He continued to offer the first-floor shops for various businesses.

Each room now contains the bare essentials, a bed and dresser, and sometimes a small black and white television set. The building has most recently been a mission house for men trying to turn their lives around. The property, which has passed through four generations of Nannie Phenix Kilby's descendants, is currently for sale. McElrath believes the old hotel and addition would make perfect showrooms for the International Home Furnishings Market. The Washington Drive (name now changed from "Street") Renaissance Group, Inc. hopes to turn the hotel into a senior citizens apartment complex and bring back the old neighborhood luster, laughter, and successful business ventures.

Today the Kilby Hotel, listed on the National Register of Historical Places, stands as a historical landmark and serves as a monument to the woman who worked so hard to build and manage it.

Information for this piece came from the following sources:
• Nickie Doyal and Alice Sink's Interview with Joe McElrath on September 22, 2003. Also, personal tour throughout entire hotel, including the 1927 addition. *NOTE:* Mr. McElrath said his great-grandmother, Nannie Kilby, was a practical nurse, wood peddler, fish seller, and hairdresser. The above job descriptions for Nannie Kilby are also included in a published booklet entitled *History of the Negro in High Point, North Carolina: 1867-1950,* edited and compiled by The High Point Normal and Industrial Club.
• Smith, Margaret Supplee & Emily Herring Wilson. *North Carolina WOMEN Making History.* Chapel Hill, The University of North Carolina Press, 1999.
• Reid, Kevin. "Historic Kilby Hotel Has Future." Greensboro *News and Record.* Sunday, April 18, 2004. Section R, pgs. 1,2.
• Alexis Gines. "The Whole Story: High Point Museum Adds More African American Artifacts." Greensboro *News and Record.* Sunday, February 19, 2006. Section R, pgs. l, 6.
• Religion & Arts Committee. "A Link Through Time." Published by First Baptist Church, 701 E. Washington Drive, High Point, North Carolina.
• "History of African American Hair and Beauty Culture." *Cosmetic magazine.* Internet article at *www.cosmeticmagazine.com/managearticle*

- "Before Barber Sops and Beauty Salons: African American Home Procedures for Hair." Internet *article at http://northbysouth.kenyonon.edu*
- "Where are 'Good Looks?'" Internet article at *http://northbysouth.kenyonon.edu.*
- Information concerning famous entertainers comes from *www.redhotjazz.com, www.ellafitzgerald,net*, and *www.pcug.org*

OLD FASHIONED TURNIP SOUP

Take two pounds veal bones to half a gallon of water, and boil to one quart. Put turnips and bones on to boil together, then strain the liquor off and send to table hot. Season while cooking with pepper and salt.

Recipe from Mrs. Abby Fisher's *What Mrs. Fisher Knows About Old Southern Cooking, Soups, Pickles, Preserves, Etc.* 1881. Digitized by Michigan State University Library.

BOILED FISH

See that fish is well cleaned. Season inside and out with pepper and salt one or two hours before putting to boil, then have your boiler with one quart of luke-warm water to receive the fish, and let it remain on a quick fire twenty minutes; if it is a very large fish it will take thirty minutes to cook.

Recipe from Mrs. Abby Fisher's *What Mrs. Fisher Knows About Old Southern Cooking, Soups, Pickles, Preserves, Etc. 1881.* Digitized by Michigan State University Library.

Lexington

Mrs. Racie Michael's Baseball Boarding House

Picture this: Mrs. Racie Michael's dining room with sixteen ravenous Lexington Indian baseball players huddled over plates heaped with rice and brown gravy, pinto beans, fresh vegetables, and homemade biscuits. Dessert—peach pie, strawberry shortcake, or angel food cake— reigned on a nearby sideboard. All for twenty-five cents.

Beginning in 1937, Lexington Indian players, who belonged to the North Carolina State League's Class D team, lived at this 218 East Second Avenue Boarding House. They occupied the five upstairs bedrooms filled with double beds. The cost: five dollars per man, per week, plus twenty-five cents for each meal. Of course, the topic of conversation at Mrs. Michael's bountiful table focused on games, hits, errors, and batting averages.

During this time, baseball evolved from an amateur pastime into organized teams and leagues. In the 1930's the first minor league teams had appeared. Their nicknames —"farm system," "farm club," or "farm team" — originated when St. Louis Cardinals' general manager Branch Rickey sent teams to small Southern towns, and major league players joked that he "was growing players down on the farm like corn." These leagues consisted of four classes, lettered A to D, based, according to one report, "on size, drawing power, and a lot of politics." The policies and procedures did not matter to Mrs. Racie

Michael and her family. They all loved baseball and supported the players. In fact, time and stats would later prove the Lexington Indian Class D team one of the best during its sixteen years' existence from 1937 to 1953.

The Michael's son Jack, who roomed with one of the players, recalls a superstition the ball players had. When they headed out on the field, they always ran to touch first base to bring them luck. The entire Michael family felt honored to have the team stay at their home, and they welcomed local team supporters who came by the boarding house to eat and to visit with catcher George Physter, shortstop Ray Rex, and pitcher Wilbur Reeser— all of whom started their baseball careers with this farm team in the mill town of Lexington in 1937.

Mrs. Michael also fed other celebrities. In 1929, the producer, director, and actor, George White, brought his famous vaudeville show, "The Scandals," to perform in Lexington. The revue, which included the best of America's popular music, fast-moving sketches, and glamorous women, resembled a less-lavish version of the Ziegfield Follies. White had so many showmen in his entourage, the manager of a local Lexington lunchroom called Racie and asked if she could feed twenty of the actors. Racie's son, Jack, recalls how the singers and dancers ate and ate. "None of them had eaten brown gravy and fresh vegetables like she cooked," he said. "Pinto beans were my mother's specialty. She baked some of the best angel food cakes. They said they had never eaten such delicious food in all their lives. The cost for their meal was twenty-five cents each, but some put in as much as fifty or seventy-five cents, and some even a dollar."

Jack Michael recalls his mother's meals: "She was only one of two places in Lexington. The other was Leonard's, and their meals were expensive. That was where the professionals would go. Their meals were about $1.50, and it was during the depression, and...not many people had that kind of money. But the doctors and lawyers could eat at Leonard's Lunch Room. We had managers from some of the stores, and students from the high school would come down and eat for twenty-five cents each. Today you can't buy a candy bar for a quarter."

"Back in those days, my two brothers and I shared an upstairs bedroom with the ball players," Jack Michael said. "My two sisters slept in a downstairs bedroom, and there wasn't any heat in either. It was healthier that way. We would get up about 7:00 and go to my parents' bedroom where they would have one of those big stoves, and we would all dress at that fire. After we left for school, my mother would clean, do our personal laundry, and start cooking dinner. She shopped for groceries at a nearby wholesale house and stored non-perishable items on the large back porch of her house. She would sometimes take a nap in the afternoon because she had worked so hard in the day. We would all have to be quiet so she could sleep."

Mrs. Michael also had a garden, and her specialty was raising beautiful chrysanthemums. Before locals attended a football game, they bought these flowers to make corsages representing their school colors.

Racie Michael did, indeed, stay busy. Proclaimed by her son Jack as "Lexington's best cook," she prepared all the meals by herself. She did have two women assistants who served the meals, cleaned the house, and helped with the laundry. Sunday noon meals, called "dinner" in the South," cost a little more—fifty cents—and drew both regular boarders and townspeople who wanted to enjoy a special culinary treat after church. The boarding house dining room table, with its thick white starched tablecloth, seated sixteen people per serving. Outside, on the porch, another sixteen people, waiting to eat, relaxed in rocking chairs. Mrs. Michael took great delight in watching people devour the food she served. She appreciated big appetites.

George White's performers stayed with Racie Michael.

"No one could make a homemade biscuit like she could," son Jack recalls. "I wish I had the recipe...I just about have tears now thinking about it."

Although Mrs. Michael had waitresses who helped serve meals, women to assist with the cleaning, and a commercial laundry to wash bed sheets and tablecloths, her work days began early. She got up before daylight, started cooking and serving breakfast, then packing lunches for those boarders who could not return to the house for their noon meal. Then she hand-washed and dried her dishes, pots, and pans before beginning preparation for a hot noon meal and thinking about what she would serve for supper.

Racie Michael and her prized automobile.

Rules abounded at Michael's Boarding House. Racie allowed no drinking, no profanity at her table, and no arguing. Occasionally, if people raised their voices during various discussions at mealtime, she would tell them to leave. The only other problems this charming lady had with her boarders resulted from some men losing their factory jobs and finding themselves unable to pay what they owed. Racie would feed and board them for two or three weeks on credit, hoping they would find work. If they did not, most would disappear with their belongings while the Michael family attended Sunday worship services or went on Sunday afternoon outings. "It happened too many times," Jack relates. "She would feed them and then they would take off. She couldn't understand how she could be so nice to feed them and them do that—leave, owing her grocery money. We never did see them any more."

Probably the highlight of Racie Michael's life occurred in 1931 when she won one of the first V-8 Fords that came on the market. Merchants in Lexington had given coupons every time someone did business with them. The night of the drawing, people filled the Carolina Theater and even lined up outside. All wanted to win. Mrs. Michael, lucky enough to be seated inside, heard the Master of Ceremonies call the winning number. She held that ticket, went to the stage, and collected her prize. From that day on, her shiny black automobile appeared in all family snapshots.

"You see the picture of her?" Jack Michael asks as he points to an old sepia tone photograph of the boarding house. "She had that hat on. She was sure beautiful. See the boarding house. There were brick walls all around. You don't see that anymore. It looks like snow in the picture, but it was taken in the summertime. See, we were all sitting around on the porch. You can see us there. I was near the door. There are two sisters and then a brother over there."

In the late 1940's, Mr. Michael accepted an engineering position at the local Children's Home, so Racie closed her boarding house. She and her husband moved to a cottage provided by the orphanage and lived there on campus until their retirement.

Information for this piece comes from the following sources:
• Nickie Doyal's Interview with Jack Michael on October 11, 2002. Picture of Racie Michael and Michael's Boarding House complements of Jack Michael.
General information about "farm teams" and Lexington Indians Baseball Team comes from several sources:
• Burk, Robert F. *Much More Than a Game.* Chapel Hill: University of North Carolina Press, 2001.
• "Band of Brothers" *http://www.minorleaguenews.com/history/baseball/2005/04/06/01.html*
• "The Independent Carolina Baseball League" *http.//www.haroldseymour.com/article.asp?articleid=19321*
• "North Carolina State League" *http://www.baseball-reference.com/bullpen/North_Carolina_State_League*
• General information about George White's "Scandals" comes from *www.pbs.org/wnet/broadway/stars/white_g.html*

ANGEL BISCUITS
(PROBABLY SIMILAR TO RACIE MICHAEL'S BISCUITS)
1 package yeast
2 to 3 Tablespoons warm water
5 cups plain flour
3-5 Tablespoons sugar
1 Tablespoon baking powder
1 teaspoon salt
2 teaspoons soda
1 cup shortening
2 cups buttermilk

Dissolve yeast in warm water. Sift flour, sugar, baking powder, salt, and soda together. Cut in shortening. Stir into yeast mixture and buttermilk. Roll on floured board; cut into biscuits. Brush with melted butter. Bake at 400 degrees for 10 to 15 minutes. Yields 4 dozen. (From Alice Sink's *Alice's Restaurant* cookbook, based on old family favorites).

Evie Thornton with the Davis triplets.

Deep River

Mama Thornton's Baby Boarding House

One September morning in 1938, Evie Gossett Thornton, a forty-five year old widow, busily prepared a noonday meal in the kitchen of her Sunny Glade Farm in the Deep River Meeting House area between High Point and Greensboro. The men who were building a new road near Mrs. Thornton's house would soon be entering her kitchen and crowding around a rectangular porcelain table for their hot dinner of stewed potatoes, pinto beans, slaw, homemade biscuits, and sweetened iced tea.

A car rumbled down an already-existing rural dirt lane, which the locals called Baby Town Road, pulled up at the back of the one-story baby boarding house, and stopped. When Mrs. Thornton looked outside, she saw an acquaintance, Jesse Davis, unloading a big wicker basket filled with nine-day-old triplets.

Mrs. Thornton, known locally as Mama Thornton, usually received babies without much prior notice. Mothers sometimes died during or soon after childbirth, and fathers who needed help often took their offspring to Mrs. Thornton's Baby Boarding House until they could make more permanent arrangements with family members. Doctors in nearby High Point and Kernersville also recommended Mama Thornton's Baby Boarding House to the families of girls who had children out of wedlock. After doctors delivered the birth mothers in their private residence, they helped make specific arrangements for these babies to be nurtured and cared for by Mama Thornton until they could be adopted by childless couples in surrounding towns. Word of mouth connected this hard-working, compassionate surrogate mother with infants who needed her. The first arrived on a December day in 1933. She was a five-month old girl, Nancy Gail Clark, who stayed for six years until a Goldsboro couple adopted her. "It was hard to give her up," Mama Thornton admitted.

This surrogate mother's biggest challenge came soon after the birth of the first set of triplets born in Burris (later renamed High Point Memorial) Hospital on Sunday, August 28, 1938. Events preceding and following the babies' births made regional news for years. Annie Montsinger Sullivan Davis, age thirty-three, an obviously pregnant woman, walked into the hospital on Saturday night with her thirty-six-year-old husband, Jesse Stanton Davis. No one, including the mother-to-be, knew she carried triplets because following the Depression, pre-natal medical check-ups were practically nonexistent in rural areas of North Carolina. In fact, throughout her entire pregnancy, Annie had arisen each morning, milked cows, prepared meals, washed clothes, canned fruits and vegetables from the garden, and tended to her regular household duties on their Kernersville Route 1 farm, which cuts across the Guilford-Forsyth county line north of High Point.

Annie was so proud of the land, handed down to her and Jesse by her husband's grandfather, Squire Davis, and of the new bedroom suite and living room set she and Jesse had saved for years to buy. Everything looked promising. Only one thing bothered her. Family members recall her lament during her uncomfortable pregnancy, "Oh, if I could just live to get this baby born." Although she had safely and uneventfully delivered their other two children at their farmhouse in rural Kernersville, she knew something about this pregnancy was very different. Perhaps she suspected multiple births because of her size and the fact that there were several sets of twins in her family. On Saturday night, August 27, 1938, both she and her attending midwife knew for certain that Annie needed professional medical attention, so her husband drove her —over the long country dirt roads—to Burris Memorial in High Point, the nearest town with a hospital.

After Dr. W.R. McCain delivered the first baby, Sara, he said: "There's another one." After the second infant, Tom, arrived, Dr. McCain announced again: "There's another one." Then Martha, the smallest, entered this world. Sara and Tom weighed about five pounds each, and Martha weighed only four and a half pounds. Annie Davis' private-duty nurse later recalled, "I can remember Annie seeing the babies and her saying she saw them," she said. "But we didn't really know if she could see them. It was real sad, but it was not anybody's fault. They didn't have the drugs they do today to fight with. It was just a different world." Relatives have told Martha that she is more like her mother. "I talk all the time," she said. "I was the only one she held because I was

A basket full of triplets cared for by Evie Thornton.

weak, and they thought it might help me. But the nurses weren't sure she could see me because they thought she was blind at the time."

Annie Davis became extremely ill with uric poisoning and died at 9:00 A.M. of kidney failure, five days after the multiple births. She was buried on the next Saturday. "Jesse, we'll keep the babies as long as you want us to until you can find someone," hospital officials told Mr. Davis. The triplets' Aunt Edna asked Mrs. Evie Gosset Thornton if she would board the infants. Mama Thornton did not hesitate. She offered to keep all three for a dollar a day, but she said it might be a good idea to wait until the new road was completed to move the frail infants. That would not happen.

When Jesse Davis went to the hospital one day and asked about the condition of his children, a nurse told him, "They're doing about as well as they'll ever do." Because Mr. Davis interpreted that to mean they might not survive in the hospital, he put all three in a wicker basket bassinet, left with them, and drove his car to Mama Thornton's, about fifteen miles from High Point.

"I knew their mother wasn't doing well after the birth," she recalled of their arrival, "but I didn't know she had died. Their father didn't think the babies were being taken proper care of, so he just up and brought them out to me. So I just went in and asked the wife of one of the men on the road crew to finish serving the meal. Then we got those three babies inside the house and I went to make some formula for them. Sara Lane looked healthy, so her milk was regular. Martha Zane, born last, didn't look quite as strong. I made her a little weaker formula.

"But, by this time Thomas Rhyne looked to be the weakest of all," she said fondly, "so I made his milk real weak."

Only a very wise and compassionate surrogate mother would know that each child required individual formulas and would take extra time to prepare them on a daily basis. Later, Carnation Milk and Gerber baby food companies donated milk and baby food for the triplets. This proved to be a tremendous financial break for Mama Thornton. Times were hard. Her husband, Eugene Thornton, had died after only fourteen years of marriage and left her to rear their three children. In 1933, a friend suggested she open her home as a baby boarding house, to support herself and her family. She decided that was a good idea.

Consequently, Mrs. Thornton's modest one-story white frame farm house, containing only two bedrooms and one bath, became a home to children who needed her. Bassinets, cribs, large wicker baskets, high chairs, baby clothes, shoes and socks filled every nook and cranny of her four small rooms. In addition to around-the-clock care of her infant boarders, Mama Thornton mowed her own yard, cooked meals, baked cakes for special occasions and sold them, planted and harvested summer gardens, milked her cows, did the laundry for everyone—including hand washing hundreds of cloth diapers— and cared for the older children. Although she worked extremely hard, she was always neat and happy. "She had pretty gray hair that had waves in it," Martha, Sara and Tom recall, "and that smile turned on all the time."

Neighbors and fellow members of nearby Deep River Quaker Church assisted by bringing chickens, fresh vegetables, and butchered meat to help feed Mrs. Thornton, her two children still at home, and all the baby boarders. After paying the agreed-upon dollar a week for the care of the triplets, Mr. Davis, a farmer, took feedbags filled with potatoes, tomatoes, or beans to Mrs. Thornton's. He also raised hogs, and when he butchered in the winter, he took the coveted hogs' heads to her. Delighted by this rare treat, she cooked the tongue and brains—she didn't throw away anything.

Jesse Davis occasionally took his two older children, Bett, ten years old, and Paul, thirteen, to Mrs. Thornton's baby boarding house. At first, the triplets' older siblings could only look at their brother and sisters through an outside window. Mama Thornton and Mr. Davis feared Bett and Paul might infect the infants with any diseases they might have picked up at school. In these times, there were few vaccines to prevent serious illnesses. Sara, Martha and Tom did not go home often, but occasionally—as they got older—their daddy or their Aunt Gladys would get them just for the weekend.

No one in the tobacco-farming Davis family had much money, as noted by the meticulous 1939 daily journal entries kept by Jesse' father, John Davis. He accounted for every penny he "took in." One entry notes a tobacco crop that yielded 1,192 pounds for which he received $110.90. He also sold homegrown sweet potatoes ($1.50 a bushel) and Irish potatoes ($1.00 a bushel), ribs (15-cents per pound) and hams (25-cents per pound), and roosters (19-cents per pound). Then he had expenses. The Davis family bought most of their staples from Hauser and Marley General Store on Wrenn Street in High Point. John Davis also recorded every penny he spent. He paid 25-cents for oranges, 15-cents for coffee, 75-cents for a gallon of molasses, 8-cents for Rinso, and 9-cents for vanilla flavoring. For 10-cents each, he also bought a Coca-Cola, tobacco, veal liver, cotton, tape, salts, celery, oysters, bread, lettuce, and dried beef. His light bill totaled $2.60 a month, and the phone "rent" amounted to $7.00. A Chevrolet cost him $25.00. Doctor McCain made house calls for $3.00 a visit. John Davis' journal also records money spent for "dress goods," organdy, thread, and lace. His daughter Nan sewed most of the baby outfits worn by the triplets. Sara and Martha still have identical dotted-Swiss dresses made by their Aunt Nan.

Christmas 1938, when the triplets were four months old, Mama Thornton recorded in Martha's baby book: "Had a tree. Received toys from Aunt Etta. Had comb and brush set. Socks from Frances Thornton and toy bears from Pauline Thornton. Toys and aprons from Aunt Flosie. Christmas greetings from Grandfather Davis. Daddy was with us Christmas Eve and Christmas night. He gave us rubber teething rings."

The triplets stayed with Mama Thornton for five-and-a-half years. They went back to their father's house in time to enter first grade at Oak View School. Sara remembers their first day at school. "There were eight grades, and the teacher took us to every room and showed us to every class. We've just always been a show," she admitted. When the school day ended, the triplets had routine chores at their father's house on Route 1, Kernersville. "We learned what work was," Martha said. While she preferred cooking and inside tasks, Sara and Tom liked to plant and harvest field crops. All was not labor, however. "We played every night, too," Sara said. "We were a happy family." Often, older brother Paul organized weekend neighborhood ball games, and everyone—big or small—participated.

The triplets adjusted well to their family homeplace, and today they give credit to their older siblings, Paul and Bett. The trio also praises Mama Thornton and her grown daughter, Pauline, who filled out baby books for them and for all the children who lived in the baby boarding house. Everyone who boarded with them received a record of his or her first tooth, favorite toys, and dates when they sat up alone, crawled, and walked. When children left Mama

Thornton's for their permanent or adopted homes, they were given their baby books to take with them. For the 130 children she boarded, Mama Thornton also recorded, for her personal enjoyment and posterity, all the names and birthdays of her charges and also their arrival and departure dates. Today her granddaughter, Lana Smith, cherishes the yellowed pages of that same little black notebook she keeps as a reminder of her grandmother's love and devotion to all her babies.

After fifteen-and-a-half years of running her baby boarding house, Mama Thornton moved into High Point and went to work sewing upholstery at one of the furniture manufacturers. Her fellow workers liked her so much they built a special curio cabinet for her 300 salt and pepper shakers. Collected from over the entire United States, the collection consisted of a variety of animals to tiny dolls to old telephones. Wouldn't you know? Evie Gossett Thornton recorded the history of each set, just as she had written and dated, in her perfect penmanship, other important events of her life.

After retiring from the furniture plant, Evie began another career— catering for weddings. At her 90th birthday party, she told well wishers—among them the Davis triplets and Nancy Gail Clark Brady, her first boarding house baby— that she was trying to phase out of the food-catering business.

"I love to cook," she confessed, "but the price of food is so high that I'm ashamed to charge enough to cover my cost. It's been two months since I've done a wedding."

That gave her more time to devote to her favorite organization, the Good Deed Club, of which she was a charter member. Members of this club pledged to assist someone in need by donating food, cards, or visits. When this ninety-year old bundle of energy was not busy cooking or cheerfully volunteering her time and talents to those who valued her friendship, she planted a variety of colorful annuals in her front-yard rock garden, and bordered her walkway with flowering bunches of candy tuft. Because of Evie Thornton's rich and interesting life, she was featured on the popular regional television program, *Roy's Folks.*

The Davis triplets, as they aged, always included Mama Thornton in their family celebrations. "We would go over and get her," Martha said. "She would spend Thanksgiving with us and Christmas Eve with us, and her family— her own three children—knew it and it was okay."

The triplets, grown and married with children and grandchildren of their own—living within a stones-throw from each other on an acre of land from their father's 70-acre farm—recall receiving regular telephone calls from Mama Thornton.

"She'd call us to come down there and help her pull weeds out of her rock garden," Martha said with a chuckle. "And she would call and say, 'I wish I knew where I could get some dirt.' She meant, 'Bring me some dirt to put around my roses.' She was a workaholic."

Were there any humorous incidents? Martha remembers well the day of Pauline Thornton's home wedding.

"She got married while we were still there," Martha said. "The day of the wedding, I poured a whole thing of face powder in a chair in the living room." She laughingly adds, "And I got whipped."

Evie Thornton, born in 1893, lived to be one hundred years old. She died April 11, 1993. Her baby boarding house has been torn down; a modern shopping center now spreads across the area that used to be Sunny Glade Farm on Baby Town Road. Sara, Tom, and Martha love to reminisce about their surrogate mother.

"She was a saint," they recall. "She always had a smile for all her kids."

Information for this story comes from the following sources:
• Personal Interview with Davis Triplets on November 12, 2002, by Nickie Doyal and Alice Sink. Also Martha Davis Stafford's baby book and recipes given to her by Mama Thornton.
• Gayle Badett's article "Mama Thornton Celebrates 90th Birthday With Memories." *High Point Enterprise.* February 18, 1993.
• Donalee Goodrum-White's article "Kernersville's Davis Triplets Then and Now." Kernersville *News.* July 11, 2002.
• Recipes shared by Lana Smith (February 8, 2004) .

Mama Thornton's Famous Recipes

CHRISTMAS SNAPS
1 quart black molasses • 1 pint shortening • 1 pint sugar • 1 teaspoon soda • 1 Tablespoon ground ginger • 1 teaspoon each cinnamon and allspice • 1 to 3 teaspoons salt • Plain flour, enough to make a stiff dough.

Roll very thin, cut in any desired shape. Bake on baking sheet until brown at 375 degrees. Makes approximately 24 dozen cookies.

CHEESE RINGS
1/2 lb. aged grated cheese • 1-3/4 sticks margarine • 2 cups plain flour • 1/2 tsp. cayenne pepper

Cream margarine and cheese together. Add flour and pepper to mixture and mix well. Fill cookie press and form rings on ungreased cookie sheet. Place in preheated oven at 400 degrees for 10-12 minutes.

A festive looking Monte Vista lit up for Christmas.

Black Mountain

The Monte Vista

Many of the boarding houses that once dotted every nook and cranny of western North Carolina have disappeared, but the Monte Vista on West State Street in Black Mountain still survives, going strong after more than eighty-five years. Even the Depression years brought paying guests. According to long-time owner and manager, Rosalie Phillips, "We were not pretentious. Survival did not depend upon keeping up with modern times." A visitor, walking into the old-fashioned lobby furnished with lovely antiques, can attest to this truth.

At the turn of the twentieth century, Rosalie's grandparents, Lucien and Rosalie Phillips, moved to Black Mountain from their cotton farm in South Carolina. They wanted their asthmatic daughter to benefit from the clear mountain air. Soon after their arrival, rumors began circulating that the Methodist Church would build a new convention center in Black Mountain, so Mr. and Mrs. Phillips bought a great deal of property in the heart of the small town. When Lake Junaluska actually became the site of the assembly ground, the Phillips' Plan Two went into operation. Lucien and Rosalie purchased an old school from the Buncombe County Board of Education, remodeled the interior, and opened a boarding house in 1919.

The Monte Vista provided rooms and meals for the many visitors who came on the train to Black Mountain. Located just a few minutes' walk from the train station, the boarding house enjoyed a booming business. Floridians came for the entire summer to escape the heat. Other guests stayed there and commuted to various nearby religious assemblies such as Ridgecrest, Montreat, and Blue Ridge.

In 1924, the Phillips family needed more room, so they built a fifteen-room building and named this addition The Farm House. Lucien and Rosalie also turned some of their purchased property into a large farm. At Camp Wachama, a short drive away, they raised their own chickens, hogs, cows, fruits, and vegetables so their guests could enjoy cured ham, fresh milk and cream, and garden produce.

South Carolina nieces Kathleen and Emily came for entire summers and earned their room and board by working at the boarding house. Their assigned duties, playing the piano and singing for guests at night, angered the Phillips's daughters Dorothy and Lucia, who had to do all the laundry. They thought the arrangement unfair.

The early days brought some of the same disturbances sometimes seen today. "A friend of my grandfather talks about a woman who stayed here all summer and didn't pay her bill," Rosalie Phillips volunteered. "And the day she was supposed to leave, she called my grandfather to her room. Later, she came downstairs and claimed rape. So she got out of her bill that way."

The Great Depression did not close the doors of the Monte Vista—quite the contrary. In 1937 Lucien and Rosalie tore down the old school house, borrowed $70,000—an astronomical sum for those days—and constructed a new three-story, thirty-six-room brick structure. This building, located behind large trees, looked down on Main Street. A rolling front yard and cozy veranda with antique wicker furniture lured guests to read, chat, or engage in a game of bridge. A Grand Opening of the new Monte Vista in 1938 drew large enthusiastic crowds eager to dance the "Big Apple," the craze of the day, and listen to the orchestra the Phillips family had hired to celebrate the momentous occasion.

The boarding house soon became the home-away-from-home for industrial leaders. Personnel from Beacon, a large blanket plant, and Kearfott, which made parts for the aerospace industry, stayed at the Monte Vista while their respective plants underwent construction. Workmen building the Terry estate, now the Episcopal Diocesan Center, headquarters for the Episcopal Church, also boarded with the Phillips family.

Clientele at the Monte Vista grew during WW II, when the Moore General Hospital, named after Dr. Samuel P. Moore, Surgeon General of the Confederacy, opened in Black Mountain. This facility contained 1520 beds and a training unit for officers, nurses, and enlisted men. Wounded soldiers went to Moore General for treatment, physical therapy, and medication. When families came to Black Mountain to visit patients, they stayed at the Phillips' boarding house. Later, when recuperating soldiers could leave the hospital for a week-end, they rented a room at the Monte Vista.

After Lucien's and Rosalie's deaths, their son Bill and his wife Marilyn took over in 1955 as new owners and managers. Marilyn, the only Mormon in town, had come to Moore General Hospital from Utah as a therapist and married

Black Mountain's Monte Vista Hotel was hailed as western North Carolina's "beauty spot."

into the Phillips family. Bill ran the farm, and Marilyn took responsibility for the house and guests. She gave charming parties for the teachers in town, planned tea brunches and dances, fed various civic clubs, and provided games and merriment. When Marilyn prepared food for special groups, she always made extra goodies so her regular guests could come downstairs and sample left-overs when a particular party had ended. Marilyn became so popular with the townspeople, they asked her to run for mayor of Black Mountain, but she refused because she said, "It wouldn't be ladylike."

Guests' comforts came first. Marilyn and Bill's two daughters, Rosalie and Carol, learned early that they could talk with adults in the lobby or on the front porch, but not in the dining room. Once Rosalie warned her younger sister, "Oh, Carol, don't cry. The guests will all leave."

Marilyn and Bill continued with the philosophy espoused by Bill's parents: Make a comfortable living while serving the community. In one form letter to potential visitors, Marilyn and Rosalie wrote, "We don't take deposits because we don't want to keep your money if you have to cancel; therefore, it is very important to telephone if you have to cancel. We haven't gotten around to credit cards; we want to serve you and have you pleased before you pay."

They did not hire staff to work at night. Instead, when they went to bed, they left the keys for unoccupied rooms on the desk with a note that people who checked in late could pay for their rooms in the morning.

Every Christmas Eve, after Marilyn had catered thirty-five or forty community holiday parties, she turned her thoughts to her family and guests. Monte Vista Party Time included refreshments, singing, dancing around the Christmas tree, and, of course, Santa's visit. On Christmas morning, Marilyn awoke her guests about 6:30, serving them steaming coffee in their rooms. Youngsters Rosalie and Carol opened their gifts while Monte Vista's boarders looked on. Marilyn said she always enjoyed the season. "It's not a party for the guests but a party with the guests," she explained, and then humorously added, "I generally plan on having the flu in January."

Elderly guests filled the rooms at the boarding house during winter months. Poet Charlotte Young, 101 years old, boarded at the Monte Vista until she moved to Stroup Rest Home in Oteen. On her 107th birthday, Miss Young autographed copies of her sixth volume of poems, smiled, chatted with friends, talked with one of her former students, and reminisced about changes during her lifetime.

"The young people now have wondered at the same things I did when I was a youth," she observed. "But they have so many wonders—a cure for polio—the telephone, which has united people all over the world—television and radio have done so much for civilization. But the greatest accomplishment I believe I have seen is a man walking on the moon."

Asked if she still created poems, she confessed she wrote her little haiku verses and gave an example. "I remember John/He helped me find my lost youth/which I'd never had."

Rosalie recalls how Miss Young and other guests became surrogate mothers: "There were about fifteen single schoolteachers who lived here. They directed my life, always telling me what to do and correcting me. Miss Thomas and Miss Fisher were colorful characters. These women checked my homework and gave me music lessons."

She also remembers the summer people. Her mother Marilyn provided entertainment every evening after supper. Bingo, clapping games like "Matthew, Mark, Luke, and John," hat parties, different theme nights, and comical womanless weddings, so popular during this time, became favorites. In 1968 Marilyn hosted a reception at the Monte Vista for a wedding party of Little People. The wedding party of Mr. and Mrs. James D. Turner received a glowing tribute in the Asheville *Citizens-Times*:

"Following the ceremony, the wedding guests attended a reception in the Monte Vista Hotel in Black Mountain, where flashbulbs popped as friends snapped pictures of the newlyweds. Mingling with the guests were members of the bridegroom's family, his mother, brothers and a sister, all of normal stature. For Turner, a gregarious and witty man, the spotlight on his wedding was

welcome because he believes it will help bring public understand of the Little People's organization and its accomplishments."

Marilyn always wanted to please her boarders. She lent an ear to budding romances, called a needed doctor or ambulance, and performed personal services. Guests loved the on-going competition of various card games. Rosalie confesses, "Because Mother was Mormon, we weren't supposed to *enjoy* playing cards; that would have been sinful. We were just supposed to be doing it to entertain the guests." One of the highlights of Monte Vista entertainment centered about a womanless wedding, written by a Florida boarder. Organ music, solos, and floral arrangements accompanied the mock wedding party, composed entirely of men. Following the ceremony, guests enjoyed a traditional wedding cake baked by Rosalie.

In 1980 Bill and Marilyn added a new sixteen-room wing for permanent boarders. When an issue of *Family Circle* magazine published an article entitled "50 Dream Vacations on a Shoestring," the Monte Vista was the first on the list with the following hook: *"Seven nights and 20 meals for $67.50 in a 1919 hotel in a small town."* Letters of reservation—to the tune of 1,200—poured in. The Monte Vista could not accommodate even a fraction of the requests, but Marilyn, with the assistance of some of her boarders, answered each request with a form letter, Chamber of Commerce brochure, and a list of other available lodgings.

When Rosalie finished college, earning a degree in chemistry from UNC, she went back home to help her mother at the boarding house. In addition

The Monte Vista's dining room offered meals served with mountain elegance.

to running a residence for regular boarders, the two hosted club meetings, wedding receptions, and bridge luncheons. The dining room with white tablecloths resembles a stately upscale restaurant, but instead of printed menus, waitresses announce the choices of the day. Carole Currie, Lifestyle Editor of the Asheville newspaper, visited one day while the Kiwanis Club met for lunch and recorded her experience:

"Choices of the day were a hot roast beef sandwich, broccoli quiche or the lunch buffet. I chose the buffet which included homemade hot tomato soup, ten salads, five hot vegetables, sweet and sour meatballs and baked chicken, homemade yeast rolls and banana muffins with butter, beverage, and dessert. My favorite of the salads was one of chopped broccoli and cauliflower with chunks of blue cheese, chopped onions, Ranch dressing and mayonnaise. There was also a delicious Rotini pasta and green pea salad. I could have made a meal of the zucchini casserole which featured the vegetable nestled in a tender custard, richly flavored with Swiss cheese. Dessert of the day was hot fudge cake, a generous slab of chocolate cake filled with ice cream and topped with a rich, pudding-y chocolate sauce. Everything was good and an incredible value for $3.50."

After Bill and Marilyn's deaths, their daughter Rosalie Phillips inherited the Monte Vista in 1989, continuing the tradition begun decades earlier by her grandparents. Having lived and worked her entire pre-college life at the boarding house, she had cultivated the expertise so vital to running the busy establishment. She hosted conventions, family reunions, weddings, receptions, writers' conferences, and at the same time, tenderly cared for her regular guests. People lingered on the porch in summertime or huddled in Victorian chairs around the living room fireplace in the winter. They still brought their musical instruments and told stories. "Plain old people," Rosalie emphasizes.

Probably the incident that caused the biggest political and religious battle in Black Mountain concerned a liquor referendum in 1978. Churches circulated petitions to close the state Alcohol Beverage Control store to kill liquor-by-the drink. On the other hand, the mayor argued that losing the $125,000 a year annual revenue would put a great strain on the town's budget. "We'd have to cut our police department and our streets department. Our entire recreation program would be eliminated," he said. Speculation indicated that the store's closure would encourage illegal bootlegging. Woodrow Propst, a 64-year-old former moonshiner commented on this possibility.

"The thought of prohibition is enough to drive a man to drink. Course, this fancy liquor don't taste half as good as the white lightning I used to make."

Although Rosalie Phillips did not comment on the referendum or conflicting opinions, she did tick off other numerous memorable incidents. "On Pearl Harbor Day, John A. Rice, the founder of Black Mountain College; my mother; and my grandmother were outside and heard that the bombs had dropped," she said. "And Billy Graham has enjoyed many Sunday lunches in our huge dining room," she added. In addition, Jay North of "Dennis the Menace" fame stayed at the Monte Vista and presented Rosalie with several autographed glossy photographs. At age seventy-five local poet Julia Hunter met her soon-to-be husband, aged ninety-five!

A few irksome individuals also surfaced during Rosalie's tenure. She simply called the police and put the troublemaker's belongings by the side of the road. Rosalie also recalls days when she had no help. By necessity, she learned to cook, scrub pots, and do laundry. She always convinced herself, "I can do this." Her self-imposed job description would shock even the most energetic person.

The day of our interview, Rosalie busied herself decorating for Christmas and making homemade candy. The evening before, she had cooked twenty turkeys and served Thanksgiving dinner to four hundred people. With a laugh, she confessed, "Last night we were full, and I rented out my bed. One of my regular boarders had gone for the holidays; she had agreed I could sleep in her room, but one of my new guests—an old man—couldn't climb the stairs. I gave him that room."

That caring philosophy typifies the eighty-five year history of the Monte Vista in Black Mountain, North Carolina. Several years ago, Rosalie sold the Monte Vista to new owners, but the tradition continues.

WANT TO GO?
The Monte Vista Hotel
308 West State Street
Black Mountain, NC 28711
Phone: 828/669-2119
Toll Free: 800/441-5400
Website: *www.themontevista.com*
Current Prices: Call or Visit Website

Family owned and operated "boarding house" type inns used to be common in every mountain town. The Monte Vista in Black Mountain is one of the few that has survived, and is still going strong. The minute you enter their spacious lobby, you know you've passed a threshold of time.

Information for this piece came from the following sources:
• Alice Sink's Interview with Rosalie Phillips at the Monte Vista on November 28, 2003.
• Undated photocopies from various newspapers in Rosalie Phillips' files:
  - "Poet, 103, Still Loves Writing."

- "Monte Vista Gets 1,200 Inquiries for 'Dream Vacation'"
- "Womanless Wedding Was Wonderful Fun."
• Lane, Carol. "Monte Vista Hotel has served Black Mountain Visitors Since 1919." The Black Mountain *Chronicle.* Winter 1992.
• "Little People's Wedding." Asheville *Citizen-Times.* June 23, 1968.
• Krzyzynski, Gene. "Homey Old Hotel in N.C. Mountains Is Unusual Bargain."
• "Monte Vista: Authentic Retreat for Budget-Wise Vacationers." Knight-Ridder Newspapers.
• Lauterer, Maggie. "'I Feel Happy,' Says Poet, 107." *Asheville Eat.* June 18, 1985.
• "Black Mountain Folks Split Over Demon Rum Referendum." *The Washington Post.* August 24, 1978.
• Currie, Carole. "Monte Vista Inn's 60th Anniversary to Be Observed Dec. 3rd." Asheville *Citizen -Times.*
    - "Monte Vista Hotel Caters to Tradition."
• Osborne, Clyde. "Monte Vista Hotel Stays Full."
• "Nothing's Changed" and "Desk Work." Asheville *Citizen-Times.* November 25, 1979.
• Duberman, Martin. *Black Mountain.* N.Y.: E.P. Dutton & Co. Inc., 1972.

ICE CREAM

One quart of sweet cream and the whites of six eggs beaten to a light froth; then beat in the eggs half teacup of sugar. Beat the cream light, and add one teacupful of sugar to cream and beat again until light, flavor with one and a half tablespoonful of vanilla, and put the whole in freezer. Put at the bottom of freezer pail a layer of ice, cover with salt, set freezer in on it and fill in around freezer with ice and salt; a layer of ice and layer of salt until full to the top of freezer; let no salt get inside of freezer. Ten minutes will freeze it.

From Mrs. Abby Fisher's *What Mrs. Fisher Knows About Old Southern Cooking, Soups, Pickles, Preserves, Etc.* 1881. Digitized by Michigan State University Library.

Ava Gardner, North Carolina's small town girl who hit the big time. This is the famous discovery photo that sent her to Hollywood.

— *Brogden* —

Mollie Gardner's Boarding House: Home of Movie Star Ava Gardner

In 1941, the night before Ava Gardner went to New York City to launch her career as a movie star, she and her friends gathered for a casual good-bye on the front porch of Mrs. Virginia Kilpatrick's boarding house in Smithfield, North Carolina.

"I'm going to marry the biggest star in Hollywood," Ava teased.

Her two best friends, Alma Kilpatrick and Rudy Howell, probably giggled at that proclamation. Sure, Ava's sister and brother-in-law had sent her photograph to MGM, and a New York talent scout had agreed to talk with her. Although the idea of their friend's interview sent chills down their spines, they knew Ava had no training or experience as an actress. Why, she even perceived herself as a "Grabtown" girl who had lived almost her entire life under the roof of her mama's various boarding houses. In 1925, Mollie Gardner and her family moved to Brogden (sometimes called Smithfield, which is actually a town nearby) or "Grabtown," a nickname for Brogden.

The story behind the nickname of "Grabtown," is almost as interesting as the movie star who lived there. According to legend and author Doris R. Canon, the little town got its name in the following manner:

"Long before the 'horseless carriage' became a familiar sight on country roads, a salesman who operated a general store on wheels made regular stops in a sparsely settled Johnston County township called Boon Hill in North Carolina's Piedmont.

"The merchant hauled his wide range of merchandise in a covered wagon drawn by four horses. When he reached a spot less than two miles from the Neuse River and eight miles from the little town of Smithfield, he tied his horses to a large oak and got down to business.

"He would take cash, if his customers were fortunate enough to have any, or he would trade for something that he could sell at other stops along the way—perhaps a few dozen eggs, a generous slab of ham, a fresh bundle of collards. Inside the wagon was almost anything that country folks might need or want: kerosene lanterns; ropes and bridles; boots and shoes; spools of thread and yard; bolts of colorful cloth for housewives to turn into dresses, aprons and shirts; blocks of salt to be licked by cattle; and peppermint candy to be licked by children. So to say that the big covered wagon was a welcome sight as it lumbered into view was a bit of an understatement. And to say that it made regular stops was somewhat misleading.

Mollie Gardner
(Photo: Ava Gardner Museum Collection)

"The man who operated the rolling store no doubt did his best to meet a regular schedule, but on many occasions circumstances caused his customers to wait for hours at the oak—and sometimes the wagon didn't show up until the next day. But regardless of whether the wagon was on time, when its wheels finally came to a halt, the customers began grabbing for goods. So it was that the wagon's stopping place became known as Grabtown."

Mollie ran Brogden Teacherage, a boarding house for single female teachers of Brogden School, while her husband Jonas farmed and worked in a near-by sawmill. At the Teacherage, six young women lived on the right side, the Gardner family resided on the left, and a living room, dining room, and kitchen comprised the central area.

Mollie's duties included the usual cleaning, cooking, washing, and ironing; however, her popularity came from much more than the completion of household chores. She soon became a mentor and surrogate mother to the teachers—many of them still teenagers—who called her Mama Gardner. On weekends, she welcomed the young women's suitors to the Gardner parlor, where couples could "court" under her supervision. Young Ava loved to hide behind the French doors and try to catch couples as they stole kisses. Mollie treated the teachers as family, not guests, and included them in holiday celebrations. She celebrated Christmas by decorating a twelve-foot tree with popcorn strings, homemade ornaments, and candles and by preparing a holiday meal.

Although the Teacherage usually accepted only single women, the Johnston County Board of Education made an exception for one of the married teachers. Maggie Williams—whose husband David was serving time for killing a law officer—gained permission to reside in Mollie's boarding house. In 1928, while Maggie taught little Ava in the first grade and lived in the Gardner home, David Marshall Williams spent his days in prison designing the Carbine rifle, which the Winchester Company produced. It made David rich and famous after his release. While in Mrs. Williams' first-grade class, Ava starred as Rose in her first stage performance, *A Rose Dream.* The operetta centered on a little girl named Rose who became lost, fell asleep under a tree, and ultimately followed elves to Fairyland. After taking in all the lovely sights and sounds of Fairyland, Rose fell asleep once again, only to be rescued by her mother from her slumber in the park under a lilac tree. Historian Doris Rollins Cannon comments, "The curtains closed to rousing applause and the audience walked into the spring night feeling proud and thoroughly entertained. After such a debut, Ava surely was justified in thinking that more plum parts in school productions would come her way—but such was not to be."

The teachers who boarded with Mollie treated her with reverence and respect. Ruth Higgins, who owned a Model A Ford, often took Mollie and the teachers for a ride in the car. About the only other entertainment—as a deserved break from Mollie's boarding house duties—came from church revivals and an occasional movie at the Howell Theater in Smithfield. Ruth took Mama Gardner and Ava to see Clark Gable and Jean Harlow star in the movie, *Red Dust.* The viewing of this romantic adventure film may have set the stage for Ava's desire to become a movie star.

Brogden teachers ate three hardy meals a day in Mollie's dining room. One of Mollie's recipes still receives raves from Cannon: "This palate-pleaser had a layer of vanilla pudding topped with a crust. On top of that was a layer of chocolate pudding. Topping the chocolate layer was a mound of fresh whipped cream enhanced with a tantalizing touch of brandy."

As Mollie's older children matured and moved away, her born-late-in-life child Ava remained at Brogden Teacherage. Mollie refused to spoil this beautiful little girl. She expected Ava to fill the firebox with wood and help with other chores, such as setting the boarding house table or assisting her father, Jonas, in his tobacco fields. Ava's main task at harvest time consisted of handing tobacco leaves to the stringer who, in turn, prepared them for curing.

Mollie also valued play time for her daughter. When the academic week ended on Fridays, Mollie supervised Ava and her friend, Clara Whiley, as they frolicked on a huge sawdust pile behind Brogden School. Mollie also encouraged Ava to invite girlfriends to spend Friday night at the boarding house. Before the children went outside to play on Saturday morning, Mollie fed them a Southern breakfast of grits, fried country ham, and biscuits with homemade syrup. Memories of her sumptuous meals surface even to this day.

"Ava liked to pour the syrup over her biscuits," Clara recalled, "...she had a bad habit of chewing her fingernails down to the quick, and in my mind I can still see her sucking the syrup off those fingers."

Even though Ava and Clara played together as best friends, they did have one serious falling out over who would play the part of the angel in the Christmas play. "Ava wanted to be the Christmas Angel," Clara said, "and one day she even left class to rehearse the part. But she found out that the role had been given to Clara, whose straight blonde hair and blue eyes looked more angelic to the teacher in charge than Ava's curly top and hazel eyes. This caused the two girls to claim other best friends for a time, but they soon picked up where they left off."

Although Mollie usually accepted Ava's tomboyish personality and her love for tree climbing and puddle sloshing, she knew where to draw the line. When one of the teachers asked Ava to be flower girl in her wedding, Mollie sewed her daughter a lovely dress, bought her new stockings and high-buttoned shoes, and styled her hair in Shirley-Temple-like ringlets. Then Mollie took her to a photographer to record the child's charm and beauty.

In 1936, Mollie, Jonas, and Ava moved to Newport News, Virginia, where Mollie opened another boarding house. After Jonas' death in 1938, Mollie and Ava both wanted to come back to North Carolina, so Mollie accepted a job as manager of a Teacherage in Rock Ridge, a small farm community only thirty-five miles away from Brogden. The Rock Ridge Teacherage, divided into two apartments on the first floor, housed a married couple—the Sheffields—on one side and Mollie and Ava on the other. Unmarried female teachers lived upstairs. With Mollie's loving disposition and sense of humor, she again became Mama Gardner to all who lived there. Dewey Sheffield, who owned a car—always

Mollie Gardner and Ava, who even as a child was a beauty.

(Photo: Ava Gardner Museum Collection)

volunteered to drive whenever his wife Emily and Mollie needed to go shopping. Appreciative of Dewey's generosity, Mollie once said, "I thought it would be a long time before we'd get to go anywhere, but it's only been three weeks and here we are going again!" Once when Emily and Mollie visited the North Carolina State Library, Molly, who carried Emily's son Dewey, said to her friend, "Emily, I think you'd better take the baby. I'm afraid my knee might give out on me." Not long after the child had been returned to his mother's arms, Mollie fell; when several students rushed to help her, Mollie was laughing. "She had a great sense of humor," Emily said.

Ava made friends easily with all the women who lived in the Rock Ridge Teacherage. One teacher who boarded with Mollie introduced Ava to Alberta Cooney on the first day of her senior year at Rock Ridge School. The young women had a great deal in common—from their almost identical looks to their grief over losing their fathers. Bonding with another girl, Margie Williamson, Ava, Alberta, and Margie soon became know as The Three Musketeers. Alberta envied Ava's natural beauty and marveled that she wore very little makeup—only a light touch of Tangee lipstick and Cutex fingernail polish.

Alberta liked to spend the night with Ava in the teacherage and holds fond memories of Mollie. "Ava's mother was the sweetest, most wonderful woman," she said. "She often made a delicious chocolate cake, and would always send word for me to come and have a piece. She told me she put grated

potatoes in the cake, but I don't know if she meant the batter or the icing."
Alberta also recalls Mollie's loving way. "In Ava's home, 'I love you' was said
freely and often."

Time passed, and Ava graduated from Rock Ridge High and enjoyed the
following summer. She attended the annual June German dance in Rocky
Mount, at Holt Lake, at the home of one of her friends, Alma Kilpatrick, who
lived in the boarding house her mother Virginia operated near the courthouse.
Ava also visited with her older sister Bappie in New York. Then, that next fall,
Ava returned to Rock Ridge and helped her mother run the boarding house.
News of the day concerned everyone. Germany had invaded Poland in
September, bringing Britain and France into the war against Germany. The next
summer Ava entered Tarboro's Tobacco Festival beauty pageant and wore a
stunning Grecian-style gown Mollie had made for her; however, the judges did
not choose her as winner. That fall, Ava and two friends, Alberta Cooney and
Margie Williamson, decided to take the train to Washington, D.C. to look for
jobs. They wore two-piece dresses with matching turbans. "We wanted to look
mature and sophisticated," Alberta admitted. They all got jobs as waitresses.

Back home, Ava enrolled in Atlantic Christian College, where she was
voted Campus Beauty. Her big break came as a mere coincidence after Bappie's
husband Larry, a photographer, had displayed a photograph of Ava in the
window of his New York Tarr Photography Studio. One day Barney Duhan, a
clerk in the legal office of Loews Theatres in New York, stopped to admire the
photograph. He liked what he saw—a girl glowing with freshness and
innocence—and decided to enter the photography studio to try and obtain her
telephone number so he could call her for a date. The receptionist refused to
release Ava's phone number, and Barney mentioned that MGM should receive a
copy of her picture. Larry and Bappie thought so, too, so they stayed up all night
preparing a portfolio which Larry personally delivered to MGM's New York
office. Studio officials liked what they saw and invited Ava to come talk with
them the next time she was in the city. After a routine interview in 1941, Ava
received a seven-year contract at fifty dollars a week, which sent her on her way
to Hollywood.

Though excited about Ava's new adventure, Mollie did not want her
youngest daughter to go alone to Hollywood, so she persuaded Bappie to
accompany her. Their first day at the MGM studios, Mickey Rooney, filming
Babes on Broadway with Judy Garland, introduced himself to Ava. Soon they
began dating, and on December 10, 1943, they married in a little white church
with only a few family members and guests present. Mollie did not attend the
wedding because she suffered from uterine cancer. She probably never saw the
headlines that proclaimed the marriage of "the daughter of a poor sharecropper
had married the biggest star in Hollywood." The marriage lasted only four
months.

Mollie died at the age of fifty-nine in May of 1943, the same month as Ava and Mickey Rooney's divorce. After Ava left for Hollywood, Mollie continued to attend to her boarding house duties at Rock Ridge Teacherage, and even after she experienced severe abdominal pain and excessive bleeding, she tried to treat herself with excessive amounts of aspirin. Only when Molly's doctor forced her to slow down did she resign from her job and move to Raleigh to live with another daughter, Inez, where she died at Rex Hospital.

WANT TO GO?

The Ava Gardner Museum is open daily from 9a.m. to 5p.m., Monday through Saturday, and 2p.m. to 5p.m. on Sundays. Admission is $5.00 for adults, $4.00 for seniors 65 and older and teens ages 13-16, $3.00 for children ages 3-12. No charge for children under age 3. Phone 919-934-5830 for more information. It is located at 325 E. Market Street in the heart of Smithfield, N.C.

Information from this piece comes from the following sources:
• Canon, Doris Rollins. *GRABTOWN GIRL: Ava Gardner's North Carolina Childhood and Her Enduring Ties to Home.* Asheboro: Down Home Press, 2001.
• Ava Gardner Museum official website, *www.avagardner.org.*

Molly Gardner's Coconut Cake
(Recipe from *Recipes and Remembrances,* courtesy of Angela Lawson,
Executive Director of the Ava Gardner Museum.)
2 sticks butter
3 1/3 cups self-rising flour
2 cups sugar
1 cup milk
4 eggs
1 teaspoon vanilla
Cream butter and sugar thoroughly (by hand). Add eggs, one at a time and beat after each egg. Add flour alternating with milk and vanilla. Bake in 4 well-greased-and-floured 9-inch pans at 375 degrees for about 25 minutes. Test with straw. Filling: 4 egg whites • 3 Tablespoons white Karo syrup • 2 coconuts, grated • 1 1/2 cups milk from coconut • 3 cups sugar. Cook sugar, Karo syrup with milk from coconut, until this spins a thread. Pour slowly over stiffly beaten egg whites and beat until almost cool. Stir coconut into frosting. Frost side and top of cake after it cools. Substitute: 2 packages frozen coconut in place of coconut and substitute water in place of coconut milk. *(This recipe was baked by Ava's mother and sisters, Inez Grimes and Elsie Creech, and sent to her on her birthday no matter where she was. Courtesy: Ava Gardner Museum Collection).*

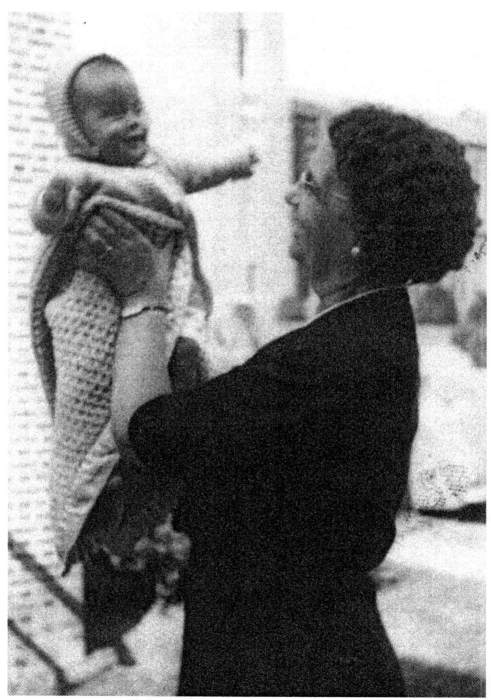
Lucille Hege Clodfelter sharing a smile with a baby.

Lexington

Lucille Hege Clodfelter's Hege Inn

The owner and hostess for this popular up-scale establishment, Lucille Hege Clodfelter, had not aspired to be an entrepreneur. As a young woman, she had clerked at W.G. Penry's drygoods store and also taught in her mother's school. She and her husband, Dr. Charles Meade Clodfelter, a practitioner, resided in the private residence on West Center Street until an illness rendered Dr. Clodfelter bed-ridden for the remainder of his life. Now the only breadwinner, Lucille needed to bring in money for herself, her husband, and their two children, Charles and Olivia.

According to one friend, Lucille "knew what it was to climb steep hills and travel rugged roads, and she knew the meaning of toil and struggle and hardship. But she never permitted these things to interfere with her joyous nature. Her smile and her determination and her unfaltering step kept her ever moving toward a better day."

She decided to open a boarding house, but first she needed a bold plan to enlarge her existing home. In 1925, she added four large open parlors across the front of the house, a dining room, seventeen bedrooms, and several suites. She named her new establishment Hege Inn, and according to one report, "the men and women who made a beaten path to its doors through the years had an affection for the old Inn that was as deep as that felt for the famous 'Wayside Inn' by the Longfellows and the Emersons and their contemporaries as they passed through Sudbury, Massachusetts, in their travels."

Conveniently located only one block east of the monument of the Confederate Soldier that towered in the middle of the intersection at Main and Center Streets, and within walking distance of the railroad station, Hege Inn's proximity to the Davidson County Courthouse provided Lexington attorneys a convenient, genteel place to board. Lucille insisted the grounds of Hege Inn emulate the beauty of the quaint little Southern town, with its lush lawns flanked by towering oaks, poplars, and dogwoods. She furnished the interior of the house with antique tables, sideboards, luxurious sofas, chairs, and gilded mirrors.

Lucille then hired a staff to create a grand and memorable experience for her "paying guests," as she called them. Cooks Rosa and Coco produced delicious Southern cooking. Georgia Mae assisted them in the kitchen and also cleaned the entire house. Elsworth provided handyman services while Roosevelt and "Little Joe" Sullivan performed various chores such as mowing the lawn and raking leaves. Lucille's staff proved so industrious and loyal, they stayed for many years—even after her death.

The Hege Inn served meals three times a day, seven days a week. Work began at 6:00 A.M. when Lucille made coffee and met with her staff to make preparations for the day. After breakfast, Lucille went to the grocery store to restock supplies. Back at the Inn, she presided over the serving of lunch and then rested for an hour or two with her knitting or reading until time to supervise the evening meal.

Starched and ironed white linens covered multiple tables in the dining room. All meals were family style. Food, served in big bowls on each table, encouraged the "all you can eat" atmosphere. On Sunday morning, Elsworth made his special hotcakes. During the week, greens, beans, field peas, and potatoes cooked on the big stove and homemade fruit cobblers baked in huge pans. No one went away hungry from Lucille's table.

Sunday noon found regular boarders and townspeople waiting on the front porch or living room for the bell to summon them to their noon meal. After-church family dinners meant fried chicken, ham, fresh vegetables, homemade bread, and fruit cobblers served a la mode. Elegant china and silver always graced each table. Lucille, an outgoing lady, loved to circulate among her boarders and Sunday regulars, and other members of her family ate with the boarders and townspeople.

Lucille also enjoyed teas, showers, and civic club meetings held in the Inn's gracious parlors. With her short brown hair coifed and curled and wearing her finest dress and shined pumps, her posture ram-rod straight, she received guests in the formal living rooms. Fresh flowers and starched organdy curtains complimented antique furnishings in each of the parlors. Lucille Clodfelter loved playing hostess to her guests.

For Hege Inn's very special teas and receptions, Lexington's legendary cook, Jessie Payne, arrived with apron and culinary expertise. "Painie," an

African-American born in 1878 of slave parents, prepared succulent dishes in the Inn's kitchen. Guests knew if Jessie Payne cooked for any celebration, the food would be elegant and tasty. Party menus included ham, potato salad, peas, perfection salad, cheese soufflé, and Devil's food cake with white icing. Or there could be chicken salad, tomato aspic, cheese straws, scalloped potatoes, and blocks of coconut cake. On special holidays, Jessie prepared turkey, dressing, cranberry salad, scalloped oysters, rice, beans and corn, mince meat tarts with whipped cream, and coconut balls.

Lucille also made sure that her guests enjoyed socializing with each other. Regular boarders enjoyed after-supper singing around an upright piano or a challenging game of bridge at tables set up in the parlors during cold weather or on the porch in the summer. According to one of Lucille's nieces, "There were probably a few poker games in the rooms, too." Whatever the activity, Lucille enjoyed mingling. She presided as charming hostess over each activity because she loved people and wanted them to enjoy elegant amenities.

Single attorneys, who had offices two blocks west in Lawyers' Row behind the Davidson County Court House, lived at Hege Inn. Circuit court judges came for an extended period of time and sometimes brought their wives. After his wife's death, Judge L.A. Martin moved into a suite at what he called "the Old Inn." He referred to his nine-year tenure as being "just as rich in nostalgic memories...as the Waldorf-Astoria is rich in memories to those who have been patrons and visitors at the famous old hostelry in New York." Unmarried women who taught at the local schools also boarded with Mrs. Lucille, as did business executives, doctors, dentists, ministers, executives, clerks, and bookkeepers. The boarders, although diversified, always put forth their best manners. According to family members, they do not recollect anyone ever becoming troublesome, noisy, or rude. Amazingly, no one ever left without paying his or her boarding tab.

According to Olivia Clodfelter Moylette, her mother charged about thirty dollars a month for room and board and rented six rooms on the first floor and eight on the second. The family occupied the third floor. Olivia and her brother Charles often slept on two sleeping porches—unless they were needed for late-arriving guests. Olivia remembers sometimes in the night she and Charles would be awakened and asked to move to their parents' room because someone had come in late and needed a place to stay. "We didn't resent this," she said, "because it was either someone they knew or someone in need." From her childhood, she also recalls her father's illness, a form of cancer. She would go upstairs to his bedroom with her dolls and get out his medical instruments; he would show her how to operate on her pretend patients.

Sometimes unmarried guests met their future spouses at the Inn. When Harvey Dick moved to Lexington to work as an accountant, Hege Inn became his home. He met and married Pearl Hege, a niece of the proprietoress of the boarding house, who had just completed college and had moved back home. Two other couples, who also met there, married in a double ceremony.

The town of Lexington grew rapidly and through the years offered a wide assortment of businesses on both sides of South Main Street. Boarders could shop at Belk, Hoover Furniture Store, Costner's Jewelers, and Fred Thompson & Company. All provided fine quality goods, friendly clerks, and personal service. The two five and dimes, Macks and McLellans—directly across Main Street from each other—sold everything from shoes to light bulbs to freshly popped corn and roasted nuts. Business executives, doctors, dentists, and bookkeepers had offices in second floor suites above the retail stores.

Three drug stores, Rexall, Mann's, and Peoples, had soda fountains. While people waited to have a prescription filled, they could enjoy an orangeade made from freshly-squeezed fruit or a fizzing Coca-Cola in a tall frosty glass or a grilled-cheese sandwich with dill pickles. The Carolina and the Granada, two theaters—one on each end of the shopping district—advertised popular movies of the times.

Women's social clubs sprang up in Lexington as early as 1898 when The Club of the Twelve organized. Later years saw the formation of many other social and cultural organizations including the Sorois Club, Entre Nous, Round Dozen, Pleasure Club, and Delphinia Embroidery Club. Often, Hege Inn hosted these meetings.

According to historians M. Jewell Sink and Mary Green Matthews, "Lexington was beginning to change...to shed its reputation of being a village worthy of the days of old Rip Van Winkle, very quiet, and very slow."

Over the thirty years that Lucille Clodfelter served the town's elite and wealthy, she never forgot the needy. "How often I have heard so many people say that whether the person who knocked on her door at night was a beggar or thief, or just an unfortunate unemployed person passing through town, no one was ever allowed to leave her door hungry," Judge Martin said, commenting on her generosity.

Until her death on Mother's Day, May 8, 1955, Lucille Hege Clodfelter continued to run her home for "paying guests." Judge Martin commented on the pathos and timely order of her passing: "Indeed her going away on this memorial day for mothers was a fitting and well-timed climax, for surely no woman in all Lexington has served and ministered as a mother to so many people for so many years." He complimented her determination and called her work a "ministry that spread out in many directions, and if any criticism could be made of her in this respect it would probably be correct to say that she did not do too little but too much, and far more than she was able to do."

After Lucille's death, her grown children, Charles and Olivia, ran the Inn for several years. When asked of her memories associated with living at Hege Inn, Olivia's daughter Sherry Pollard had many to choose from.

"There are so many many stories to tell!" she declared. "The hobos coming to the back door always got a hot meal. Sitting on the back porch snapping beans or shucking corn. Elsworth's long service at the Hege Inn and his mother, Mina's, before that. I was told her mother was a slave. Sitting on the front porch waiting for the dinner bell to ring, we would play car polo, each one choosing a different color car to count. After dinner, standing around the old upright piano singing

A sign from the Hege Inn now on display at the Candy Factory in Lexington.

songs together (there was no TV then). The Public Library was next door. All kinds of folks living at the Inn—Miss Ada Simpson, who taught me third grade and the Duke Power boys Mama always kept on the third floor. And there were the folks that came just to eat. Meals were at a set time and all were alerted by the brass hand bell tingling. All meals were served in big bowls on each table with all you could eat. Coco made the biscuits and I put them on the baking sheet. I have her old wooden rolling pin."

Grace, charm, and dignity still reigned supreme at Hege Inn under Olivia and Charles' management. The old staff of six remained. Coco and Rosa cooked; Georgia Mae served and cleaned; Elsworth continued to complete handyman chores, and Roosevelt and "Little Joe Sullivan" assisted in a variety of ways. Today Hege Inn is a lingering nostalgic memory, and those former boarders still alive today, no doubt, cherish recalling its heyday. But all good things must come to an end. The old boarding house proved no exception. In the mid-to-late 1960's, after Mrs. Clodfelter's children closed the establishment, the wrecking crews demolished the building. Gone was what L.A. Martin called "an institution" because "the reputation of her place was known far and wide and was patronized by people from every section of the state."

Information for this piece comes from the following sources:
- E-mail interviews with Olivia Clodfelter Moylette (Daughter of Lucille Hege Clodfelter), Sherry Pollard (Granddaughter of Lucille Hege Clodfelter), and Jan Berg (Granddaughter of Lucille Hege Clodfelter).
- Nickie Doyal's' interview with Catherine Dick in September 13, 2003.
- "Roswell King and Olivia Earnhardt Hege." Section 551. *Davidson County Heritage,* 269 (From photocopy)
- Broughton, Vickie. "Hege Inn Was a Place for Socializing, Good Food." Turning Back the Clock. Lexington *Dispatch* . September 1989. (From photocopy).
- Martin, L.A. "Lingering Memories of Hege Inn." Source unknown, but believed to be from his personal files. (From photocopy).
- Sink, Jewell and Mary Green Matthews. *Pathfinders Past and Present: A History of Davison County, North Carolina.* High Point: Hall Printing Company, 1972.

RECIPE FROM JESSIE PAYNE'S COOKBOOK
(Compliments of Jean Leonard)

RUSSIAN TEA
(As Written)
1/4 lb. tea
Put on stove in white porcelain pot.
1-1/2 gal. water
3 cups sugar
In other pan
2 T. cloves
2 T. spice (whole grain) in bag.
Steep [sic] in qt. boiling water
Put tea in bag and steep [sic] in about 1 qt. boiling water 3 to 5 minutes. Have ready juice from 1-1/2 doz. oranges, 1 doz. lemons. When ready to serve add tea to hot water. To each pot of tea, [add] 1/2 c. orange juice, 1/4 c. lemon juice, 1/2 c. spice juice in tea. Serve at once, piping hot.

Charlotte

The Greenwood's Boarding House

The 1944 Charlotte City Directory lists Charles H. Greenwood and wife Zera F. living at 1535 Elizabeth Avenue. In the mid 1940's, Elizabeth Avenue boasted large and exquisite homes within walking distance of the town's square. The neoclassical revival Hawley House at 923 Elizabeth Avenue, designed by architect Leonard L. Hunter and built in 1906 by a wealthy cotton merchant, became Mrs. Morehead's Boarding House in the 1930's. Guests paid $7.50 a week for a room and two meals daily. Later, before the boarding house was demolished in 1990, its name changed to "The Clary."

At 926 Elizabeth Avenue stood the East Avenue Tabernacle, a brick church with a large circular sanctuary, a dome, a balcony, and a neoclassical entrance designed by architect J.M. McMichael. Also on Elizabeth Avenue, the Charlotte Kindergarten occupied a tall, rambling two-story house with gables and a wrap-around front porch. Other kindergartens and private schools were housed in the teacher's private residence.

Elizabeth is the only old neighborhood in Charlotte named for a woman, Anne Elizabeth Watts. In 1897, Charles B. King established a Lutheran college for women and honored his mother-in-law by naming the institution Elizabeth College, after her. Although the college moved to Salem, Virginia in 1915, the fashionable neighborhood retained its name and was where such local leaders as William Henry Belk, founder of the Belk Department Stores, lived.

Elizabeth became a part of Charlotte in 1907. The Charlotte *Evening Chronicle* of April 16, 1910, refers to this section of the city. "The breezes of heaven blow their freshest, the light of the sun is at its brightest in this favored neighborhood," the newspaper declared.

Today, Elizabeth Avenue's two-story Greenwood Boarding House no longer stands, but in 1945, it loomed large and comfortable with a wrap-around front porch, rocking chairs, and swings. Four to six girls boarded in the five upstairs bedrooms. The proprietors expected lady-like behavior from their boarders, and no one ever disappointed them. The Greenwoods, a married couple in their early 50's, executed a rather strange form of management. Mr. Greenwood always cooked and served all the meals, and the young women enjoyed their big breakfasts of ham, eggs, oatmeal, and biscuits.

The girls rarely saw Mrs. Greenwood around the house; she did not eat her meals or socialize with them. When she did appear, she wore fancy clothes and diamonds. She dressed fashionably and had her short curly hair fixed. Apparently she made cameo appearances, passing through the dining room while her female boarders ate supper and asking how everyone's day had gone.

Occasionally the Greenwood's female boarders would skip supper at the boarding house, and go to a diner called Minute Grill for the delicious pork chops served there. Once the young women boarders openly rebelled against the food prepared by Mr. Greenwood. After being served green beans one time too many, the young women decided they had had enough. One night each girl put a big heaping spoonful on her plate, but then left the table at the end of the meal with the beans still untouched. They didn't get green beans for a long time after that.

In 1945, women chose to live at the Greenwood's boarding house so they could be near their jobs at Quartermaster's Depot, a government agency begun in 1941 in the one million-square-foot former Ford Motor Company plant on Statesville Avenue. During World War II, the Depot collected, bundled into units, and distributed reusable salvage items to thirty-seven Army posts in four states. Materials included everything from small items such as paper, wood, wool, aluminum, used lumber, nails, and steel scrap, to larger pieces including telephone poles, sewing machines, sewer pipes, milk cans, wheel barrows, scales, and blasting machines.

At Quartermaster's Depot women worked in Civil Service positions from eight until five o'clock, earned about $37 a week, and bought war bonds every time they received a pay check. In fact, employees of the Depot set a 1944 national record for their purchase of these bonds. Patriotism abounded.

Quartermaster female employees worked hard at their jobs while they waited for their sweethearts to finish their tours of duty. They enjoyed fraternizing with their single female friends who lived with them at the

Greenwood's boarding house. During the work week they usually came home tired, so after supper they went upstairs and took showers or baths in one of the two bathrooms. Then they read magazines, preferring one about movie stars like Betty Grable. They may have listened to Radio Station WBT. Announcer Charles Crutchfield had formed a group called the Briarhoppers to play old fiddle tunes, hymns, and heart songs. In the mid-1940's, the Briarhoppers broadcast weekly coast-to-coast from WBT on the CBS shows *Carolina Hayride* and *Carolina Calling.* Famous Briarhopper musicians included singer Fred Kirby; banjo player Shannon Grayson; and multi-instrumentalist Arthur Smith.

When the women who boarded at the Greenwood's had finished their work week, they enjoyed various events in Charlotte. Both the Imperial and Carolina Theaters offered the newest movies in air-conditioned comfort. During this time, actor Randolph Scott, who had grown up in Charlotte, emerged as a top box office draw. Portraying the good guy in the white hat, he was always the hero in his cowboy roles.

The S&W Cafeteria on West Trade Street advertised good food and low prices, "with the quality and flavor like an extension of the boarding house." McCrory's or Woolworth's lunch counters became a favorite gathering spot for downtown shoppers.

A trip to J.B. Ivey and Co. Department Store on North Tryon Street for a Saturday of window shopping possibly brought forth talk about Mr. J.B. Ivey, the son of a Methodist minister, who covered the store's windows with dark shades on Sundays in respect for the Sabbath. Or an afternoon spent in Efrid's Department Store, also located on North Tryon Street and famous for having the first escalator in the region, provided a nice change of pace. Shoppers could find there, according to one advertisement, "ladies clothing, straw hats, Octagon Soap, Gail & Ax Snuff, colorful parasols, lace curtains, and Marseilles bedspreads." Especially exciting was the Efird and Belk competition for lavish Christmas decorations.

The Public Library of Charlotte and Mecklenburg County had a quiet, furnished reading room available for reading or viewing educational films. Bowen's Drugstore, on South Tryon Street, provided the perfect atmosphere for the young women to relax as they sat and talked at little ornate ice cream tables, while enjoying a soda, lemonade, or sarsaparilla ordered from the soda fountain counter.

According to articles in the August 15, 2005, Greensboro *News & Record,* Betty Austin had another interest—an extremely important Army private named Dominick Bruno, whom she had glimpsed only once, but known as a pen pal for four years. They had fallen in love through their correspondence. Their relationship began like this: Betty, a fifteen-year-old student at Marshville High School, rode the bus home from school one day. She and her friends noticed

Jake Houston's photo of Betty and Bruno's VJ-Day kiss was famous.
(Photo: Charlotte Observer)

from the rear window a young Army private driving an armored military car. The girls waved, the driver waved back, and then Betty impulsively scribbled a note and tossed it out the opened window just before she got off the bus. The note said, "Miss Betty Ross Austin, Route 1, Box 53, Peachland, N.C. Please write me someday and tell me your address."

Dominick Bruno stopped his vehicle, picked up the note, and waved again. When he returned to his Army base in Montgomery County, he did write. That letter became the first of over five hundred that he sent the girl he had only glimpsed as she got off the school bus. Dominick Bruno served in four campaigns in Europe and Africa, but he always carried with him Betty's first little note. After his discharge from the Army on August 3, 1945, Dominick visited his parents in New York City and made plans to go to Charlotte, where Betty then lived and worked. She thought he would arrive on Saturday, August 10, so after work on Friday, she went back home to borrow her father's car for the weekend.

Dominick arrived early—on Friday night—at the Greenwood's. Someone informed him that Betty would not return until the next morning, so the young man spent the night in the front porch swing of the boarding house. Betty arrived, as scheduled, on Saturday morning. Wearing old clothes and sporting curlers in her hair, she realized how terrible she must have looked. She waltzed right past her soldier boy and sprinted inside the house and up the stairs to change into the pink two-piece linen suit, hat, gloves, and pumps she had brought for their first real face-to-face meeting.

"When she walked down those sweeping stairs, she was a vision," Dominick said. "I thought, 'Oh my gosh, look at what I've got here.'"

National news that same day revealed that a second atomic bomb had been dropped on Nagasaki. When Japan's surrender followed, Betty and Dominick went to Charlotte Square to join in the victory celebration on August 14, 1945. As the couple kissed, Charlotte *Observer* photographer Jake Houston captured the moment in a picture that made the front page of the newspaper. Even today, the Austin-Bruno kiss rivals the famous Alfred Eisenstaedt's photo of the sailor and nurse embracing in New York's Time Square. Celebrating over sixty years of marriage to Dominick, Betty says, "You know, of all the kisses, I still love that kiss in 1945 the best."

Information for this piece comes from the following sources:
• "For Soldier and N.C. Girl, This Kiss Wasn't Just a Kiss." *News & Record.*
   August 15, 2005.
• "Charlotte Quartermaster's Depot" *www.cmstory.org*
• Morrill, Dan. *Historic Charlotte: An Illustrated History of Charlotte &
   Mecklenburg County.* San Antonio: Historical Publishing Network, 2001.

- Kratt, Mary & Mary Manning Boyer. *Remembering Charlotte:Postcards from a New South City, 1905-1950.* Chapel Hill: The University of North Carolina Press, 2000.
- Hanchett, Tom and Ryan Sumner. *Charlotte and the Carolina Piedmont.* Charleston: Arcadia Publishing, 2003.

COCONUT PIE

One coconut fresh, draw off the milk, then place the nut in a hot oven and let it stay long enough for the shell to pull off; then grate with the nut juice one teacup of powdered white sugar, one tablespoonful of butter and lard rubbed together until creamed, then take the yelks [sic] of four eggs and beat into sugar and butter until perfectly light; grate the rind of one lemon into it, and squeeze the juice of the lemon into the creamed butter and sugar; beat the white of four eggs light, and add also to creamed butter and sugar, and stir them well, add also one-half teacup of sweet milk. Will make three pies. Use a half pound of flour for the pastry, one tablespoonful each of butter and lard—you only want crust at the bottom of plate, and bake in quick oven.

From Mrs. Abby Fisher's *What Mrs. Fisher Knows About Old Southern Cooking, Soups, Pickles, Preserves, Etc.* 1881. Digitized by Michigan State University Library.

Erlanger Village

38 Mill Street

In 1942, Erlanger Mills hired Mrs. Lucinda Caroline Carrie Clayton to manage Erlanger Boarding House, located at 38 Mill Street. This sprawling structure had three floors and twenty-three rooms. An oil stove heated the living room, while a wood stove in the kitchen doubled as heater and cook stove. Mrs. Clayton telephoned in her grocery list to Conrad and Hinkle in nearby Lexington, and within a few hours an employee of the store delivered her order. The Clayton family resided on the first floor. Single male and female cotton mill workers—and occasionally a married couple— occupied bedrooms on the second floor of the big house and shared the one upstairs bathroom. Boarders ate most of their meals, served family style, at the dining room table where Mrs. Clayton and her two helpers, Emma and Christine, placed large bowls of meat, vegetables, bread, and banana pudding.

Nancy Clayton Meeks, daughter of Mr. and Mrs. Clayton recalls her mother's writing a regular column, "Erlanger News," for the Lexington *Dispatch*. "My mother was active in the church, and at election times, she was politically involved," Meeks relates. "She and daddy were very political...Republicans. She was active in getting the registration list up to date, making sure everyone was registered. Mama was outspoken. Daddy should have been a lawyer; he was very much into politics...once when they were so involved in the registration books, they got a threatening phone call. But it didn't seem to phase them. It didn't scare them out of doing what they were doing. Daddy just wanted to get all those who were not eligible to vote off the registration books."

The boarding house at Erlanger Village.

Nancy Meeks vividly remembers a Baptist and a Methodist church across the street from each other. Each sponsored various community events. Two newspapers, *The Erlantern* and the *Erlanger Community* printed announcements of up-coming events. "We had ice cream dinners on the front lawn. And everyone would be invited," she says. "I remember the women of the church would have a hot dog sale. They would be a nickel each, and there would be a big bucket filled with ice bottles—not cans in those days. And I remember one woman grating cabbage for slaw. To this day I can still see her grating the slaw."

Mrs. Clayton, a woman small in stature, but large in spirit, ran her establishment in accord with Erlanger Mills's "etched in stone" model-village philosophy. If anyone drank alcoholic beverages or misbehaved in any way, Mrs. Clayton "would give him a good talking to." Her daughter Nancy recalls a few lines of a song her mother used to sing when she was distressed about something or when one of the boarders had misbehaved: *Old faithful, on the range together, in all kinds of weather.* "When she sang that song, you knew she was bothered. You knew to tread lightly," her daughter says.

Planning for this model village began in the early 1900's, when the Erlanger family of New York wanted to build a mill to produce cotton cloth needed to manufacture men's B.V.D. underwear. By 1913, Abraham and Charles Erlanger had bought a two-hundred-fifty-acre plot of land just north of the city of Lexington in an area of North Carolina known for its mild climate, rural environment, hills and valleys, and pine forests.

Howard Davis Townsend of Cabarrus County built a cement dam on the nearby creek. Two-horse wagons hauled dirt to fill existing ditches. Talented tradesmen, master builders, and masons contributed their time and talents to build the mill and surrounding houses. Rocks for underpinnings, chimneys, and steps came from nearby Swearing Creek.

Erlanger Cotton Mills Co. opened on March 24, 1914, and the production of cloth began for the B.V.D. Company. Officers and superintendents arrived to fill various positions, and laborers came from all over North and South Carolina to work on the production line. While houses sprang up for married men and their families, single males also needed a place to live. Mill officials opened a boarding house at 38 Mill Street. Through the years, people have incorrectly referred to this structure as a "hotel," "motel," "inn," or "lodge." The establishment meets the definition of " boarding house" because the men (and later women) stayed for extended periods for a nominal weekly fee, which included a place to sleep, a shared bathroom with tub, sink, and toilet, hearty family-style breakfast and supper five days a week in the large dining room, plus a brown-bagged dinner of sandwiches to take to the mill when the whistle blew for noon break.

Officers hired Mr. and Mrs. Jay Moon, the first in a succession of couples who ran this establishment. Generally, while the husband worked in the cotton mill during the day, his wife supervised the shopping, cooking and serving of meals, packing daily lunches, and cleaning. African-American women, who lived with their husbands on a surrounding parcel of land, arrived daily to help clean and cook. Company policy also dictated that any needed house painting and yard work would be provided free of charge. Mill owners paid all the bills.

Potential workers liked the reasonable rent of twenty-five cents per room per week (including water, sewerage, and lights) that attracted families to the new single dwellings at Erlanger Mill Village. Printed bills advertised the village:

WANTED by OCTOBER lst to 15, 1916

Cotton Mill help of all kinds, especially Spinning room help. Best of wages. Work runs well either day or night on 30s warp and 40s filling yarns. Weavers make as good wages as the best in this section. Doffers make from $8.00 to $11.00 per week at night. Good Spinners run from eight to twelve sides. Mill runs five nights and pays for six. Transportation furnished good families. Pay off every Saturday. We have modern Y.M.C.A., equipped throughout with amusement room, reading room, shower baths, etc. Also first-class Sunday School and day School with night School. Lunch room with Hot Coffee in the Mill for all night help.

FOR FURTHER INFORMATION APPLY TO ERLANGER COTTON MILLS CO.

In addition to affordable housing and good wages, residents of Erlanger Mill Village enjoyed other perks. A general store, post office, billiard room, swimming pool, and barber shop added to the amenities. Word spread quickly that residents always took care of each other in times of crisis. Women moved their personal sewing machines to the Y.M.C.A. and established a make-shift production line to produce clothing when any neighbor needed assistance; the mill provided cotton material free of charge with which to sew these garments. If someone in the village suffered misfortune, a bounty of food rapidly filled the kitchen of that family. Law enforcement officers, under the leadership of Constable Shirley Fritts, maintained strict order in this peace-loving community, and anyone not obeying the law would find himself—and his entire family— immediately leaving the village.

The community grew quickly, and mill owners insisted upon the best facilities and trained personnel to provide villagers with a good education, health and physical fitness benefits, and extra-curricular activities.

The Erlanger family, owners of the mill, established a school for the children. In 1920, Florence C. Fox, a specialist with the U.S. Bureau of Education came to the village to supervise the principal, teachers, and curriculum. In addition to their classroom lessons, young girls received instruction in home economics, where they learned to cook, sew, and can meats, fruits, and vegetables. Teachers gave reading and writing lessons to adults in special night classes. A teachery opened with seventeen rooms available for single female school teachers, both those in the village and those employed in the City of Lexington school system. For a five-cent fare, a jitney bus transported these women where they needed to go.

Mill officials hired C.M. Oliver as director of the village Y.M.C.A. Oliver provided supervised physical activities for both children and adults. A modern facility for its time, this building had an amusement room, reading room, and showers (women on one side; men on the other). Officers also allocated money to build beautiful playgrounds and common areas for recreation. About 1920, Mr. Howard Davis Townsend organized the first mill baseball team, called "The Cussless Team." This group of men took baseball playing seriously. Townsend—who scouted various colleges in the state—offered summer mill jobs to the most outstanding players and immediately recruited them to play ball for Erlanger.

In addition to baseball, other sports provided physical activities. The men's basketball team won the Southern Textile Conference Tournament in Greenville, South Carolina, in 1933. Players included Jack Childers, Lincoln Link, Willard Ball, Jake Sowers, Red Essick, Carl Everhart, and Carl Lee Barnes. Women enjoyed tennis competitions on a newly laid tennis court. Volleyball became a popular sport for both sexes.

Erlanger Mill officers authorized the building of a community cannery, where families could preserve the vegetables they had grown in their summer gardens. Tutored by a professional horticulturist, women learned how to increase the yields in their gardens and how to have something growing throughout the year. Contests sprung up to see how much the women could can; one year the total was 15,835 quarts. A special piggery and a poultry yard, located on the periphery of the village for sanitary purposes, allowed residents to raise pigs for pork and chickens for eggs.

A dairy managed by Mr. Jim Swing operated under extremely high sanitary standards. Owners of the mill, understanding the nutritional value of milk, insisted upon absolute cleanliness for the barns, cows, and workers. The dairy eventually furnished the mill lunchroom, the community store, private residences, and the Mill Street Boarding House with dairy products delivered by horse and buggy.

A village nurse, Mrs. Jessie Setzer, had an office in the Y.M.C.A. but spent much of her time visiting homes, caring for new mothers and their infants. Her services were available twenty-four hours a day. An annual "Baby Day" provided free physical check-ups for the youngest residents. The mill paid for flu shots for everyone. In addition to having around-the-clock medical attention, a dentist office, conveniently located in

Help! Help! Help!!

Go to Sunday School Sunday and See
WHAT YOU ARE NEEDED
To Help Do.

We want to have a picnic for the benefit of our community Sunday School, and we want you, no matter what class you attend, to be present and "HELP" decide WHERE and HOW it must be done. If you have never been to Sunday School before NOW is the Time to start. If you used to go and through carelessness have stopped NOW IS THE TIME TO START AGAIN. We need you and we believe that you need us.

We would be glad to see every mother that is in the entire community present, with as many members of their families with them as possible.

The Band will Play. The Choir will Sing
—AND—
Mr. Earl Gosnell will render a solo–"Is My Name Written There." Mrs. W. T. Solomon and Miss Lettie Hudson will render a duet–"Must I Go Empty Handed."

BRING EVERYBODY YOU CAN GET TO
COME WITH YOU.
SEND THE OTHERS AHEAD   BE PROMPT 9:30 A. M.
W. H. BROWN, Supt.

F. O. Sink Job Print, Lexington, N. C.

A notice calling announcing a concert by the Erlanger band to benefit the Sunday School.

the basement of the Methodist Church, provided dental care. Good health—in all areas—became a top priority.

Everyone in the community looked forward to special events and holidays. "Erlanger Day" always drew a huge crowd. Many considered this gathering the highlight of the year. Residents and guests enjoyed barbecued chicken, special entertainment such as The Arthur Smith singers, beauty contests, and parades with floats. While men visited various textile exhibits, the ladies displayed their finest crocheted and embroidered handiwork and their ever-popular knotted bedspreads.

On October 20, 1921, Mr. W.M. Jolly organized the Erlanger community's first band. A strict disciplinarian, Jolly insisted band members adhere to all his rules. He severly chastised band members if they arrived at practice late or without their instruments. The band played at Erlanger's special events, and they ultimately received an invitation to play at a state-wide convention in Hendersonville, North Carolina. An old handbill invited one and all to a special Sunday school meeting where the band was performing:

Help! Help! Help!!
Go to Sunday School Sunday and See
WHAT YOU ARE NEEDED
TO HELP DO.

We want to have a picnic for the benefit of our community Sunday School, and we want you, no matter what class you attend, to be present and "HELP" decide WHERE and HOW it must be done. If you have never been to Sunday School before NOW is the Time to start. If you used to go and through carelessness have stopped NOW IS THE TIME TO START AGAIN. We need you and we believe that you need us. We would be glad to see every mother that is in the entire community present, with as many members of their families with them as possible. THE BAND WILL PLAY. THE CHOIR WILL SING and Mr. Earl Gosnell will render a solo—"Is My Name Written There." Mrs. W. T. Solomon and Miss Lettie Hudson will render a duet—"Must I Go Empty Handed."
BRING EVERYBODY YOU CAN GET TO COME WITH YOU.
SEND THE OTHERS AHEAD. BE PROMPT.
9:30 A.M.

W. H. BROWN, Supt.

Hazel Bowman Barnes, a former pastor's daughter, reflects on the happy days and church-related activities of Erlanger Village. "Our lives were centered around the church, and the church fulfilled our spiritual needs and our social life. It seemed the whole church came, all ages and there was always enough homemade ice cream for all. Afterwards, the adults would have their own lawn party throughout the village, and their laughter could be heard. The village was like one big happy family."

People of the community came together, not only to have a good time, but to raise money for worthy war causes. Charitable contributions from workers often resulted from management challenges. The most popular contests between the day and night shifts determined which group could purchase the most war bonds and war stamps during World Wars I and II. Throughout the years, mill employees also contributed generously to the Red Cross and Jewish Relief.

As glorious as Erlanger Mill Village may sound, unfortunately, the Great Depression did not spare the mill or its workers. Layoffs and pay cuts happened here, just as they did everywhere else. Then, instead of recovering from the Depression, conditions worsened. About 1930, when men's underwear changed from one to two pieces, the Erlanger family lost its contract with B.V.D., causing the mill to abruptly change to the manufacture of shirts, bathing suits, dresses, and pajamas. But management did not relax the old rules and standards. When Mr. Jack Childers came on board as textile designer about 1932, he upheld the philosophy of providing excellent working and living conditions that the company had always espoused. Subsequently, Erlanger Mills became a model for the world-wide textile industry. Representatives from across the globe came to inspect the well-ventilated mill, note the workers' white uniforms, white hats with a blue stripe, and marvel at the cleanliness of the surrounding village.

Times changed. The City of Lexington absorbed Erlanger Village in September of 1940. The mill school closed. Between 1953 and 1963, when upkeep became more and more expensive, owners of the company sold individual houses to occupants for $500 a room. Some paid cash, but others financed; not one single foreclosure resulted. After the death of Milton Erlanger in 1969, his heirs sold the cotton mill to Parkdale Mills.

The years since 1969 have changed Erlanger from that beautiful community of yesteryear. Residents no longer enjoy ice cream socials, hear laughter pealing across the once beautifully manicured lawns, or root for their favorite baseball players. The flowers and gardens have disappeared. The old house at 38 Mill Street has lost its wide porches, its fresh coat of paint, and its gentlemanly boarders. Time has taken its toll.

One of the most poignant remembrances, written by someone identified only as "Bootsie," recalls Erlanger Village then and now.

"Sunday supper is over with," Bootsie wrote. "It's growing dark and katydids are winding down, ending their course for the day. The men are on the porch already, the women still cleaning up, washing and talking. Not much happening, the murmur of talk punctuated occasionally by the lonely tap of the screen door...Do you remember when we did not lock ourselves in at night? Yes, an ordinary street, a quiet street...more people than cars going by. People to say "howdy" to and invite to set a spell...Yes, a quiet street with those old-fashioned street lights that celebrated the night. Mostly the murmur was simply talk, grownup talk, family talk, talk we never really listened to as kids...but I think we did hear with far more than our ears. I felt I had to go back...to the good times and good places. Oh, the roads had changed a bit, bypassed some things and bulldozed others. There was even a new steel and concrete bridge over the Southern Railway...but I sure did miss the clumpty, clumpty, clump of the wooden one it replaced. I was here. Erlanger Mill Village. 301 Olympic Street. I was home. I circled the block several times. I stopped. I cried. Some of the houses

were simply gone, all were changed, and only a few stirred memories in me. 301 Olympic Street was the worst of the lot. There was no front porch swing because there was no front porch. The roof was held up by hastily placed 4x4's. There was no back porch at all, and the trees I once flew in were cut down to useless stumps. Trash and mud and filth were everywhere. I fled. Why did I have to go back? Now I know. No, there is no such thing as closure, since nothing ever closes. I had sought to go home again, while blinded to the fact that I had never left.

> *'Bootsie, come and wash up. Elwood will be home for supper directly.'*
> *'I'm coming Maw, I'm coming.'*
> *And I am."*

Every autumn, descendants of those first village mill workers have a reunion. They laugh and they cry. They reminisce, and they share old photographs. Although most do not return to the community of their childhood, they still remember and talk about the parades, ballgames, swimming pool, gym, and cozy homes with large well-kept yards. They prefer it that way.

Information and direct quotes for this piece came from the following sources:
• Informal interviews with people at Erlanger reunions.
• On-going informal discussions with former Erlanger Village resident Mickey Byrd.
• An e-mail from Helen Linder
• An apparently self-published (undated) booklet entitled *The North Lexington Baptist Church "They Came From Everywhere"* by Joyce White Melton, Clerk and Historian.
• Nickie Doyal Interview with Nancy Clayton Meeks on May 8, 2003.
• Website: Essay entitled, "The Porch," found at *www.angelfire.com/nc3/bootsie/ porch3*

Erlanger Nurse Jessie Setzer's Famous Corn Bread
(From the Bread Section of an old, undated cookbook owned by Alice E. Sink)
1/2 cup plain flour
3/4 cup cornmeal
1 heaping teaspoon baking powder
1/2 teaspoon soda
1 Tablespoon sugar
1/2 teaspoon salt
3 Tablespoons oil
1 cup buttermilk
Bake in iron skillet 30 minutes at 400 degrees.

High Point

Mrs. Eva Carter's Boarding House

Born August 22, 1918, Eva Carter came from a South Carolina tobacco farming family. Having had little education, she could not read. Neither could she drive. She spelled her great-granddaughter Amy's name "Ame." Keeping a formal set of books or tallying financial statements eluded her, but Eva Carter could count money and run an efficient boarding house.

The equation was simple—she took the cash she collected from boarders and then bought needed supplies. Her son, J. P. Elliott, recalls his mother's determination and savvy.

"She taught herself how to run a business because she had three husbands who did not support her," he declared. "She did this to survive and was able to make enough of a living. At one time she had as many as twenty-five boarders at the same time."

Although Eva Carter ran boarding houses for thirty-seven years in different High Point locations, grandson Mike Elliott remembers best the large, old residence on Kivett Street where his grandmother began keeping boarders in the late 1950's. Pecan trees flourished in the back yard and shaded dirt parking spaces. The front lawn consisted of a small twenty by twenty foot grassy area, which Eva mowed with an old-timey lawn mower. She had a harmless fetish for new curtains and loved to change window dressings in her boarding house—new and different styles and colors. Because she seldom left the residence, redecorating probably enriched the routine of her life.

Eva Carter in her kitchen.

Eva's hard work and tenacity impressed all those with whom she came in contact. She spent her days cooking in her large commercial-style kitchen filled with stainless steel sinks and several ovens. A huge coffee pot, holding 30-40 cups of fresh brew, always sat in one corner of the dining room. When Mike helped his grandmother restock the drink box in the hallway, he always received a free Nehi grape soda for payment of his labors, after she unlocked the chest with her secret key,

Boarders enjoyed family style meals in a dining room where three rows of metal-legged tables and vinyl-bottomed chairs seated 36 people. The family, including Eva, always ate with the paying guests, which included out-of-town men employed in the factories and mills, and tree-trimming crews. In addition, she always prepared meals for the holidays.

"Sometimes we would have at least 50 people eat lunch for a holiday meal," grandson Mike Elliott recalls. "It took us at least three hours to clean the dishes. Then it was time to start supper."

Great-granddaughter Amy Elliott recalls exchanging gifts at Christmas. "All her money was spent on gifts for others. Even little stuff meant a lot to her."

Either cornbread or biscuits accompanied every meal. Mrs. Carter made biscuits using flour, pure lard and buttermilk. She worked them up by hand in a large stainless steel bowl. Choosing not to use a drinking glass or traditional cutter, she shaped them all by hand and put them on two huge baking sheets. When they turned golden brown, she took them out of the oven and buttered them. Twice a day she fixed at least three dozen homemade biscuits.

For the most part, her menu was simple: dried beans, potatoes, collards, turnip greens, and ham. She bought everything in large commercial containers at the local Big Bear grocery, just down the street from her Kivett Street boarding house. She neither kept a garden nor raised chickens. A quart jar of Cheyenne peppers always appeared on her table.

Eva Carter got up at 4:00 every morning so she could have breakfast ready by 5:00. Then she would wake the men up and get them off to work. With the help of her grandson, she packed sandwiches for the men to take to their jobs. They used luncheon meat which came in a can about 12 inches long. Mike recalls cutting off a huge hunk, probably 4x4 inches, and slapping it between two slices of bread. He put the sandwiches in paper sacks, ready to be retrieved by the men before they left for work.

Mrs. Carter did have an adult helper named Shorty, a gentlemen who earned his room and board by keeping the kitchen clean and straightening the house. Once a week, Mrs. Carter and Shorty would go upstairs, strip the beds, launder the sheets, and clean the rooms. She did her own laundry, hung bed linens on the backyard clothesline to dry, and washed all her dirty dishes by hand. Shorty lived in a little room that measured approximately eight feet by eight feet, and shared this space with extra cases of Nehi's.

The other boarders—usually about fifteen men—lived upstairs, two, three, or even four to a room. Although Mrs. Carter's descendants don't have a clue as to what she charged, they do remember that rates varied for different sleeping arrangements. Prices increased as years passed, but family members agree that early rates for room and board probably started at twenty-five dollars a week. Amy Elliott sums up her grandmother's philosophy: "She was always here if you needed her. She loved Jesus. She loved to cook. I was her little helper when I was five. She called me that. She always acted like she wasn't struggling, never asked for help. Always said 'Jesus will make it happen.' She was a short little redheaded lady with no temper. If my brother or I needed discipline, she would just smile and shake her head."

According to her family, boarders generally respected Eva Carter even though she ran her boarding houses "with an iron hand." She always treated boarders as her children, giving them advice, "whether they wanted it or not," according to one family member. Occasionally, though, men would come back to the boarding house after an evening of drinking. A strong-willed woman of Irish descent, Mrs. Carter would be testy with them. "You know I won't have this in my house," she would say, and, for the most part, they would straighten up.

When male boarders tried to slip their girlfriends into Eva's home, she always caught them. The guys then tried a new approach. Without asking Eva, they borrowed her quilts, covered their ladies so they would stay warm, and persuaded them to sleep in their cars. Somehow, Eva always knew what had transpired because the next morning she went out to the vehicles, snatched her quilts off the women, marched inside, and told the guilty parties to get out.

Although a petite woman, she could lay down the law and make her point. "This is my house," she would spat. "This is where I live."

She scolded, but then did favors for them. Her boarders trusted this woman; they gave her their checks, and she took them to the bank, cashed them, and returned the money one hundred percent.

Grandson Mike Elliott notes, "I guess the biggest change I saw in her was when she got religion when I was about twelve years old. I mean here was a lady who smoked once in a while, kept her hair cut short. She joined the Holiness Church and it was like...the next day it was long dresses and long hair. A whole new version of her personality."

This conversion happened when she was about 50 years old. "It wasn't a bad thing," Mike says. "It was just a change that I saw in my grandmother."

Even after her religious conversion, Eva Carter still loved to sing colorful songs while she worked. She had learned this favorite while growing up in Nichols, South Carolina:

> *Redbird, redbird, sittin' on a pine,*
> *One's chewing tobacco*
> *But he can't have mine.*

Mike Elliott has fond memories of his grandmother. "She made it a point never to spank me because I was the only grandchild," he says. "It was kind of ironic because my other grandmother told me I was the meanest thing ever born. Grandmother Elliott would always hug and kiss me. 'You know you're my little baby,' she would say. I can remember as a kid her asking if I'd come up and help her run the boarding house. As an adolescent—maybe ten, eleven, twelve—I remember standing at the sink helping wash dishes with her. She always wore dresses with aprons.

"She was tough, but she was sweet. 'You're my little heart string,' she would tell me—even as an adult. She always had little surprises for me, and she'd bawl like a baby when she gave them to me. She was a very sweet lady."

Until her health declined, Eva Carter ran boarding houses for a total of thirty-seven years. "She ran a tight ship," one of her Steele Street neighbors, David Southern, said. "She was always doing things for people. She'd bake a cake or whatever. She was always working in that two-story house, painting the porch and banisters even after she was in her 80's."

Amy Elliott recalls life after boarding house days for her great-grandmother. "She traveled to Wichita, and I remember how she liked body powder, so I bought her three for Christmas. She acted like it was the best present." Amy also remembers taking Eva to the K&W Cafeteria for dinner. "She loved to eat, but she hated Mom's spinach balls."

Eva Carter lived her final months at Britthaven Nursing Home, where she entertained everyone by dancing a jig and singing some of her old ditties.

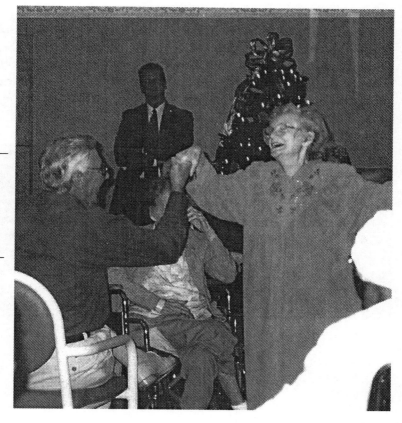

Eva Carter enjoyed singing and dancing even when she was living in a nursing home.

She would move her arms and belt Baha Men's hit, "Who Let the Dogs Out?" to whoever would listen. The next minute "she'd go up and down the halls and witness to people," her former Sunday School teacher, Evelyn Nance, recalls. "She would witness to you in a minute."

Long-time friend Polly Driggers remembers Eva's last request: "Polly, would you cook me some green beans?"

Eva Carter died on April 16, 2002, at the age of 83. Her pastor, Reverend Riley Puckett, of High Point Church of God eulogized Carter's life. "It was hard to realize how powerful her influence was in our church until she was not there," he said. "She was a mainstay in the seniors group, the Christian Classics. She didn't take leadership roles, but she was right in the middle of what was going on and helping make every church project a success. I know in recent years she lived on a fixed income, but it didn't matter what kind of fund-raising project we were in, she was always giving. I couldn't figure out how she was always coming up with money to help the church when she didn't have much herself."

Puckett concluded by referring to her life as filled with "prayer, giving, and loving." He called her an "Energizer Bunny."

Information for this piece came from the following sources:
• Nickie Doyal's Interview with J. P. Elliott (Eva's son) on September 20, 2002.
• Nickie Doyal's Interview with Mike Elliott on January 18, 2003.
• Nickie Doyal's Interview with Amy Elliott on September 27, 2002.
• Burchette, Bob. "Boarders Toed Line at House: Eva Carter's Strict Standards
  Remained Unchanged for 45 Years." *The News & Record (Piedmont Triad,
  N.C.),* May 1, 2002.

BREAKFAST CORN BREAD

One teacup of rice boiled nice and soft, to one and a half teacupful of corn meal mixed together, then stir the whole until light; one teaspoonful of salt, one tablespoonful of lard or butter, three eggs, half teacup of sweet milk. The rice must be mixed into the meal while hot; can be baked either in muffin cups or a pan.

From Mrs. Abby Fisher's *What Mrs. Fisher Knows About Old Southern Cooking, Soups, Pickles, Preserves, Etc.* 1881. Digitized by Michigan State University Library.

Mayodan

Odessa Holt's Boarding House

Listening to drunken laughter from the room above, Odessa Holt crept up the plank stairs of her boarding house. Night enveloped her, but the steel revolver she clutched gave her comfort. Rowdy talk came from the bedroom. She opened the door and leveled the gun at two people sitting on the bed.

"Get out of my house now," she demanded.

"Don't shoot," yelled one as he scrambled over empty liquor bottles and dove under the bed.

Odessa poked the gun under the edge of the bed and repeated her demand.

The two reluctantly scurried out of the room. On the stairs one of the men turned and threatened, "I'll be back."

Odessa Holt did not have time to obsess over the incident. She needed to get back to bed. Morning came early.

At 4:30 A.M., Odessa arose, dressed, and began her day by asking the Lord to help her do right. She worked alone in her kitchen cracking six dozen eggs, "getting a big coffee to boiling and smelling so good," frying bacon or ham, setting out cereal, jams, and jellies, and making her famous hand-pinched biscuits with Davis Mill flour, lard, and milk. Grandson Jeff Bullins, who slept in a downstairs bedroom with his parents, still remembers those early mornings when he headed for the kitchen to grab a fresh hot biscuit.

Odessa Holt

Odessa stood in the entrance of the dining room door and collected a dollar from each boarder as he filed through to enjoy the bounteous family-style breakfast. When everyone had eaten, Odessa handed each man a bag lunch before he left for Mayodan's Washington Mill, where his daily job would demand all his strength and energy. Odessa cleared away the plates, cups, platters, and bowls and began preparations for dinner and supper.

"I've fixed enough pinto beans to swim down to the river and back," she said in an interview when she was 101 years old. Shopping at the A&P and the Park and Shop, Odessa redeemed coupons to get the best deals on vegetables and staples. She killed, plucked, cleaned, and cooked several chickens and turkeys each week. Desserts came from Berrier's Bakery across the street, where on Saturday night Odessa bought "over-bakes" for half price.

All this work and responsibility might seem believable for a young woman; however, Odessa Holt had already turned 50 years old in 1952, when she began managing the seventeen-room boarding house for Washington Mill, the largest and probably most important economic engine in the area.

Actually, the mill—first called Mayo Mills, a textile manufacturing plant—came into existence in 1896, the same year as the town of Mayodan (claimed in Ripley's *Believe It or Not* as "the only town in the world with that name"). Textile manufacturer Francis Henry Fries built a cotton mill near the Mayo River in order to have ample water power to operate necessary machinery. Simultaneously, a group of realtors organized the Piedmont Land and Manufacturing Company, purchased 300 acres of land, and began laying off Mayodan's streets and selling lots for homes.

Roanoke natives Hohn and Sarah Ault erected the town's first commercial building. Fries purchased Robert Lewis' homeplace and hired Mrs. Eliza Higgins to operate a boarding house and the first Post Office. Howard E. Rondtaler, one of the new town's surveyors, held the first church service on the porch of Mrs. Higgins Boarding House, but later moved worshippers to Ault's Drug Store. From these early meetings, Mayodan's Moravian Church evolved with Rondtaler as the first minister. Children attended the first public school, located in the Moravian Chapel. Later, on February 16, 1899, Mayodan (named after the Mayo and Dan Rivers) boasted a charter as an incorporated town with 225 residents.

With the Mayo Mills up and running, Colonel Fries then went a couple of miles north and started building a new cotton mill and a new town which he named Avalon. So, here—just before the turn of the twentieth century— two cotton mills operated just two miles apart. Skilled adult men averaged $2.50 per day and unskilled men, seventy-nine cents. Skilled women received $1.30 and unskilled females, sixty-six cents daily. If workers produced inferior products, mill officials docked their salary, which "always kept the employees a week behind in their pay."

Because there were no laws prohibiting child labor, youngsters worked the same twelve-hour shift as their parents. According to one historian, "Wages for children ranged from about $1.37 per week to a high of $6.56 for teenagers

Surveyors in the late 1800's. The farm house later became part of the Mayodan Hotel.
(Photo: Jeff Bullins Collection)

doing adult jobs. These wages were customarily turned over to the head of the household. Guy Poole recalls working...for twenty-five cents per day and 'giving it all to Daddy.'"

An interesting chain of events followed. For approximately fifteen years, the two mills operated separately in the adjoining villages. Then on June 15, 1911, a machine in the Avalon Mill caught fire. Historian Ola Maie Foushee records her remembrance of that evening:

"At about 5:55 that afternoon, Grover Cobbage left his spinning frames to change his clothes. John Willie Richardson was monitoring Cobbage's looms when he noticed a little smoke coming from one of them. Quickly he grabbed a bucket of water and threw it on the loom, only to make the fire worse. Fortunately the work day was nearly ended and the mill almost emptied by the time it was realized the whole fourth floor was belching flames and smoke that could be seen miles away. It was the largest fire Rockingham County had experienced."

Although the mill had what was considered the best water system and automatic sprinklers in the South, the pump mysteriously failed, and the mill went up in flames. Colonel F.H. Fries estimated the loss at $250,000 but reported that he had enough insurance to rebuild the mill. Then, his plans changed. He would not rebuild. He soon announced the relocation of the entire community to Mayodan. Since Fries owned every Avalon house except one, families had no options. They watched in sadness as fifty mill houses left, one by one, on logs and rollers drawn by horses and mules to Mayodan. Avalon residents followed to work in the Mayo Mill (later renamed Washington Mills). A first-hand description of their poignant exodus follows:

"Like bands of gypsies or displaced persons, Avalon families trudged along the road with their possessions. There were no moving vans then—just a few wagons for hire. Older people and little children rode in the wagons while the others walked alongside."

Because of the Avalon Mill fire in 1911 the population of Mayodan suddenly doubled, and Washington Mill provided jobs for many people. Polly Case worked there from 1948-1996 with small breaks in between. She started at ninety-six cents an hour as an inspector in the sewing section. She would look at t-shirts, and if she found no flaws, she sent them on to be packaged. Later she worked as a time keeper in the office. She remembers getting a Christmas ham from the company and a catalogue from which she could choose one gift.

"People I worked around were like family," Case says. "I had a wonderful supervisor—never one to make you feel he looked down on anyone."

Another Washington Mill employee, Daisy Ore, began work on July 5, 1933, when she was only fifteen years old. After she started her new job, she boarded in town during the week. Her brother would pick her up on Fridays and take her home to Walnut Cove, about twenty miles away. On Sundays he would take her back. She received $6.50 in cash each week, and paid $3 a week for board at Mrs. Pearl Lunsford's, and then Annie Martin's. In the 1940's she moved to Mayodan. Ore started out folding men's underwear and later packed sleepers for J.C. Penny's and Montgomery Wards. During World War II, she stamped men's two-piece underwear (long-sleeved tops and long bottoms) with a government stamp and tied them together for shipping. "During the earliest years the bathrooms were in two rooms," Daisy recalls, "one for the men and one for the women. But the toilets were just one long board with holes cut into it."

The Mayodan Hotel in 1919.
(Photo: Jeff Bullins Collection)

Marilyn Nance worked at Washington Mill from 1953-1955, and again from 1972-1976. The first time she boxed sweatshirts and received $1.03 an hour. The second round she worked as many as fifty hours each week in shipping and packing. Large floor fans and open windows (no air-conditioning) cooled the mill during summer months. She remembers a meeting that dealt with a new opportunity to buy mill stock, but she decided not to purchase any.

"There was a doctor in the main office at the mill," she said. "He would take care of accidents that happened to employees. One time a woman had part of her arm cut off in the spinning department. Otherwise, just generally cut fingers and the such."

By 1951—when Mrs. Odessa Holt agreed to manage the boarding house for Washington Mills employees—both the mill and Mayodan had grown. Mrs. Holt, who ran a grocery story at the time, recalls one neighbor chiding her for accepting the new job. "You made a mistake giving up the store," the woman said. Odessa Holt also remembers clearly her own response: "Old lady, we'll just see about that." And see about that, she did. Two years later, she bought the structure for $900 and continued, as owner, in the same manner until her retirement 30 years later.

Odessa's hard labor and careful management proved profitable. In the earlier days, one bedroom slept three or four men and cost $5.00 a week, per person. Boarders and walk-ins from the community paid about $1.00 for each meal. Extra revenue came from Thursday night Lions Club suppers prepared and served by Odessa. Life flowed smoothly until drunken stragglers began sleeping on the front porch or boarders "skipped" without paying. Odessa had solutions for both. She walled in the large front porch and converted it to bedrooms, thus eliminating non-paying vagrants while bringing in additional income. After taking a walk across the street to the police station and reporting missing guests, Odessa usually received money due her when officers tracked down offenders, collected back rent, and personally delivered cash to her. One night, after Odessa's husband died, she heard some men talking loudly upstairs. She went up, opened the door, and saw liquor bottles everywhere. She left, went to the police station, and returned with an officer. As the policeman escorted the rowdy men down the stairs and out of the boarding house, one of the men said, "I'll get you yet!"

Most of the borders were quiet and respectful. When asked in an interview, when she was 101 years old, if she divided men and women by different floors, her vague response, that "People were not mean and dirty then...or not the men who stayed with me," needed no fancy interpretation. Clearly, this woman balanced total control with a kind heart. Occasionally, men separated from their wives came to stay at the boarding house. Odessa remembers one man in particular, who was so stressed by his separation from his wife that he could not sleep. "He wanted company to talk to," she recalls.

Although she worked extremely hard, Odessa Holt always found special time for her church and her family. For fifteen years she taught the 10-12 year old Sunday school class. She cared for her daughter, Katherine Bullins, who had contracted polio and suffered paralysis from the waist down. Each Sunday night Odessa's extended family, including seven grandsons, ate supper in the boarding house dining room and then gathered in the family quarters to watch *The Ed Sullivan Show.*

In 1980 Jeff Bullins bought the boarding house from his grandmother, but for the next two years she continued to run it in the same way she had for the previous 28 years. When she turned 80, she got up one morning and knew she had done enough. Jeff sold the house and Odessa Holt moved next door, where she still lived at the time of her visit with the authors of this book.

Information for this piece comes from the following sources:

• Nickie Doyal and Alice Sink Interview with Mrs. Odessa Holt (101 years old) and her grandson, Jeffrey G. Bullins, on September 26, 2003; and subsequent telephone interviews for clarification with Mr. or Mrs. Jeff Bullins.
• Powell, William S., Editor. *Dictionary of North Carolina Biography*. Chapel Hill: University of North Carolina Press. Copyright 1979-1996.
• *http://www.westernrockinghamchamber.com/id22_m.htm*
• *httn://www.netpath.rc net//la mayodan.htm* "Information About Mayodan"
• Foushee, Ola Maie. *Avalon*. Chapel Hill Books, 1977.
• Nickie Doyal's Interviews with Polly Case, Daisy Ore, and Marilyn Nance (former Washington Mill employees). June 5, 2006.

More Recollections

of North Carolina's

Boarding Houses

and the

Women Who Ran

Them

Martha Hinton's Boarding House

The following excerpts are from the Ferrge Papers, #4258, Fol. 2. and are direct quotes from the oral history transcript/interview of December 9, 1938, written by Travis Jordan, Southern Historical Collection, The Library of The University of North Carolina at Chapel Hill.

I will call her Martha Hinton although that is not her real name. When she opened the door in answer to my knock I said nothing for several seconds, for the expression on the woman's face was so unexpected that it startled me.

I had come to see a good woman, a woman warmed and tendered by the fire of religion, but Martha Hinton's face is the coldest, most relentless and stpic [septic] face I have ever seen. It is as unyielding as a block of granite. Her hair, a dingy white is coarse and bristly, growing low down on her deeply corrugated forhead [forehead] giving her a furtive, repellent look. She wears it brushed straight back coiled in a big knot on top of her head, and there are bangs standing up and back from her forehead stiff as the bristles of a brush. Her grey eyes are cold, even belligerent and as uncharitable as frosty ice on a winter morning. Long lines cut deep grooves at each corner of her mouth; deeply marked feathery wrinkles spread over her cheeks whose parchment skin is brownish and tough looking as thick wrapping paper, and her poorly fitting upper false teeth slips from her gum when she talks, keeping her busy pushing them back into place with tongue, making a clicking noise.

She stood holding the door knob with her hand with the door only half open, looking at me. Her thin lips were clamped together as close and unsmiling as a the [sic] bit of a steel trap, and there was no gleam of cordiality on her austere face nor in her frosty eyes.

"What do you want?" she questioned, without any salutation whatever.

She took me into the house...As we went into the hall which was dark and stale smelling with inside blinds and doors closed tightly as prison cells, Mrs. Hinton said abruptly, "This is my house. I worked and paid for it myself by keeping boarders. I've lived right here for fifty years. Since my husband died I stay here by myself...I don't board anybody any more, I'm too old to cook and no nigger is going to be messing in my kitchen and carrying off my things."

She led the way into a combined sitting and dining room where a coal fire burned in an open gate. The four box [sic] windows to the south held potted plants and a big pot of Christmas cactus sat on the dining table heavily laden with pink buds. The large room was crowed and cluttered with miscellaneous furniture. A big, worn leather-covered rocker sat beside the hearth and next to the radio whose voice was silent. A leather couch sat...beyond the table, a sideboad littered with dishes, newspapers, paper bags and what-not stood beside the door, a china closed[sic] crowded to overflowing was in one corner, and on the table in a rusty cage a green and yellow parrot popped its bill and croaked hoarsely.

The house itself is old style with five rooms up stairs and five down. A hall runs from the front door on to the back porch, with the stairway in the rear. Everything is old, cluttered and unkempt for Mrs. Hinton keeps no regular help, only a Negro man comes about twice a week to fill up the wood and coal boxes on the back porch. Nothing about the place is in order. An accumulation of every conceivable article is scattered in dusty muddles about the halls and rooms. Only the beds have a clean, well kept appearance. There is no steam heat, the rooms are heated by stoves and fireplaces. Small electric light bulbs hang high from the center of the ceiling with cords to pull on the current. There are no wall buttons.

The furniture is old, shabby and frazzled with an occasional antique. The only modern thing in the house is a gas stove and electric lights and Mrs. Hinton resents both. "I didn't want them" she told me, "and if I had been at home they wouldn't have been put in. I was sick in the hospital once and when I got back home Joe, my husband, had the stuff in here. For a long time I wouldn't use them. I had been using lamps and a wood stove all my life and it was sinful to be spending money for gas and electricity." We left the kitchen and went back into the dining room.

"Sit down," she said, pointing to a hard, uncomfortable rocker on the other side of the hearth. The sun came through the south windows making bright patches on the drugget of a drab, taupe color and showed up clearly the thick coating of dust on the dark painted floor. Too, it fell across Martha Hinton, making a soft halo of her white hair—a halo that contrasted strangely with the harshness stamped on her face.

"I was born July 20, 1859," Martha Hinton said.

Then the story of her boarding house days begins to unfold. After the first husband had died, Martha and her three children went to Durham to live. "I married again," she says. "He was Joe Hinton and he was seven years younger than I was, and like my first husband he drank liquor. He was the type of man who laughed too much and laughter is frivolous. He wasn't serious about anything and he played the fiddle, even played the fiddle at dances and all my begging couldn't make him stop. When I told him the Lord would punish him for fiddling he would throw back his head, laugh and say, 'What you talking about, Martha? I bet when I play "Old Dan Tucker," the Lord himself gets out on the heavenly floor and swings the angels around to beat the band.'

"A little over a year after my second marriage, Elwood, my youngest son, was born. I made up my mind then I would never have another child and I told Joe I wouldn't. That was forty-six years ago and I never slept with Joe again. It is [a] sin having so many children. There ought to be a law that a woman couldn't have but two...Joe, he began to run with other women...He continued to serve the devil and I continued to serve the Lord. As he kept spending his money on other women I didn't want anything he had so I started taking boarders. I made a living for myself and the children and saved enough to buy this lot and build this house."

Martha could not understand why her children wanted fine clothes, worldly adventures, and freedom. "I was a living example of uprightness," Martha self-righteously affirms. She continues: "Debt is sin. The trouble with folks these days is that they have too big notions. A man with a ten dollar week income has a twenty dollar week notion, so he goes in debt. I don't believe in giving money to the poor; I don't believe in *giving* anybody anything, make them work for it. I never give a beggar food nor clothes. The other day when it was snowing a man came to the door. He was a young white man with only one leg and a pair of crutches and he asked me for a pair of old shoes. I told him I had shoes left by my late husband but they were not for him. I told him I was old; twice as old as he was, that I worked to make a living and that he could do the same thing if he got out and worked instead of begging. Free giving to people isn't charity, it's just aiding them in their laziness and such doesn't please the Lord...I have lived too close to the Lord for remorse, and I am still a good woman."

The interviewer interrupted her to ask if she remembered anything about the Civil War. "Yes," she said slowly, "I remember a little bit. Not when it begun, but it must have been about 1864 that I remember things happening. I was about five years old then. I had three uncles who went but Father was too old and Brother was too young to go, but in 1864, along toward the end of the war, they sent for Father. I remember when the messenger came for him. He rode up in the yard on a big brown horse, and when he saw Father he threw up his hand and touched his cap, and Father did the same thing. I didn't know what it meant but I thought it must be something awful for [mother] fell across the kitchen table and began to cry. I had never seen her cry before and it scared me. Brother fell across the bed and began to cry too. I crept over in a corner and sat down on a stool, and Sister who was washing dishes dropped a blue platter and broke it all to pieces. The slaves all came running and began to moan and cry: 'Oh, Marse John, oh, Marse John." Some of them fell on their knees and began to pray.

"Father told the officer that he was too old to go and that he could prove it by the birth record in the Bible, but the officer told him he would have to go with him to Raleigh to prove it. So, Father tore the sheet that held the birth dates out of the Bible and saddled his best horse. Mother had stopped crying by then but the slaves were still moaning and carrying on and I was still huddled in the corner on the stool. Father told us all good bye and rode off with the officer. It took almost a week then to go from Person County to Raleigh on horseback for the roads were muddy and bad.

"When he got to Raleigh and proved he was fifty years old going on fifty-one, they didn't take him. In four or five days he came back. He came back in the night and next morning a noise woke me up. It was just about day, time for the slaves to be at the stables feeding. I remember I sat up in bed scared at all the noise that was going on, and the window panes were so red with the day break that I thought the house was on fire. I woke Sister who was sleeping with me and we jumped up, pulled on some clothes and ran down stairs. The house was full of slaves all singing praises loud enough to wake the dead. 'Marse John's come home, Praise de Lawd, Praise de Lawd, he's come to stay, Praise de Lawd, Praise de Lawd,' they sang.

"Sister ran in Father and Mother's room with me right behind her. Father was in bed and Mother knelt beside him, praying, and the Negroes were praying too and shouting. I remember the two little Negro house boys, Lewis and Charlie. They were kneeling at the foot of the bed; had pulled the covers loose at the foot and were kissing Father's feet."

She began to tell about her family. "I grew up in my father's house wanting for nothing...I never went to school much...No, I don't believe in too much education. I don't believe in anything that takes you away from the Lord...There was only four books allowed in my father's house, the Bible, almanac, McGuffy's Fourth Reader and a Blue Back Spelling Book...We never went anywhere except to church. We rode horseback to the little log school house three miles away where services were held every fourth Sunday. That was when women rode horseback decently, not straddle the immodest way they ride now. Then we rode sideways and wore long skirts that hid our legs for in those days a woman's ankle was sacred from a man's eye, and we wore our hair done up in nets to keep it from jostling down. I never saw a paved street until I was over thirty years old.

"I married first when I was seventeen. I married a country doctor named Marshall but I always called him Doctor. He was a good doctor but he wasn't good to me, for he drank liquor and wouldn't follow the Lord's teachings. We went to live in a two room log cabin...The nearest neighbor was three miles away and from early fall when the rains began until spring the roads were so muddy you couldn't go anywhere...Many is the time when the doctor would be away from home days at a time and I would be in the cabin night and day with not a soul to speak to...Then the children began to come." Martha Hinton leaned nearer the fire. A strange expression flitted across her face, and she gazed deeply into the glowing coals.

"I hated having children," she added vehemently, "hated carrying them, it seemed so vile and indecent, it's a punishment the Lord puts upon women for some sin they've done. I've often wondered why He punished me by giving me seven children. I've never done any wrong, I've always been a good woman...To think that my own people, my husband, children and grandchildren should have brought shame, disgrace and dishonor upon me when I spent my entire life in doing for them...I have always been a righteous, good woman without turning a fraction of an inch from the wayside, and in spite of all the trouble sent upon me I pray for strength that, like Job, I may endure with increasing faith...Then look what the World War did to me. It took Elwood my youngest son...There were plenty of men to go without Elwood and he was all I had left.

"No, I've never been cold nor hungry, nor without a roof over my head, but I've had enough trials, tribulations, shame and disgrace heaped upon me by the actions of others to have laid me in my grave...I have lived too close to the Lord for remorse, and I am still a good women."

The interviewer rose to his feet. The green parrot popped his bill. "Get going, get going," he croaked hoarsely. After Travis Jordan left Martha Hinton's house, he noted, "...the air was fresh and clean. As I looked back at the big old house with the tightly closed prison-like blinds, Martha Hinton closed the door without saying good bye and I heard the key turn in the lock."

Lill Camp

Raleigh

Lill Camp's Remembrances of Camp Family Care Home
aka Lill's "Boarding House"

My first person was Gilbert Brown," Lill recalls of her boarding house days. "He was thirty-nine years old when he came to live with me, and he died when he was 69 and a half. He died in a chair right here in the house. He was with me thirty years. He was born in Manhattan. He lived with his mother until he had a seizure and fell off the bed. His mother sent him to the hospital. It was learned he had a mental problem, and he was then sent to Eastern Long Island Hospital. He finished school there at the hospital. He was a pantry boy during that time and then helped or worked in the morgue.

"At that time I was living in a nice four-bedroom house at 3430 Great Neck Road, Amityville, New York. A friend was talking with me and said, "Why don't you go over to the hospital and see if there isn't a resident that needs to live outside the hospital? So we went over, and I talked with the doctor and he told me about Mr. Gilbert Brown. He said, 'He is a nice man; he will respect you. But don't let him go out with girls. He's never been with girls.'

"At this time New York did not require me to be licensed. I only needed to sign a responsibility paper. I received monthly payments from the State of New York.

"I brought Mr. Brown home with me, and he stayed with me for thirty years. When I got him, he had spent twenty years at the hospital. He was

American Indian. He was my right hand man. He sat in the passenger side of the car. One day in 2002 he fell asleep in a chair in my house, and he was gone. He was a wonderful man. He even bought presents for me. I'm wearing a pair of shoes he bought for me.

"The second man was Wilton Mak, another American Indian. He was from D.C. He was in the same hospital as Mr. Brown and had been there also for twenty years. He didn't like to work, but he wanted to look nice. We got along okay. He was a heavy smoker and he didn't like girls. He did go to church and went along on our different vacations. I always drove. My nickname was 'Road Pig.' I drove an Oldsmobile, an automatic. Mr. Mak eventually developed lung cancer and died in the house in 2000.

"The third man was from Petersburg, Virginia. Edward Ryles. He was Black. A mother's boy, but he didn't want to live with her. During his early life he had joined the Navy and been to California. Then it was discovered he had a mental condition, and he wandered away from his mother and she had him put into the hospital. The hospital told me he was a wanderer and he was. He was in the hospital for twenty years also. He would wander off, and I would have to call the police and have them fetch him. He went with us on our vacations and errands also."

In the mid-1970's, Lill moved her household south. "On July 25, 1975, I brought all three men and myself and moved to North Carolina. After being in North Carolina for six months (January 10, 1976) I applied for my license to have people in my home. The state checked me out. They went back twenty years into my history and gave me an 'A.' I got my license in 1977. During that short time I held down a part-time job to help meet expenses, and the State of New York still sent me the checks for the men's care. After I got my license, I could no longer hold an outside job. My job then became taking care of my people.

"After moving down here, we took a trip and on that trip stopped to see Mr. Ryles' sister in Virginia. Apparently the sister talked with her brother and either told or asked him to stay with her. But nothing was said to me. After sometime back home in North Carolina Mr. Ryles (this was in wintertime) about 4:30 in the afternoon put on a double pair of socks, a shirt, two coats, and a toboggan and shoes and he walked away and he didn't come home that night. I called the police and reported him missing. Nothing happened. Then over three months later a niece came through town and stopped and said she saw Mr. Ryles at the bus station. I called his family and the police but nothing.

" Five years later the phone rang. It was his mother. She said a man had read in the newspaper about a man in the hospital in Raleigh and said that was her son. I'm assuming she called the hospital. They asked me if I could do something. His toes had been frozen and were amputated. He had been missing for five years. He had gotten chilled and frozen somewhere. The hospital asked if he could come back with me and I said, 'Yes, his bed is still open.' In 1980 he came back to my house. He never left the yard again unless he was in the car with me or I walked with him. He joined the church and became an Adventist. But then he developed lung cancer and died about 2001.

"When I moved down here, the house I bought only had one bathroom. I needed another one so I had the house remodeled and a new bathroom added. I got a female patient. Betsy Jones. She lived with me for about five years until around 1982 or so. She was a very nice lady. Very friendly. Liked to go around with me. I took her to New York on vacation to my brother's house. She had Alzheimer's. Every day she had to call home to Durham to her daughter Ida. One night she took all my brother's clothes out of his closet and had a good time. When I decided to make another trip to see my brother in New York and called Ida (Betsy's daughter) to see if her mother could go with me, Ida said she could take her in to live with her. So that's where she went."

Camp Family Home Care could be considered an extension of more institutionalized adult health care. However, Mrs. Lill made her residence seem more like a boarding house. Her caring concern proves that she took special interest in her clients. She included them as part of her family, taking them on trips, reporting to the police when they strayed from her home, and keeping in touch with the residents' families. Maybe Lill's compassion and motherly attitude came from her experience at other jobs she had held. According to her biography, Lillie Webb grew up fast in Wilson, North Carolina, so in 1939 she moved to New York City where she lived for fifteen years. Then she moved to Amityville for another twenty-one years. What did Lillie Webb Camp do during those thirty-six years in New York state? In addition to pursuing her hobby of horticulture and antique collecting, she helped rear dozens of children. Lill's own words illustrate her industrious nature, her caring compassion, and will to succeed.

"I was born in poverty with little education," she said. "I went north to New York to work with Jewish families in 1939 as a teenager with no/little education. The Jewish families had fled Europe because of Hitler's advance. I worked for several different Jewish families. If I had stayed here, I could have made thirty-five to fifty cents a day, or go to New York and live with the family, eat their food, and still make $1 a day. So I went to New York. In 1972 I was able to finish junior high school up there."

In July of 1975, when Lill came back to North Carolina to be with her family, she was fifty-seven years old and, as she expressed it, "I didn't want to come home in a box." From 1980 to 1984 she went to high school and then one year of technical college. When she finished, she was sixty-eight years old.

Back home, Lill worked hard. During business days, she had two assistants help with the laundry. She tended a large vegetable garden of tomatoes, peas, cucumbers, cabbage, string beans, mustard greens, rutabaga—

but not corn. "I don't like corn," she admits. Married at one time, her husband died ten years ago. They had no children. Lill takes pleasure in going out to lunch once a week at McDonalds or Subway. She has been a faithful member of the Seventh Day Adventist Church and attends services on a regular basis.

She arose at 6:00 a.m. daily and prayed, asking for blessings, before preparing breakfast. Her menus varied little. On Mondays, she prepared cereal with fruit; Tuesdays, a different cereal and fruit; Wednesday, an omelet with green peppers and onions...and on throughout the week. She did not serve coffee, only tea, milk, and juice and shied away from desserts because those contained too much sugar for older people. Lunch consisted of a turkey sausage roll made into sandwiches, broccoli and rice, and tomatoes or hot dogs, black eyed peas, cabbage, bread, and milk or diet soda. She treated guests with ice cream only once in a great while. For dinner she prepared roasted chicken, rice, string beans, macaroni, beets, and bread. Sometimes she added pound cake for dessert. Although she learned to cook from her mother and then the Jewish families in New York, she has no written recipes. As if she did not have enough to keep her busy, Lill has volunteered many years as craft leader with children at Vacation Bible School.

Mrs. Camp ran the Camp Family Care Home in North Carolina for thirty-four years, closing the boarding house in June of 2006 at the age of eighty-eight. To celebrate her retirement, she went to the Department of Motor Vehicles. Although family members joked she was a "road hog," Lill contends she had a perfect driving record for fifty years. She went up to a clerk at the DMV and said, "I've got a double 44 in my purse, and I am turning my license in. And so I did. Why spoil a beautiful driving record."

Artist and photographer Rick Doble took a picture of Lill Camp to illustrate the cover of the 1984 book *Rainbow Roun Mah Shoulder* by Linda Brown Bragg. This novel portrays an African-American woman who overcame her humble beginnings to become a successful business person. The same holds true for Lill Camp, who has done well enough to buy three additional houses, which she rents. Ironically, one of the residences houses a day care facility for the state. In his autobiography, Rick Doble says: "When my step-mother died and my father had to be moved from Florida, he stayed at her [Lill's] boarding house where he died." Note that Mr. Doble referred to Lill's home as a "boarding house," not a state-supported institution for old, feeble adults. What a moving tribute to Lill!

Information from this piece came from several sources:
• Telephone interviews with Nickie Doyal on June 7, 2006, and again on June 11, 2006.
• Doble, Rick, "Life Story." Online autobiography. *www.rickdoble.net/lifestory/ 3thirties*

Charlotte

Aunt Zonie (back row center) and her family.

Dot George's Remembrances of Her Aunts' Boarding Houses

D ot Stephens George remembers her childhood visits in the 1920's and 30's to her great aunts' boarding houses. She referred to Aunt Zonie's boarding house on Cedar Street in Charlotte as "full-fledged." At least five employees worked in the huge kitchen. One woman made all the bread; one mixed and baked cakes; another made pies. Two additional helpers prepared vegetables and cooked various meats.

Arizona, nicknamed Zonie, donned a hat and gloves when she went downtown. She wore a black dress, always with a corset, and applied her make-up and lipstick with precision. Zonie's meticulousness carried over to her boarding house management. Dressed in her finest apparel, but covered with an apron, Zonie presided with dignity and grace over her long dining room table. Starched white tablecloths held pre-set plates, silverware, glasses for iced tea or water, and cups for coffee. Often people waited in the parlor or on the front porch in rocking chairs or swings for a "second seating." Zonie's entrees included pork roast, stew, or special liver mush, which, according to Dot, "came straight from the hog's head."

Dot George

For a short time, Dot's Great Aunt Nan also ran a boarding house on Cedar Street, just two doors from Zonie. Tenderhearted and compassionate, Nan could never turn away a hungry stranger. Beggers began marking Nan's gate with symbols signaling that the lady of the house would provide food to anyone who asked. During the depth of the Depression, Nan apparently closed her boarding house and went to work in the alterations department of Belk in downtown Charlotte.

Living on the east side of the city, young Dot walked downtown every Saturday. "I went into Belk and Aunt Nan would always buy me a sundae for twenty-five cents in the basement of Belk," Dot recalled. "Then she'd give me $2.00 to take back home with me, and that was the money that she gave us [her entire family] for eating the next week."

Dot then recalled her Aunt Juanita, who also ran a boarding house. "And Juanita lived to be ninety-nine," she said. "At age nine-two she still had her driver's license. And the highway patrolman stopped her and said, 'Mrs. Mulligan, do you know how fast you were going?' and she said she did not. When he told her, Juanita said, 'Thank you,' stepped on the gas, and kept on going."

Information for this piece comes from the following source:
• Nickie Doyal's personal interview with Dot George on September 2, 2002.

High Point

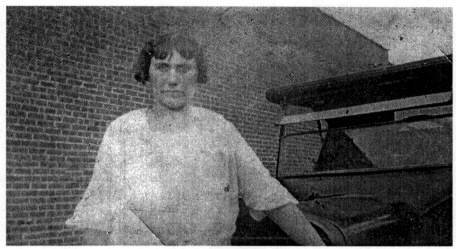

Mae MacCarter

Mae MacCarter's Boarding House

The dining room, kitchen, and living room of the Innis Street house seemed huge to Lucille Comer and her four sisters, the young stepdaughters of Mae MacCarter. Daily housekeeping chores were never the girls' responsibility; Mae took care of everything—cooking, cleaning, grocery shopping, laundry, and ordering groceries from a nearby neighborhood store. The boarders slept upstairs, and the family lived on the first floor. William MacCarter had a garden and grew vegetables, which his wife canned. He also raised hogs in the back yard and killed them for pork chops, roasts, bacon, and sausage.

Hard times during Depression days brought hungry transients to MacCarter's boarding house. William MacCarter had always told his family never to let anyone go away hungry. One day a man came to the door and asked to buy a biscuit for a nickel. Lucille's Aunt Edy invited him to come in, sit down at the table, and eat. He did. "Do you live by yourself?" he asked.

Edy said no, but then mentioned that the boarders usually left on the weekends. "Do you have a gun?" he then asked, glancing at the old gun rack on the wall. "Yeah," Edy said, "but it's broke."

A boarder poses outside the boarding house.

That night when everyone prepared for bed, Herman, Lucille's brother, told her, "I'm going to set up and wait until Dad comes and talk to him." Later, Herman came into the bedroom occupied by the five sisters and said, "Ya'll be quiet; there's somebody in the kitchen."

When he said that, all five girls, dressed only in their petticoats, tore out of their bedroom, down the long center hallway, and bolted towards the front entrance. Just as they reached the door, they saw shadows come out of dining room into the hallway. Again they ran and jumped off the front porch. Herman, one step behind the girls, picked up a piece of loose curbing and hit one of the intruders in the head. The fight was on. One of the men cut Herman and another shot at him, but missed. Then they ran. After William arrived home and heard of the night's bizarre events, he called the police, but the men had already gone by then and were never found.

MacCarter's Boarding House saw happy times and several budding romances. Lucille and two of her sisters, Nannie and Charlie, met their future husbands at Mae's.

William died three years after his marriage to Mae. She kept the boarding house going for a few more years and then moved to Winston-Salem. "She was a good woman...in every way," Lucille said in a recent interview. "A big built woman, ordinary, straight hair. She kept her hair cut short. Wore regular cotton dresses and no apron." When asked about rules, Lucille smiled and replied, "She let us do what we wanted to do."

Information for this piece comes from the following source:
• Nickie Doyal's personal interview with Lucille Comer on Octoer 24, 2002.

Remembrances of Boarding House Landladies

Brenda and Keith Flippin met in 1965 while attending Winston-Salem Business College. They lived in separate boarding houses a couple of blocks apart. One residence admitted females, and the other, males.

"A typical day in my boarding house days began at 6:30 a.m. with our landlady ringing a bell and calling, 'Girls, time to get up. Breakfast is ready,'" Brenda recalls. "Breakfast usually was eggs, bacon or sausage, toast, coffee, milk and juice. Once a week we had pancakes, and cereal was always available.

"There were ten girls living in the house. We were all students at Winston-Salem Business College. Can you imagine ten eighteen-year-old girls and one bathroom? Most of us took our bath—no shower—at night, but one or two would wait until morning, which made it difficult for the rest of us.

"Classes were from 8 a.m. - 1:30 p.m., so we were out of the house around 7:30. We had to walk one-half to three-fourths of a mile to school; none of us had a car. After classes were over, we usually stopped at a grill next door to school for lunch. We then headed back to school to study or home to watch either 'The Guiding Light' or 'Another World.' There was only one TV in the house, so whoever got home first was in charge of the television.

"Dinner was around six. Again, we were summoned by the bell. After dinner, we finished homework, watched TV, played card games, or just hung out. Curfew was 10:30 p.m. If we had to be out later than that, we had to get permission from the landlady. Otherwise, we were locked out!

"One night I had to iron some clothes and went downstairs to use the iron. The ironing board was set up in a large room that had windows on three sides. There were no curtains on the windows. I kept hearing noises outside, but could not see anything. I felt as if someone was out there watching me. I could hardly wait to get those clothes ironed and out of that room. I never went back in there—even in day time.

"During the summer of 1965, the house was being painted on the outside. When the painters showed up the second day, they found footprints on the roof of the front porch. Some of the girls had climbed out the window and met the guys from the 'boy boarding house.' Needless to say, this was reported to the school, and the 'ringleader' was transferred to another house.

"After a year of keeping ten girls, the landlady ended her contract with the school and went back to having only male boarders.

"Girls were just too much trouble."

Keith Flippin recalls his 1965 stay at the men's boarding house.

"Breakfast at our boarding house was all you could eat. Eggs, bacon, sausage, gravy, and homemade biscuits. The cook's name was Charlie, and he sure could cook. The maid's name was Margaret. She was quiet and very sweet. We called our landlady Ma. Three meals were served every week day. People could come in from off the street and eat for a dollar. The food was always good, and there was a lot of it. The football team from Wake Forest University sometimes showed up at meal time. On weekends, Charlie would bake cakes and leave them out for the boarders to eat.

"There were eight or ten business college students living there and a few barber school guys. We paid $32.50 a week. There was another man living there who had a 'real job.' He was a computer expert and a gambler and an alcoholic. Every Friday he would go to a local hotel and play poker all weekend. He drank so much that he paid one of the students to dispose of all his bottles.

"Ma had only one rule in her boarding house. NO WOMEN ALLOWED."

• Information for this piece comes from the written remembrances of Brenda and Keith Flippin. June 2006.

The Baldwin Sisters' Boarding House

During the winter, female teachers boarded with the Baldwin sisters. After they left for the summer, males lived in the house during Ellerbe's peach season. Some of the men managed various packinghouses, and some had government jobs, inspecting the fruit. Every orchard had its own packinghouse and required both a manager and an inspector on site.

According to Rebecca Howell, great-niece of the Baldwins, the oldest sister went by the nickname Sissy. "She was as broad as she was tall and kind of like a Chairman of the Board," Howell relates. "Aunt Sissy laid down the rules." One of the family stories that still circulates today concerns Sissy taking charge when church offerings fell behind the expected budget amount. At the end of Sunday services, she approached members of the congregation and asked them to "turn their pockets out" so she could collect additional money. Sissy also had a gentle side. Rebecca Howell recalls, "When we were kids and she wanted us to perform a chore for her, she'd say, 'Do this or that and I'll give you a little pretty.' She treated us children with generosity—much like a grandmother."

The middle Baldwin sister, Aunt Jane, stood tall and stately. A business woman, she always dressed neatly. The youngest of the trio, Aunt Mamie, expected proper behavior from everyone. The great-nieces knew not to say "Gosh" around her. Although Mamie did not have good health, she lived to be ninety-three, longer than her two sisters.

The outside of Baldwin's Boarding House (no longer standing), located on Church Street, had German wooden siding and a large front porch where everyone liked to sit on summer evenings and watch the blossoming of night - blooming plants.

The inside of the Baldwin house had a long first-floor hallway. On the left, heavy sliding oak doors opened into a parlor, which contained a player piano, sofa, and chairs. A huge dining room contained tables and chairs for guests' eating pleasure. Downstairs, the three sisters shared one bedroom and bath and occasionally rented the spare room next to theirs. Upstairs, seven bedrooms and one bathroom accommodated seasonal boarders. The Superintendent of the hosiery mill, a permanent guest, had his own private bedroom and bath.

Peach managers and inspectors, who worked in the Ellerbe peach orchards approximately eight weeks each summer, left the Baldwin's after breakfast and did not return until supper. They put in long, hot hours, taking advantage of the daylight to harvest, grade, and pack peaches. Rebecca Howell explains the process: "At first the fruit was brought in and run through what was called a defuzzer. Then from there the peaches went through rollers that sized them. At this point there were also young girls and women who would line up around the peaches on the rollers and pick out the bad ones. The inspectors would also walk along these lines and make sure everything was processing correctly."

Next came grading. The rollers would automatically size the fruit and dump it into bins. Each bin held a different peach size. Again, the inspectors made sure all this happened correctly. Then young girls, called "ringers," selected the prettiest peaches and put them—one layer deep— upside down into a large ring (with bottom). Then men would set an open ended barrell-like basket on the ring. Next, they put a paper liner around the inside of the basket, filled the basket with loose peaches, and then set it aside. When they flipped the basket over, the prettiest peaches on the first layer would be right side up, with the rest of the fruit resting beneath. As their final step in this process, inspectors would rubber stamp the size of the peaches—#1, #2, or #3—on individual baskets under the name of the orchard. And off to market they went in railroad boxcars located near the packing houses.

After a busy day in the orchards and packinghouses, boarders returned to the Baldwin Sisters' home for a supper of good country food, made from recipes memorized by Sissy, Jane, and Mamie. Chances are they had peach pie or peach cobbler or homemade peach ice cream for dessert.

Information for this piece comes from Nickie Doyal's telephone interviews with Rebecca Howell and from those North Carolina Agricultural Department agents who patiently explained the 1950's peach packing process to us.

Mayberry

Barney Fife and Mrs. Mendelbright's Boarding House

A nyone who watches *Andy Griffith* episode 104 on television will appreciate the special relationship between Barney and the Mayberry, North Carolina, boarding house owner, Mrs. Mendelbright.

According to *Andy Griffith* fan Joey Fann, the plot of this poignant show is as follows: "Barney is evicted from his room at Mrs. Mendelbright's Boarding House after being caught violating her rules regarding cooking and high wattage bulbs. With nowhere else to go, he moves in temporarily to the back room of the courthouse. When he goes back to beg for his room, he learns that Mrs. Mendelbright is about to sell her home in order to pool assets with her new boyfriend, Mr. Fields, whom she plans to marry. Something about the whole deal doesn't smell right to Barney. Andy finds out Mr. Fields is a con man, and he and Barney save Mrs. Mendelbright from financial ruin." Afterwards, Barney has a tearful reunion with Mrs. Mendelbright and gets his old room back.

Just another example of art imitating life?

Information for this piece comes from Joey Fann in an e-mail dated June 25, 2006, and sent to Nickie Doyal.

May Coble Thompson

May Coble Thompson's Boarding House

May Coble Thompson, made of real tough stuff, never got angry at anything or anyone, according to her daughter, Sara Forrest Hunt. Mrs. Thompson's boarding house at 5 East Main Street in Thomasville looked like a rich woman's mansion with huge rooms and rich oak paneling. Big sliding doors led to the dining room, which held six tables and thirty-six chairs. Both front and back stairways went to the second floor.

Pat Jobe, Mrs. Thompson's grandson, finds one particular feature of the house innovative for its time. "The detail Mama provided that I found most fascinating was that a communication system had been set up in the house so that boarders could speak to the kitchen from their rooms," Jobe explains. "Mama said the boarders would push 'pearl buttons' in their rooms, and they could communicate through speakers on the wall."

Regardless of the residence's size and elegance, Sara remembers the lack of privacy with so many boarders in the house. She recalls getting up at 5:00 every morning to help prepare and serve breakfast, consisting of eggs, bacon, sausage, toast, and cereals, before she left for school. "We worked all the time," she related. "I had debating team, and I would stand in the kitchen and practice while everything else was going on. It was a hard life. You do what you have to do."

Sara Forrest Hunt

Her mother served three meals a day, seven days a week. She set prices and determined the foods she would serve, including country ham and gravy, fried chicken, vegetables, and homemade breads. Although paid help assisted in washing the dishes and tidying the house, cleaning the bedrooms became a family task. After linens went out to a local laundry, the clean sheets, towels, pillowcases, and wash cloths came back as "wet wash," and Sara Forrest and her younger sister, Ruth Merelyn, had to hang everything to dry on the backyard clothesline.

Once a boarder complained about his room. Mrs. Thompson said, "I'm very sorry, but I can't ask anyone to do another thing." Boarders either did their own personal laundry or sent it out and had it done for eighty cents, according to Sara Forrest.

"Mother could sit down and go to sleep for fifteen minutes and be ready to go again," she recalls. Another task always waited.

Grandson Pat Jobe recalls another interesting snippet, told to him by his mother, Ruth Merelyn Thompson Jobe: "She said the house was called a boarding house because men lived there. In addition to the men were teachers, all female, of course, and the house would have been called a 'teacherage' had the men not been living there."

Information for this piece came from the following source:
• Nickie Doyal's personal interview with Sara F. Hunt on October 10, 2002.
  Pat Jobe's e-mail to Alice E. Sink on October 6, 2002.

Mount Airy

The Thompson Boarding House

If the walls of Maggie Thompson's boarding house could talk, they would take you back to the early years of the twentieth century. Scottish immigrants and their families have just enjoyed a delicious meal and desserts. The men bring out their bagpipies, and soon old Scottish melodies fill the house and spill onto the front porch and yard.

Maggie Thompson and her husband James opened a two-story Victorian boarding house in Mt. Airy in 1907. Scottish immigrants, who came to work at the nearby North Carolina Granite Quarry, soon filled the many rooms. That same year, an article in the *Charlotte Daily Observer* referred to Thompson House as "one splendid boarding house, just completed...and adds much to the appearances out at the quarries. This house is elegantly fitted and is handsomely furnished." Hand-carved woodwork, high ceilings, gingerbread trim and brass fixtures contributed to the elegance. The wraparound porch on the first floor and smaller porch upstairs provided places to enjoy the fresh air and sunshine.

Saturday nights at Thompson Boarding House soon became a social center for Scottish workers and their families. After eating a meal prepared by Maggie Thompson and the other Scottish women, everyone enjoyed bagpipe music, native songs and stories, sword dancing, and poems written by their revered Robert Burns. One historical account describes the immigrants and their

James and Margaret Thompson

families in this way: "They tripped the light fantastic toe till the wee sma hoors anont the taw!"

To Mount Airy, the granite cutters and their families brought their Scottish culture— celebrations, religious fervor, love of education, volunteerism, and social reforms.

Today Thompson House, located at 804 East Pine Street in Mount Airy, North Carolina, is a bed and breakfast. In the entrance hallway, a 1910 portrait of James and Maggie's daughter, Christobel, symbolizes the charm, hospitality, splendor, and beauty of those Scottish days of another century.

WANT TO GO?

New owner Reverend Phyllis Kaplan, welcomes visitors. Reverend Kaplan is a registered nurse, professional counselor, and healing practitioner. She can conduct wedding ceremonies, wedding vow renewals, and other ceremonies of celebration.

The wrap-around porch of Thompson House has plenty of rocking chairs. A large formal dining room and an old fashioned parlor offer a place to relax. Each guest room has an antique bed, dresser, and chair. Cable television and phone jacks in each room provide entertainment and laptop computer hook-up. Each room has a modern private bath. Area attractions include antique shops, the mountains of the Blue Ridge Parkway, Pilot Mountain, Downtown Mt. Airy, the Andy Griffith Birthplace, the Andy Griffith Playhouse, and The World's Largest Open Face Granite Quarry. You may reach Reverend Kaplan at (336) 719-0711 or toll free at (866) 719-0711. Her e-mail address is: *morningsun79@aol.com.*

Information for this piece came from the following sources:
• Telephone conversations between Nickie Doyal and Reverend Phyllis Kaplan.
• E-mails to Nickie Doyal from Fern and Steve Hammond. (Fern's great grandmother was Maggie Thompson). October 6 and 10, 2003.
• Brim, Randle. "Scots Drawn to Mount Airy for Granite, Stayed to Change Community Flavor." *Simple Pleasures.* December 2002.
• *www.bbonline.com/nc/thompsonhouse*

About the Authors...

Alice E. Sink

Nickie Doyal

A lice E. Sink is the published author of three books and numerous short stories, articles, and essays in anthologies and in trade and literary magazines. Her M.F.A. in Creative Writing is from UNCG. She is Associate Professor of English/Communications at High Point University in High Point, North Carolina, where she received the Meredith Clark Slane Distinguished Teaching/Service Award in 2002. The North Carolina Arts Council and the partnering arts councils of the Central Piedmont Regional Artists Hub Program have awarded Mrs. Sink a grant designed to share *Boarding House Reach: North Carolina's Entrepreneurial Women* with our state's men, women, and children.

W hen Nickie Doyal's youngest daughter went off to college, she did too. Nickie graduated from High Point University at the age of 56. She has been published in the literary magazine *Apogee*, written articles for the *Chronicle*, and placed in the short story category of the Phoenix Festival. Nickie began work on *Boarding House Reach: North Carolina's Entrepreneurial Women* during her senior year. She graduated summa cum laude, and received the "Best All Around" award from the university's English Department. Currently she is a realtor in Greensboro, N.C., where she lives with her family.

Books

If you enjoyed this book,
check out more great
North Carolina
history titles at

---

www.dramtreebooks.com.

We tell the stories that tell the
North Carolina story!

Printed in the United States
201069BV00005B/40-66/A

9 780978 624866